HISTORICAL PAPERS *of*
THE TRINITY COLLEGE
HISTORICAL SOCIETY

SERIES XXXII

The Religious Press in the South Atlantic States, 1802-1865

An Annotated Bibliography with Historical Introduction and Notes

BY

HENRY SMITH STROUPE

DUKE UNIVERSITY PRESS
DURHAM, NORTH CAROLINA 1956

HISTORICAL PAPERS OF THE
TRINITY COLLEGE HISTORICAL SOCIETY
SERIES XXXII

HENRY SMITH STROUPE

The Religious Press in the South Atlantic States, 1802-1865

An Annotated Bibliography
with
Historical Introduction and Notes

DUKE UNIVERSITY PRESS
DURHAM, NORTH CAROLINA 1956

 CAMBRIDGE UNIVERSITY PRESS, LONDON, N.W. 1, ENGLAND. LIBRARY OF CONGRESS CATALOG CARD NUMBER 55-12244. PRINTED IN THE UNITED STATES OF AMERICA BY THE SEEMAN PRINTERY, INC., DURHAM, N. C.

To

Elizabeth Denham Stroupe

Preface

As in ante-bellum days the term "religious press" is used here to include newspapers and magazines assigning half or more of their space to religious matters. Many periodicals that combined religion with literature, general news, or other interests were classified by their editors as belonging to the religious press. Both denominational and nonsectarian publications, whether issued by private individuals or by church bodies, are included.

The area studied consists of Virginia, the Carolinas, Georgia, and Florida, and West Virginia before 1861. The date 1802 is that of the opening number of the first religious periodical known to have been published in the South Atlantic States. The date 1865 not only marked the dividing line between the Old and the New South but was also a turning point in the history of the religious press. Every periodical that had not already done so suspended publication at the close of the Civil War, some never again to appear. Many of those that resumed publication had different titles, editors, or publishers, or began new series.

The portion of this book entitled "Historical Introduction" narrates briefly the founding of the leading periodicals, explains why they were started, and analyzes their problems, their objectives, and their relations with each other. The attitude of the religious press toward several notable historical events is described.

In the annotated bibliography, arranged alphabetically by title, each of the 159 publications known to have appeared in the South Atlantic States before 1865 is described. Nine others that were proposed but apparently not published are listed. Where known, the following information is given for each publication by formula: title, including variations; place of publication; date of first and last issues; periodicity; format, including number of pages and columns; circulation; editor; and publisher (owner of both the periodical and the printing equipment) or proprietor (owner of the periodical but not of the printing equipment). Each sketch also identifies the editor and denomination, states what type of material the periodical contained, and gives sufficient general information to round out a brief history of the publication. Finally, each sketch locates extant files, either by references to published works in which they are listed or to libraries holding them. The writer has discovered many titles and files not listed in the principal reference works relating to the subject. In recording the holdings of libraries scattered issues are listed by date. Brackets indicate for the dates enclosed incomplete files in which the issues are too numerous to list individually. Thirty-five publications of which no copy has been found are known from contemporary evidence to have existed. Files, some complete, others scattered, of the remaining 124 publications constitute the principal source of information used throughout the study. The average life before 1865 of the entire 159 was found to be five years and seven months.

I wish to thank the staffs of the following libraries and depositories for their assistance in locating materials: American Baptist Historical Society, Charleston Library Society, Confederate Library and Museum, Crozer Theological Seminary, Duke University, Erskine College, Foreign Mission Board of the Southern Baptist Convention, Furman University, Historical Foundation of the Presbyterian and Reformed Churches, Lenoir-Rhyne College, Library Company of Philadelphia, Library of Congress, Lutheran Theological Seminary, Newberry College, North Carolina Department of Archives and History, North Carolina State Library, Presbyterian Historical Society, Public Library of Wilmington, North Carolina, Union Theological Seminary, University of Georgia, University of North Carolina, University of Richmond, University of South Carolina, University of Virginia, University of West Virginia, Virginia Baptist Historical Society, Virginia State Library, Wake Forest College, Wofford College, and Yale University.

To the Carnegie Foundation for the Advancement of Teaching I am indebted for a portion of the funds used in travel and the preparation of the manuscript. I owe special debts of gratitude to Professor Charles A. Sydnor, Department of History, Duke University, for helpful suggestions regarding organization, and to Mr. Carlton P. West, Librarian, Wake Forest College, for a critical reading of the manuscript.

Wake Forest College H. S. S.
May 15, 1952

Contents

THE RELIGIOUS PRESS IN THE SOUTH ATLANTIC STATES, 1802-1865

Historical Introduction

The First Religious Periodicals

Although Thomas Prince, Junior, had founded the *Christian History* in Boston as early as March 5, 1743, and published it weekly until February 23, 1745, as a chronicle of the progress of the Great Awakening, when Henry Holcombe launched the *Georgia Analytical Repository* of Savannah in 1802 he was making the first effort, as far as is known, to publish any kind of religious periodical in the South Atlantic States.[1] A native of Virginia, Holcombe grew up in South Carolina, where his formal education ended when he was eleven years old. Later he became a Baptist minister. After serving in the Revolutionary Army, he had charge of several small churches in South Carolina before moving in 1795 to Savannah. In the Georgia city he became a popular preacher, active writer, and aggressive civic leader, founding, among other institutions, the Savannah Female Orphan Asylum.[2]

Holcombe observed that the ecclesiastical history of Georgia

[1] Despite its lack of variety, the *Christian History* is usually regarded as America's first religious periodical. See Frank Luther Mott, *A History of American Magazines, 1741-1885* (3 vols.; Vol. I, New York: D. Appleton and Company, 1930; Vols. II and III, Cambridge, Mass.: Harvard University Press, 1938), I, 78. See also Lyon N. Richardson, *A History of Early American Magazines, 1741-1789* (New York: Thomas Nelson and Sons, 1931), p. 58. Two other religious magazines appeared prior to independence. Christopher Saur published two volumes of *Ein geistliches Magazien* in Germantown, Pennsylvania, between 1764 and 1772 and John M'Gibbons published two numbers of the *Royal Spiritual Magazine* in Philadelphia during 1771. In 1789, the year the *Arminian Magazine,* the first sectarian periodical, was founded, religious magazines were still rarities in the United States. At the turn of the century the idea of a religious newspaper was, according to a contemporary, still nowhere entertained. See David Benedict, *Fifty Years among the Baptists* (New York, 1860), p. 25.

[2] John D. Wade, "Henry Holcombe," *Dictionary of American Biography,* IX, 133.

remained not only unwritten but unknown, that morals were of the lowest order, and that the general state of the region looked gloomy to those interested and concerned. Feeling that human laws alone were ineffective against crime and sin, Holcombe decided that a religious periodical would strengthen them by building up moral support. Friends advised him that since "learning and religion, here, are in their infancy," Georgians should depend upon outsiders for published materials. This he refused to do, contending instead that the arts and sciences in any region must have a humble beginning and that it would be foolish to delay introducing his periodical until he became qualified to conduct it with taste and ability, for that time would never come.

Holcombe voiced as widely as possible his aim of "contributing towards the maturity of both literature and piety" and his determination to be impartial toward all denominations. He reminded Georgians that the difficulties and dangers of settling a frontier country had now largely disappeared, and that the only remaining obstacle to the growth of enlightenment was the "want of inclination."[3]

Dedicated to Josiah Tattnall, Junior, Governor of Georgia, and printed by Gurdon I. Seymour, Philip D. Woolhopter, and Francis Stebbins, the first issue of this bimonthly magazine appeared with the date May and June, 1802.[4] Holcombe was listed as both editor and proprietor. After six numbers the periodical had to be abandoned because the "literary spirit" in the people was insufficient to sustain it.[5] Later aspirants to a publisher's career may have remembered Holcombe's experience. In any event, no evidence of further efforts to publish a religious periodical of any kind in Savannah during the ante-bellum period has been discovered.

The *Georgia Analytical Repository* contained biographical notes, historical sketches of all the churches in Savannah, proceedings of benevolent and religious associations, accounts of revivals, and essays on civil government. Especially valuable is the discussion of the proceedings which led to the organization of the

[3] *Georgia Analytical Repository,* Preface (dated May 25, 1802), Vol. I.

[4] On Jan. 1, 1802, Holcombe had submitted his plan for the periodical to Governor Tattnall in writing, asking the privilege of dedicating the publication to him. The governor viewed the plan "with pleasure" and granted Holcombe the unrestricted use of his name. See Henry Holcombe, *The First Fruits, in a Series of Letters* (Philadelphia, 1812), p. 81.

[5] *History of the Baptist Denomination in Georgia.... Compiled for the Christian Index* (Atlanta, 1881), pt. 2, p. 274.

General Committee of the Georgia Baptists (later the Georgia Baptist State Convention), as well as the story of the first efforts to mitigate the severity of the penal code of Georgia, the account of the Savannah Female Orphan Asylum established by Holcombe, and the several descriptions of camp meetings.

A year after the demise of Holcombe's periodical, a group of Presbyterian ministers founded a second religious periodical in the South Atlantic States, the *Virginia Religious Magazine* of Lexington. Approved by the Synod of Virginia, which declared a vehicle of communication essential to the prosperity of the church, the periodical obtained three hundred and fifty subscribers and survived for three years. Religious news items, biographical sketches, accounts of revivals, and essays on moral questions were printed. Of the last a typical illustration may be found in an attack on horse racing as the most destructive vice of the day. If "A Spectator's" description of the fighting, gaming, reveling, and lewdness at a series of races in 1805 is correct, his opinion regarding their destructiveness is well founded.[6]

During the succeeding decade a half-dozen religious magazines of slight importance and short duration appeared in scattered locations. Samuel K. Jennings of Virginia offered the nonsectarian *Lynchburg Evangelical Magazine* to represent those who accepted the statement "God willeth every man to be saved" as a comprehensive summary of the evangelical view. The *Christian Mirror* of Charleston also appeared without a sectarian label. Although octavo in size, it was published weekly and called a newspaper. In 1815 John Alburtis began printing in Martinsburg, Virginia, a short-lived Episcopal weekly called the *Lay-Man's Magazine*. The editor, who completely concealed his identity from present-day readers, sought to "commence a crusade against pride, profligacy, lukewarmness and ignorance."[7]

The Benevolent Movement

The progress of the Great Revival in the South and West shortly after 1800 was furthered by the favorable attention which it received in the news and editorial sections of the earliest publications. In turn, after a few years the spiritual impulse generated by the revival expressed itself in missionary activity, in the found-

[6] *Virginia Religious Magazine,* I (Oct., 1805), 267-269.

[7] *Lay-Man's Magazine,* Nov. 16, 1815.

ing of academies, colleges, and seminaries, and in the establishment of philanthropic organizations for publishing Bibles and encouraging Sunday schools. Most editors of religious periodicals were favorably disposed toward these activities also, admiring them collectively as the benevolent movement.

The editor of the *Monthly Visitant; Or, Something Old,* founded in Alexandria, Virginia, in 1816, directed the attention of his readers to these "doings of the Lord" by reporting the operations of numerous benevolent societies.[8] Andrew Fowler, the first missionary sent out by the Society for the Advancement of Christianity in South Carolina, used his *Sunday Visitant: Or, Weekly Repository of Christian Knowledge,* Charleston, to explain the rites and ceremonies of the Episcopal Church as a means of directing the new religious enthusiasm into that church.[9]

Presbyterians Take the Lead

Whereas Episcopal editors such as Fowler usually remained moderate even in their support of the benevolent movement, Presbyterian editors, who at this time outnumbered those of other denominations, seized every opportunity to praise the new ventures in Christian benevolence. John Holt Rice, founder of several educational and benevolent societies and editor of the first outstanding Southern religious journal, took the lead. After he had established the first Presbyterian church in Richmond (1812) and settled down as its pastor, he began issuing a weekly religious newspaper called the *Christian Monitor.* His principal purpose was to communicate "religious intelligence," which he defined as "accounts of Revivals of Religion; the proceedings of Bible and Missionary Societies; the labors of Missionaries; and, allowing a little latitude to the expression, remarkable occurrences in the life and death of Christians."[10]

Unable to retain a printer, Rice brought the publication to a close after the completion of two volumes. In January, 1818, however, he sent to his former subscribers the first number of a much larger periodical entitled the *Virginia Evangelical and Literary Magazine,* which, with alterations in the title, appeared monthly for the next eleven years. Rice defined *evangelical* as pertaining

[8] *Monthly Visitant; Or, Something Old,* I (July, 1816), 2.

[9] *Sunday Visitant: Or, Weekly Repository of Christian Knowledge,* Jan. 3, 1818.

[10] *Christian Monitor,* Richmond, July 8, 1815.

to the system of doctrines which assumed the total depravity of man, that is, the necessity of regeneration by the Holy Spirit; justification by faith alone; and the requirement of holiness as a qualification for happiness. He maintained that the study of the history of religion and literature since the Protestant Reformation would show "that learning and philosophy are handmaids to religion whose services ought not to be disregarded." Accordingly, he introduced the term *literary* to permit essays on agriculture, inland navigation, the construction of roads, schools, "and whatever our correspondence will furnish for the promotion of internal improvements."[11]

In 1820 Rice reviewed for his readers the *Memoirs of Dr. Joseph Priestley to the Year 1795 Written by Himself; With a Continuation . . . and Observations on his Writings,* by Thomas Cooper, using the review to attack the recent election of Cooper to a professorship in the University of Virginia. He quoted Cooper as denying the immortality of the human soul, freedom of the will, the eternal duration of future punishment, and the doctrine of the Trinity. Rice believed Cooper an atheist filled with "arrogance and self conceit," lacking the "character of a true philosopher," and unworthy of teaching young citizens. Having helped found the university, Rice felt that he would "sin against the common good" should he fail to take notice of Cooper's views.[12] Other religious leaders joined Rice, and together they were able to persuade the Board of Visitors to accept Cooper's resignation.

After depending upon hired printers for three years, Rice secured the aid of Nathan Pollard, proprietor of the Franklin Press. Together they conducted the magazine, the former as editor and the latter as publisher, an arrangement which continued until 1827. Pollard meantime had founded in 1822 a weekly newspaper containing accounts of the progress of all denominations and entitled the *Family Visitor.* Five years later, at the beginning of 1827, it became the *Visitor and Telegraph,* Richmond, upon absorbing the *North Carolina Telegraph,* published in Fayetteville during 1826 by Robert Hall Morrison.[13]

Pollard's popular religious newspaper decidedly injured the prosperity of the *Literary and Evangelical Magazine,* leaving it

[11] *Virginia Evangelical and Literary Magazine,* I (Jan., 1818), 2-8.

[12] *Ibid.,* III (Feb., 1820), 64, 72.

[13] The *North Carolina Telegraph,* Dec. 29, 1826, described the sale of the subscription list to Pollard.

with fewer subscribers in 1828 than formerly. Rice, occupied with many other duties, had by this time relinquished the editorship as well as the ownership to Pollard and Amasa Converse. In July, 1828, the latter became sole editor and proprietor of both the *Literary and Evangelical Magazine* and the *Visitor and Telegraph.*[14]

Born in New Hampshire and graduated by Dartmouth, Converse became well-known in Virginia as teacher, editor, and minister. Finding the editing of both publications burdensome, he abandoned the *Literary and Evangelical Magazine* at the close of 1828 to devote himself exclusively to the form of journalism which both he and his patrons, mostly Presbyterians, preferred, that is, the newspaper the *Visitor and Telegraph.* The Synod of Virginia, then supporting Converse, regarded a newspaper as indispensable for the communication of information to the people.[15]

Other Denominations during the Twenties

Although not so active in religious journalism as their Presbyterian contemporaries, members of other denominations also established periodicals during the twenties. A score of years had elapsed between the founding of Holcombe's *Georgia Analytical Repository* and the appearance of the second periodical published by a Baptist in the South Atlantic States, the *Roanoke Religious Correspondent; Or, Monthly Evangelical Visitant.* Founded by John Jenkins at Danville, Virginia, in 1821, the work failed to attract enough support and ceased to appear after the completion of two volumes.[16]

The earliest Baptist publications with a continuous history throughout the ante-bellum period were the *Evangelical Inquirer* of Richmond and its successor, the *Religious Herald.* When the demise of the *Latter Day Luminary,* published in the nation's capital, left Virginia Baptists without a periodical, Henry Keeling, a young Baptist minister, decided not to depend on the North to supply the need. Instead, he launched the *Evangelical Inquirer* in 1826, emphasizing that it was designed for Southern

[14] Notice of the sale of Pollard's interest in the two publications appeared in the *Visitor and Telegraph,* July 26, 1828, at which time it had twelve hundred subscribers.

[15] *Literary and Evangelical Magazine,* XI (Nov., 1828), 610.

[16] *Roanoke Religious Correspondent; Or, Monthly Evangelical Visitant,* Milton, N. C., II (Oct., 1823), 145. Jenkins moved the publication to this North Carolina town in June, 1823.

consumption. Making the unprecedented profit of "several hundred" dollars on the venture, he, with the help of several Baptist laymen, enlarged his journalistic project by replacing the monthly magazine with a weekly newspaper, the *Religious Herald*.[17]

Keeling was importantly aided by William Crane, a Virginia Baptist leader, when the latter invited William Sands, an expert printer, to come from Baltimore to Richmond to publish the new paper. With money lent by Crane to Sands, Keeling and Sands on January 11, 1828, founded the *Religious Herald* as the unofficial organ of Virginia Baptists. When, three years later, Sands insisted that Keeling, the editor, assume a portion of the financial responsibility for the paper, he resigned the editorship and left the publisher in sole charge. Now editor as well as publisher, Sands soon established himself as a leader in the denomination and made the *Religious Herald,* which had an average of 2,756 subscribers, one of the three leading Baptist papers in the Seaboard South.[18]

Southern Methodists entered the field of religious journalism in 1825 when the South Carolina Conference founded the *Wesleyan Journal* in Charleston. Although this official weekly, with William Capers as the principal editor, was well received, the conference agreed two years later to combine it with the *Christian Advocate* of New York in order to avoid the "danger of collision" which existed when there were separate papers.[19] The *Christian Advocate and Journal,* under which title the two papers were merged and published in New York, retained a strong influence in the South until the forties.

The Protestant Episcopal Church, a member of which had issued the *Lay-Man's Magazine* in 1815, waited a decade before launching a second periodical, the *Gospel Messenger and Southern Christian Register,* a monthly magazine which served as the official organ of the Bishop of the Episcopal Diocese of South Carolina from 1824 until 1853. The leaders in editing and financing this publication, the expenses of which were greater than the income from its three hundred subscribers, were Bishops Nathaniel Bowen and C. E. Gadsden.

Another publication destined to have a long run appeared in

[17] *Virginia Baptist Preacher,* Richmond, I (Jan., 1842), Preface.

[18] The other two were the *Biblical Recorder* in North Carolina and the *Christian Index* in Georgia.

[19] *Wesleyan Journal,* March 3, 1827. See also W. M. Wightman, *Life of Bishop Capers* (Nashville, 1858), pp. 249-250.

Charleston during the twenties when Bishop John England founded the *United States Catholic Miscellany.* A native of Ireland, England became Bishop of the struggling Diocese of Charleston in 1820 and was soon recognized by many as the leading Catholic clergyman in the United States.[20] England hoped to make his newspaper, the first Catholic periodical founded in the United States, a national organ, but could not win the necessary support from the hierarchy.[21] Although never self-sustaining, the *United States Catholic Miscellany,* with an average of about eight hundred subscribers, survived until the fire of December 11, 1861, destroyed its office and one-half of all Charleston.

A few periodicals issued by members of minor religious groups also made their appearance as early as the twenties. The *Unitarian Defendant,* probably edited by the eminent Unitarian clergyman Samuel Gilman, was published in Charleston during 1822. A year later Alexander Campbell, nominally a Baptist at this time but later the founder of the Disciples of Christ, began publishing at his farm on Buffaloe Creek in Brooke County, Virginia, a monthly periodical called the *Christian Baptist.* This magazine and its successor, the *Millennial Harbinger,* became important media for the communication of Campbell's teachings, and soon raised the Disciples of Christ above the status of a minor group. Jacob Frieze, a Universalist minister from Rhode Island, came to Wilmington, North Carolina, where he founded the *Liberalist* and organized a Universalist State Convention. Michael Smith, another Universalist minister from the North, began the *Star of the South* in Milledgeville, Georgia, to assure his readers that no man would be punished in hell, that all would be saved. The leading Southern Universalist editor was Otis A. Skinner, who launched the *Southern Pioneer and Gospel Visiter,* published simultaneously in Baltimore and Richmond, in 1831 and continued it for six years.

Sectarianism Predominant, Growth Rapid

Prior to the 1830's most religious periodicals had used nonsectarian titles and, even though edited by men attached firmly to

[20] Peter Guilday, *The Life and Times of John England* (2 vols.; New York: The American Press, 1927), I, 473. See also Theodore Maynard, *The Story of American Catholicism* (New York: The Macmillan Company, 1943), chap. xiii.

[21] Paul J. Foik, *Pioneer Catholic Journalism* ("United States Catholic Historical Society Monograph Series," no. XI; New York: The United States Catholic Historical Society, 1930), p. 75.

a particular denomination, had appealed with some degree of success to all groups. During the thirties loyalty to a denomination began to receive greater emphasis, with editors more frequently making their positions known in the titles of their publications. A wider use of the word *Southern* in titles and the more frequent insertion of articles in defense of slavery reflected the trend of thought in political matters.

The decade of the thirties witnessed rapid expansion both in circulation and in the number of religious newspapers and magazines published, with more new publications being launched in that decade than in the three previous decades combined. A majority of the early publications had been monthlies in magazine format, but those begun during the thirties and afterwards tended to be weeklies, most of which were large folios of four pages. With few exceptions, the weekly, usually described as a religious family newspaper, enjoyed wider circulation than the more specialized and therefore less popular magazine or review.

An example of a monthly magazine that defied the trend by outstripping its weekly contemporaries in circulation is to be found in the *Millennial Harbinger,* successor in 1830 to the *Christian Baptist.* Within a few years Campbell was sending forth over three thousand copies monthly, but it should be added that in January, 1844, he reported his impecunious or disinterested subscribers $42,-700 in arrears. During the fifties Campbell's subscription list reached eight thousand. Meantime his followers had founded several state and local publications. One of these, the *Christian Publisher* (continued by the *Christian Intelligencer*), opposed the heresies of John Thomas and served as the organ of Virginia Disciples from 1836 until the Civil War. Reuben Lindsay Coleman and James W. Goss were the chief editors. The opponents of John Thomas also found an able advocate in John T. Walsh, who founded the *Spiritualist* in Richmond in 1844 and later began the *Christian Friend* in Wilson, North Carolina.

The John Thomas referred to above was an English physician who migrated to Richmond, where in 1834 he founded the *Apostolic Advocate* in support of Campbell's teachings. Thomas and Campbell soon disagreed, however, producing a schism among the Disciples, with followers of Thomas forming the Christadelphian denomination.[22] Thomas later published the *Herald of the Future*

[22] H. K. Carroll, *The Religious Forces of the United States Enumerated,*

Age, which contained his calculations of the date for the imminent second coming of Christ.

Soon after the migration of the *Wesleyan Journal* from Charleston to New York, some Southern Methodists became unwilling to leave the field of religious journalism to the North. Accordingly, in 1831 G. Capers founded the *Georgia Christian Repertory* at Macon and the following year Ethelbert Drake began the *Christian Sentinel* in Richmond. The latter, after changing titles several times, became the *Richmond Christian Advocate,* one of the South's leading religious newspapers. Leroy M. Lee, a vigorous writer, was editor for the twenty years following 1839. In 1840 the paper became the property of the General Conference of the Methodist Episcopal Church.

In the effort to satisfy the desire of Southern Methodists for a paper of their own, the General Conference, at the request of Southern delegates, had in 1837 established the *Southern Christian Advocate* at Charleston.[23] With William Capers editor for the first three years and William M. Wightman for the next fourteen, the paper was in capable hands. The General Conference of the Methodist Episcopal Church, South, took it over in 1845 without confusion and continued uninterrupted publication until near the close of the Civil War. Resumed in the summer of 1865, the *Southern Christian Advocate* is still published as the Methodist state paper for South Carolina. The circulation during the antebellum period averaged four thousand copies weekly among subscribers about equally divided between South Carolina and Georgia.

Baptists Take the Lead

Among all denominations whose statistics are known there was rapid growth in numbers of communicants and an increase in organized activities during the thirties. Such expansion was most pronounced in the case of Baptists, who founded institutions of higher learning, began active support of missions and other benevolences, and greatly strengthened their efforts in the field of re-

---

Classified, and Described (New York: C. Scribner's Sons, 1912), p. 89. See also J. Z. Tyler, *Rise of the Reformation in Richmond and the Distinctive Peculiarities of the Disciples* (Richmond, 1882), p. 20.

[23] *Southern Christian Advocate,* June 24, 1837. See also Mason Crum, *The Southern Christian Advocate: An Historical Sketch* (published by the author, 1945), p. 17.

ligious journalism. Baptist newspapers and magazines published in the 1830's exceeded in number not only those of Methodists but those of Presbyterians, the leaders before 1830.

As late as 1830 Southern Baptists were still largely dependent on the North for religious and other periodicals.[24] The *Religious Herald,* it is true, had recently begun its weekly appearances in Richmond but with a circulation confined largely to Virginia. A decade before Virginia Baptists founded this unofficial denominational organ, the Baptist General Convention for Missionary Purposes had sent Thomas Meredith from Pennsylvania to North Carolina as a missionary. Having decided meantime to make Eastern Carolina his permanent home, Meredith published during 1833 and 1834, first at Edenton then at New Bern, the *North Carolina Baptist Interpreter,* a magazine designed to further the interests of the recently founded North Carolina Baptist State Convention and to oppose the teachings of Alexander Campbell. His first venture having gained a favorable reception, Meredith enlarged his enterprise by establishing in New Bern a weekly newspaper called the *Biblical Recorder.* Transferred in 1838 to Raleigh, a more convenient location for mail service, the *Biblical Recorder* is still published as the organ of North Carolina Baptists. Meredith enjoyed considerable prominence and as an editor was said to be the equal of any man in the United States in his day.[25]

The year Meredith began his *North Carolina Baptist Interpreter,* the *Christian Index,* the third outstanding Baptist paper, migrated from Philadelphia to Washington, Georgia. This periodical had been founded as the *Columbian Star* at Washington, District of Columbia, in 1822 by Luther Rice and other officials of Columbian College, now George Washington University. It was later transferred to Philadelphia, where William T. Brantly, a native of North Carolina, became editor and proprietor and changed the name to *Christian Index.* When Garrison's *Liberator* and the Nat

[24] In that year the following periodicals were being received by the reading room of Furman Theological Institution: *Baptist Magazine, Baptist Preacher, Baptist Tract Magazine, Charleston Observer, Christian Watchman, Columbian Star, National Preacher, United States Catholic Miscellany,* and *Youth's Companion.* See *Minutes of the State Convention of the Baptist Denomination in South Carolina,* 1830, p. 13. Of these only the *Charleston Observer* (Presbyterian) and the *United States Catholic Miscellany* were published south of the Potomac.

[25] William Cathcart, ed., *The Baptist Encyclopaedia* (Philadelphia, 1881), p. 785.

Turner Insurrection began to divide the nation, Brantly's pro-Southern views caused the loss of many Northern subscribers. Deeming continued survival in Philadelphia unlikely, he sold the subscription list and good will to Jesse Mercer, the Georgia philanthropist.[26] Although Mercer wrote rather poorly and by his own admission did not find editorial duties congenial, his name gave prestige to the paper. In 1840 he donated it to the Georgia Baptist State Convention, under whose direction it was published until 1861. With Samuel Boykin as editor and proprietor the paper flourished during the Civil War; others have continued it to the present.

South Carolina Baptists also launched a paper during the thirties when William Henry Brisbane, a young Charlestonian, founded the *Southern Baptist and General Intelligencer,* which, despite the hearty recommendation of the Baptist State Convention, soon languished.[27] Basil Manly and William T. Brantly, now returned to the South, followed Brisbane as editors for a short time, but in 1838 James S. Burges, who listed himself as publisher, sold the subscription list to Thomas Meredith, publisher of the *Biblical Recorder,* and the two papers were merged under the title *Biblical Recorder and Southern Watchman.*[28]

Finding their state without a denominational organ of its own, a group of Baptist leaders founded the *Southern Baptist Advocate* at Charleston in 1843, but it had to be suspended at the close of the first volume for lack of patronage. Then came T. W. Haynes' *Carolina Baptist,* founded in 1845 at Greenville. Transferred to Charleston the following year, this periodical was superseded by the *Southern Baptist,* which, with an average of 1,600 subscribers, survived until the eve of the Civil War.[29]

Primitive Baptists Object

Although most church people supported the benevolent movement with its many philanthropic societies, some opposition de-

[26] *Christian Index,* Philadelphia, June 29, 1833. Publication in Washington, Georgia, began Sept. 14, 1833.

[27] *Minutes of the State Convention of the Baptist Denomination in South Carolina,* 1835, p. 7.

[28] *Biblical Recorder and Southern Watchman,* Raleigh and Charleston, March 3, 1838. The title of the Charleston paper had been changed to *Southern Watchman and General Intelligencer* in 1836. Meredith dropped *Southern Watchman* from the title of his paper in 1842 because of plans being formed for a new paper in South Carolina.

[29] *Southern Baptist,* Charleston, Oct. 27, 1860.

veloped, especially among those known as Old School or Primitive Baptists. Soon after Baptists who favored missions, educated ministers, and Sunday schools began actively to establish newspapers and magazines, Old School Baptists entered the field of religious journalism in opposition. Their first Southern periodical was the *Primitive Baptist,* founded in 1836 by Joshua Lawrence and Mark Bennett at Tarboro, North Carolina. Transferred to Raleigh in 1848, this vigorous organ of Old School Baptists, who withdrew from the North Carolina Baptist State Convention during the 1830's, survived until 1879.

A few months after the launching of the *Primitive Baptist,* Gilbert Beebe transferred his *Signs of the Times,* the oldest Old School Baptist periodical in the United States, from New York to Alexandria, Virginia. It remained in the South only four years, but in 1851 William L. Beebe, son of Gilbert Beebe, established the *Southern Baptist Messenger* in Lexington, Georgia. As the unofficial organ of Old School Baptists in the Deep South it flourished until the war began, when there were about 2,500 subscribers.[30] By this time John Clark had founded *Zion's Advocate* to combat the heretical Arianism which he saw in the teachings of the Beebes. His large following of Old School Baptists maintained that they were a "separate and distinct" group from those led by Gilbert Beebe.[31] The antimissionary movement reached its peak during the 1840's, after which its appeal gradually weakened.

The Presbyterian Schism

As Presbyterians divided into New and Old Schools during the thirties, Amasa Converse tried to maintain in his *Southern Religious Telegraph* the appearance of neutrality. But, to cite a critical contemporary editor, the "mask" came off in 1837: "The Southern Religious Telegraph has, at length, given up the profession of 'neutrality' and hoisted the New School flag. The editor, in jumping off the fence, exclaims, 'there can be neutrality no longer in any part of the church.' "[32] The New School found little support in the South Atlantic States, causing Converse to lose about 25 per cent of his

[30] United States Census, Manuscript Returns, 1860: Georgia, Social Statistics, Newton County.

[31] *Zion's Advocate,* Front Royal, Va., Jan. 3, 1857.

[32] *Southern Christian Herald,* Cheraw, S. C., July 7, 1837.

3,000 subscribers, including nearly all those from North Carolina.[33] These circumstances prompted Converse to abandon his adopted Southland in 1839, purchase the subscription list of the *Philadelphia Observer,* and in the City of Brotherly Love combine the two papers under the title *Religious Telegraph and Observer.* He pointed out that Philadelphia would be a more advantageous location from which to serve his growing constituency in the Middle West and that the cost of publication would be less. One condition of the union stipulated that slavery not be discussed. "It is," wrote Converse, "a political subject, on which, in our view, the judicatories of the church have no right to interfere—and cannot interfere without doing great injury."[34]

The leading Old School editor in the South at the time of the schism was Benjamin Gildersleeve of Charleston. A native of Connecticut, Gildersleeve had been graduated from Princeton Theological Seminary before migrating to the South, where for more than a half-century he was an outstanding minister, teacher, and journalist. His first venture in journalism came in 1819 when he founded at Mount Zion, Georgia, a weekly newspaper called the *Missionary.* Avoiding strict sectarianism, Gildersleeve reported the transactions of various charitable societies, Baptist associations, Methodist conferences, and Presbyterian synods. The *Missionary* was superseded in 1826 by the *Georgia Reporter and Christian Gazette,* published by B. Gildersleeve and Company in Sparta, Georgia, for less than a year.[35]

The short life of this paper was the result of Gildersleeve's removal to Charleston to begin a new religious journal. Two Presbyterian ministers, B. M. Palmer and George Reid, had founded the *Southern Evangelical Intelligencer* at Charleston in 1819 to print the news of the progress of benevolent enterprises but had soon left it in the hands of William Riley, a printer. When Riley and others invited Gildersleeve to transfer his

[33] A Presbyterian clergyman from North Carolina wrote the editor of the *Southern Christian Herald* (Aug. 18, 1837) that his state would sustain the last General Assembly—that "The Southern Religious Telegraph has lost its influence among us; it will not be able to do much more mischief in this Synod." That year the Synod of North Carolina adopted resolutions denouncing the *Southern Religious Telegraph* and recommending the *Watchman of the South,* newly founded Old School paper. See *Minutes of the Synod of North Carolina,* 1837, pp. 34-35.

[34] *Southern Religious Telegraph,* Richmond, Jan. 9, 1839.

[35] *Georgia Reporter and Christian Gazette,* Oct. 2, 1826.

Georgia Reporter and Christian Gazette to Charleston and combine it with Riley's paper, he readily accepted. This merger resulted in the founding on January 6, 1827, of the *Charleston Observer,* a weekly which soon became the South's largest and most influential Presbyterian newspaper. Gildersleeve, who had acquired Riley's financial interests, was both editor and proprietor; John Cudworth did the printing. The Synod of South Carolina and Georgia recommended the new paper as serving the best interests of the Presbyterian Church. Some Congregationalist patronage was also attracted.[36]

Amasa Converse's announcement in 1837 of his support of the New School immediately prompted William S. Plumer to establish in Richmond an Old School paper called the *Watchman of the South.* This weekly absorbed three other Presbyterian papers and with 4,200 subscribers claimed, apparently justifiably, a longer subscription list than any political or any other religious newspaper published in Virginia.[37] On July 10, 1845, Plumer announced the sale of his paper to Gildersleeve, who transferred the *Charleston Observer* to Richmond and combined it with the *Watchman of the South* to form the *Watchman and Observer.* Better mail connections at Richmond was the reason given for the transfer.[38]

The Development of Specialized Publications

Among the larger denominations, the prime objective of leaders interested in religious journalism was the establishment in each state of so-called "family weeklies," most of which contained four large folio pages filled with material designed to appeal to all members of a family. When in 1837 the *Southern Christian Advocate* and the *Watchman of the South* joined papers already in existence this objective had to a considerable extent been reached. New state weeklies continued to appear occasionally throughout the ante-bellum period, but a majority of the publications founded after 1837 were specialized types. These included periodicals made up of sermons, those devoted to missions or Sunday schools, soldiers' papers, juveniles, and some maintained almost exclusively for religious controversy.

[36] *Charleston Observer,* Sept. 27, 1828.
[37] *Watchman of the South,* April 23, 1840.
[38] *Watchman and Observer,* Aug. 14, 1845.

The earliest periodical devoted to sermons was the *Virginia and North Carolina Presbyterian Preacher,* which Colin McIver founded in 1828 at Fayetteville, North Carolina. Sectarian titles were still so infrequently used that McIver felt the need of explaining that he did not plan to attack the doctrines taught in other branches of the Christian Church but to illustrate those held by Presbyterians.[39] In 1833 Lewis Eichelberger founded the *Evangelical Lutheran Preacher and Pastoral Messenger* at Winchester, Virginia, to supply the rapidly growing English-speaking portion of his denomination with sermons.

In several instances the editors of general religious weeklies also issued monthly periodicals containing sermons. William H. Stokes, editor of the *Christian Index,* began the *Southern Baptist Preacher, Or, Sermons by Living Baptist Ministers in the South* in 1839, but twenty-five months was required to secure and publish the twelve sermons of which the work consisted. In terms of longevity, the most successful venture into publishing sermons was Henry Keeling's *Virginia Baptist Preacher, Original Monthly,* Richmond, 1842-1859.[40] After witnessing repeated failures by others, Charles F. Deems launched the *Southern Methodist Pulpit* "to disprove what has already been said, that neither for love nor money could we secure a dozen sermons a year from Southern Methodist preachers."[41] Notwithstanding prophets of failure, Deems managed to acquire sufficient sermons and over two thousand subscribers, writing in his valedictory, "We do not die of neglect."[42]

The principal missionary magazines were those issued at Richmond by various boards of the Southern Baptist Convention. Thrown upon their own resources by the division of the denomination in 1845, Southern Baptists were quick to realize the need of such publications. The next year they founded the *Southern Baptist Missionary Journal,* organ of the Board of Foreign Missions and the Board of Domestic Missions. Three years later the Board of Foreign Missions established as its special organ a low-priced monthly folio entitled the *Commission,* which acquired eight thous-

[39] *Virginia and North Carolina Presbyterian Preacher,* I (Jan., 1828), cover.

[40] Keeling stated in the issue for Jan., 1843 (II, 1), that he had 2,000 subscribers. This was three or four times the usual circulation of such periodicals.

[41] *Southern Methodist Pulpit,* Richmond, I (1848), 19.

[42] *Southern Methodist Pulpit,* Greensboro, N. C., V (Dec., 1852), 379.

and subscribers.[43] These two publications were combined in 1851 to form the *Home and Foreign Journal,* which continued for a decade and had at one time fourteen thousand subscribers, the largest number listed for any religious periodical issued in the South Atlantic States.[44] Meantime, in 1856, the Board of Foreign Missions, in order to have more space, had again established a special organ called the *Commission; Or, Southern Baptist Missionary Magazine.*

The *Calvinistic Magazine* constitutes the principal example of a periodical established primarily for religious controversy. After an earlier series had been published at Rogersville, Tennessee, the magazine was revived in 1846 at Abingdon, Virginia, for the avowed purpose of refuting the "slanders and disabuse" of Methodists, who for twelve years had been allowed a "clear field to abuse and misrepresent Presbyterians, and to decoy into their own church the members of Presbyterian churches and families."[45] The revival of this Presbyterian periodical induced Russell Reneau of the Methodist Episcopal Church to establish the *Arminian Magazine* "for the purpose of hurling back the assaults of the notorious *Calvinistic Magazine,"* to which, in his opinion, adequate reply had not been made.[46]

Slavery Divides the Baptists

The most important event in American church history during the forties was the division of the Baptist and Methodist denominations into Northern and Southern churches. In 1845 Northern opposition to slavery and consequent Southern resentment divided the Triennial Baptist Convention into Northern and Southern Conventions. The religious press of the South helped to bring about the separation by reporting events in the North that irritated Southerners and by affording Southerners a medium through which their comments on these happenings could return to the North.

Feeling ran high in the Southern Baptist press on the eve of the meeting of the Triennial Convention at Baltimore in 1841. Basil Manly, expecting an argument on the slavery issue, suggested in the *Christian Index,* January 1, 1841, that Southern delegates meet in advance, reach an understanding, and thus act as

[43] *Southern Baptist Missionary Journal,* Richmond, V (July, 1850), 28.
[44] *Home and Foreign Journal,* Richmond, X (Aug., 1860), 7.
[45] *Calvinistic Magazine,* III (Jan., 1848), 1.
[46] *Arminian Magazine,* Rome, Ga., I (Jan., 1848), 18.

a unit. With Northern Baptist churches, associations, and conventions resolving that the admission of slaveholders to the communion table was sinful, William H. Stokes, editor of the *Christian Index,* demanded that the Triennial Convention stop such activities out of respect for Southerners "whose feelings have been wantonly outraged":

> These wounds cannot, must not be healed slightly. It were vain to cry peace! peace! when there is no peace. The South, at least Georgia, never will submit to this. Our position is taken.... The ultraists must cease to revile us, and those brethren who would be thought neutral, must cease to connive at their conduct, if we ever go on together as we have done, in the great enterprises of the day.[47]

Manly's suggestion was followed and the Baltimore gathering, in spite of this bitterness, succeeded in effecting a temporary reconciliation. Thomas Meredith joyfully told his readers that the convention had adopted a resolution on tests of church fellowship which excluded the idea that slaveholding was incompatible with church fellowship.[48] Stokes was equally pleased to write on May 28, 1841, that the requests of Southern delegates had been met, that "the abolition storm has passed over, and the union of the great body of American Baptists is as yet preserved."

But the storm had not passed. As a matter of fact, from this time until 1844, when the Triennial Convention next met, antislavery agitation among Northern Baptists, particularly in New England, increased. News of this agitation reached Southerners through the Baptist press. Until 1844 most editors continued to hope that slavery would cease to plague the convention. In the spring of that year, however, an inflammatory circular sent out by the Anti-Slavery Missionary Society, which was willing to continue co-operation with the convention only if the latter ejected all slaveholders, convinced William Sands and others that separation was inevitable.[49] The convention in session at Philadelphia in 1844 renewed hope of peaceful settlement by disavowing fellowship with abolition societies, but the New Hampshire Baptist Convention quickly blasted this hope by officially disapproving slaveholders as missionaries. As a test case, Georgia Baptists recommended that the Baptist Home Missionary Society

[47] *Christian Index,* Penfield, Ga., Jan. 29, 1841.
[48] *Biblical Recorder,* Raleigh, N. C., June 13, 1841.
[49] *Religious Herald,* Richmond, March 14, 1844.

appoint James E. Reeves, a slaveholder, as a missionary. After his rejection Thomas Meredith was the only Baptist editor of the South Atlantic States who favored delaying the formation of a Southern organization. He wanted to give the Triennial Convention itself an opportunity to act.[50]

Meantime, the Foreign Mission Board of the Triennial Convention, in reply to a question from the Alabama Baptist Convention, had insisted that it would not send out a slaveholder as a missionary. While the answer was pending, Joseph S. Baker of Georgia commended the Alabama Convention for requiring the board to state its position and with great concern asked, "What position will Virginia take? The North seem to think that they can keep her in tow." Sands allayed his fears:

> Virginia will never sever herself from the South, on this question. . . . But we do not intend to be precipitate. . . . If the Board do appoint a slaveholder, our brethren in Georgia and Alabama have been too hasty. If they refuse, the act of breaking asunder the North and South will be their own. . . . But we can assure brother [*sic*] B. . . . Whilst we have the control of the Herald, we shall unwaveringly defend and advocate the interests of this portion of the confederacy.[51]

The action taken by Virginia when the reply of the Foreign Mission Board became known indicates that Sands voiced accurately the sentiments of Virginia Baptists. The Board of the Virginia Baptist Missionary Society withdrew from the Foreign Mission Board and recommended the holding of a meeting in Augusta, Georgia, in May, 1845, of all who were aggrieved. The object of the meeting would be the formation of a Southern organization. Sands gave the *Christian Index* credit for having suggested some months earlier the creation of a Southern Convention.[52]

As Southern Baptists moved to implement this suggestion only the *Biblical Recorder* demurred. "We must be permitted to say," wrote Meredith, "that this whole matter, from beginning to end—from the Alabama resolutions to the Virginia circular, is a most unnecessary, if not a most unwise and hurtful proceeding."[53] Sands regretted on April 3, 1845, that Meredith was causing North Carolina to remain aloof after the other Southeastern States had fallen

[50] *Biblical Recorder,* Raleigh, N. C., Nov. 2, 1844.
[51] *Religious Herald,* Richmond, Dec. 26, 1844.
[52] *Ibid.,* March 13, 1845.
[53] *Biblical Recorder,* Raleigh, N. C., March 29, 1845.

in line. Two weeks later he devoted six columns to the attempt to convert Meredith, pointing out that abolitionists regarded him as an apologist:

> He must perceive that the South, except North Carolina, which has not yet spoken, think further co-operation impossible, and a Southern Convention desirable. . . . Under these circumstances, will not brother [*sic*] M. withdraw his opposition—lay aside his views, . . . and lend us his aid in forming an active and efficient Southern organization.[54]

Baker's leading editorial for April 25, 1845, offered to Meredith impressive evidence that fanaticism in the North continued to increase. He wrote regarding Meredith:

> Really it seems to us, while our brother's heart appears to be right, his usually clear mind is suffering from some extraordinary obscuration. For our part we never were *cooler* in our life; nor have we discovered, in any of the proceedings at the South induced by the action of the Boston Board, any scintillations of an undue excitement.[55]

Meredith gradually accepted the prevailing view. In his principal editorial for April 26, 1845, entitled "We Will Not Oppose," he stated that since many readers had asked him not to oppose the projected Southern organization he would co-operate even though he preferred union if it could be had on "honorable terms." The Southern Baptist Convention was organized in Augusta as proposed and Meredith became a loyal advocate.

Formation of the Methodist Episcopal Church, South

The same type of sectional agitation that produced the Baptist schism also divided the Methodist Episcopal Church in 1845. Many Northern Methodists had become critical of slavery by 1837, but Southern leaders, of whom William Capers, editor of the *Southern Christian Advocate,* was a spokesman, opposed a division of the denomination. He wrote:

> In the present state of the country we believe it to be of the utmost importance to the country itself, that the churches be kept together. Let the bonds be once severed which hold the churches of the North and South together, and the union of these states will be more than endangered, it will presently be rent asunder.[56]

[54] *Religious Herald,* Richmond, April 17, 1845.
[55] *Christian Index,* Penfield, Ga., April 25, 1845.
[56] *Southern Christian Advocate,* Charleston, Dec. 8, 1837.

But Capers's wrath was aroused two years later by an article in *Zion's Watchman* of New York. Written by a Northern Methodist preacher who had spent the winter as the guest of a family in Georgetown, South Carolina, the article described the alleged mistreatment of slaves by several South Carolina families. Capers said he knew these families to be of "unexceptionable standing in the best society" and asked what would be the results of such outrageous attacks upon them:

Shall men come among us from the North, disclaiming abolitionism for a cloak of maliciousness, and in the sacred character of ministers of the Gospel, enter our families and partake of our hospitality that they may go home with their mouths full of abominable lies, to publish our names and our wives' names in characters as black as their own hearts? Is this to be endured?[57]

As charges and countercharges continued to fly, the Anti-Slavery Convention of the New England Methodist Conference adopted resolutions denouncing slavery as a sin and stating that "reformation or division" were the only alternatives. This provoked William M. Wightman to declare himself in favor of division if the General Conference adopted regulations critical of slavery:

We shall, however, wait. . . . It is believed by some, that it is the wish especially of the radico-abolitionists, to torment us till we are driven to secession. This might save them a deal of trouble, . . . but we shall scarcely afford them any such gratification, so long as there is no attempt at invading our constitutional rights.[58]

After the General Conference in session at New York in May, 1844, upheld the decision of the Baltimore Conference suspending a minister who refused to free his slaves, the columns of the *Richmond Christian Advocate* and the *Southern Christian Advocate* were filled with resolutions of individuals and ecclesiastical bodies in the South favoring a separate organization. Wightman came out unreservedly for separation in an editorial entitled "The Separation Necessary and Justifiable." He now held an optimistic view of its political consequences:

The prospect for peace and amicable relations, is infinitely better with a separation than under a forced and nominal union. And if so, the safety of the country is to a much greater extent bound up with a division of the church, than a continued union. The

[57] *Ibid.,* Dec. 6, 1839.
[58] *Ibid.,* March 10, 1843.

division of the Methodist Church will demonstrate this fact to the country, that Southern forbearance has its limits, and that a vigorous and united resistance will be made at all costs, to the spread of the pseudo-religious phrenzy called abolitionism. Thus a check will be put upon a movement which, more than all other causes of discord put together, threatens the political union.[59]

Delegates from the Southern states met in Louisville, Kentucky, on May 1, 1845, to separate formally and organize the Methodist Episcopal Church, South.

Growth and Expansion during the Forties

Although the Baptist and Methodist schisms held the spotlight during the late thirties and early forties, a number of new religious periodicals concerned primarily with other matters appeared. In the *Southern Churchman,* founded at Richmond by William F. Lee in 1835, Episcopalians, whose papers had much less to say about slavery than those of Baptists and Methodists, had a weekly comparable in circulation to the weeklies of the larger denominations. Transferred to Alexandria, Virginia, about 1840, this paper appeared under a succession of able editors until the close of the Civil War. It had to be returned to Richmond during the war and is now published there. The Diocese of Virginia, acknowledging in 1848 the "importance of weekly religious papers in the present condition of the Church," recommended the *Southern Churchman* to the "confidence and patronage of the Diocese," and urged members to use every effort to increase its circulation.[60] The only other prominent Episcopal weekly in the South Atlantic States was the *Church Intelligencer,* founded later at Raleigh, North Carolina.

Through the pages of the *Christian Warrior,* founded at Richmond in 1842, Daniel D. Smith, a champion of Universalism, defied the religious press of Richmond to prove the validity of the doctrine of never-ending punishment.[61] William H. Hughart established the *Western Baptist* to further the cause of the Disciples of Christ in Southwestern Virginia. James Boyce launched the *Christian Magazine of the South* in an effort to weld together the three thousand Associate Reformed Presbyterians scattered over

[59] *Ibid.,* Nov. 22, 1844.

[60] *Journal of the Convention of the Protestant Episcopal Church, in the Diocese of Virginia,* 1848, p. 49.

[61] *Christian Warrior,* Richmond, May 28, 1842.

the South. William H. Barnwell sought to strengthen the Episcopal Church in South Carolina by making his newly founded *Episcopal Protestant* "decidedly evangelical and protestant" in tone.

Two important family newspapers appeared in 1844—the *Christian Intelligencer* and the *Christian Sun*. The former was founded in Charlottesville, Virginia, as the organ of the Disciples of Christ in that state, and under the editorship of R. L. Coleman pursued a more moderate policy toward other denominations than had earlier Disciples of Christ publications. Daniel Wilson Kerr established the *Christian Sun* in Hillsboro, North Carolina, to further the interests of the North Carolina and Virginia Christian Conference. Kerr had been associated for a time with James O'Kelly, one of the founders of the Christian Church.[62] Transferred to Virginia in 1855, the *Christian Sun* is still published in the interests of the Southeastern Convention of Congregational and Christian Churches.

By the end of the forties most of the principal denominations had effected the establishment of an official or unofficial organ for each state. Among the Methodists the weeklies owned by the denomination formed official organs of communication, while most privately owned periodicals lacked both official and unofficial standing. Although privately owned, most major publications issued by members of other denominations were adopted by church bodies as their unofficial organs. Only a small number of non-Methodist publications failed to obtain endorsement of some kind from church bodies.

Seldom was there open rivalry between the denominational organs, official or unofficial, and the purely private ventures. Often the latter, though published in the same state, were too remote or too weak to challenge the primacy of established journals. Western Virginia Baptists, for instance, did not hurt the *Religious Herald* with their repeated efforts to publish papers in their part of the state. One of these publications was the *Baptist Recorder*, edited during the late forties by Joseph L. Walker in Fairmont. It was followed by Simeon Siegfried's *Mountain Messenger and Baptist Recorder*, Morgantown, which, by including columns of general news, managed to survive a decade even though it had only

[62] J. Pressley Barrett, ed., *The Centennial of Religious Journalism, 1808-1908* (2nd ed.; Dayton, Ohio, 1908), p. 357.

four hundred subscribers the first year. J. L. Reynolds and H. K. Ellyson published the *Baptist Guardian* in Richmond for a year, advertising it as a religious family newspaper, not the organ of any group and not designed to hurt the *Religious Herald*.[63] Two North Carolinians established Baptist papers in areas where few subscribed to the *Biblical Recorder* and after the death of its publisher gave their subscription lists to his widow. These were W. E. Mann, who published the *Baptist Messenger* in Elizabeth City, and James McDaniel, whose *Religious and General Intelligencer* flourished in Wilmington for two years.[64]

Circulation in 1850

The earliest year in which circulation figures can be studied with some degree of thoroughness is 1850, when the federal census enumerators began gathering this information.[65] Most publications were launched with a few hundred subscribers. Some soon became self-supporting; others lost part of their original patronage. The two extremes in circulation were two hundred and fourteen thousand. Joseph S. Baker issued the first number of the *Baptist Chronicle* without a subscriber but finally secured about two hundred.[66] The *Home and Foreign Journal*, published by the Southern Baptist Convention at twenty-five cents a year, attained the fourteen-thousand mark.[67]

The average circulation increased from decade to decade, reaching the highest figure just before and during the Civil War. The twenty-eight religious newspapers and magazines appearing in the South Atlantic States in 1850, which may be regarded as an average year for the period 1830-1865, had 49,381 subscribers, an average of 1,764 for each publication.[68] Subscribers were distributed among the denominations as follows:

[63] *Baptist Guardian*, Richmond, Dec. 15, 1847.

[64] *Biblical Recorder*, Raleigh, N. C., Jan. 25, 1851.

[65] The printed returns for 1850 and 1860 give only total circulation figures for newspapers and magazines, but Joseph C. G. Kennedy's "Catalogue of the Newspapers and Periodicals Published in the United States, Showing the Town and County in which the Same are Published, how often Issued, their Character, and Circulation. Compiled from the United States Census Statistics of 1850," published in *Livingston's Law Register for 1852* (New York, 1852), contains circulation figures for individual publications.

[66] *Christian Index*, Penfield, Ga., May 7, 1841.

[67] *Home and Foreign Journal*, Richmond, X (Aug., 1860), 7.

[68] At the same time, the *Macedonian*, Baptist missionary monthly published in Boston, had 30,000 subscribers; the *Pilot*, the *Puritan Recorder*, and the

Denomination	Number of Periodicals	Average Circulation
Baptist	12	1,929
Catholic	1	700
Christian	1	825
Disciples	2	4,000
Episcopal	2	775
Methodist	3	2,400
Presbyterian	5	1,300
Unclassified	2	725

The population of the South Atlantic States in 1850 totaled 4,752,837. There was, therefore, disregarding the few who resided outside the area, one subscriber to a religious periodical in every ninety-six persons. No direct relation existed between the numerical strength of a denomination and the number or circulation of its publications. Among the major denominations the Presbyterians had the largest number of publications and subscribers in proportion to numerical strength, the Baptists were second, the Methodists third. Although the Presbyterians fell short of their aim of placing a church paper in every Presbyterian home, there were 6,500 subscribers among the 35,476 communicants in 1850, a ratio of one to 5.46.[69] The ratio of subscribers to communicants among all denominations in 1850 was about one to ten.

The Prosperous Fifties

From 1850 until the Civil War the publishers of religious newspapers and magazines shared in the general prosperity of the times. During the decade of the fifties, forty-two new publications were added to the twenty-eight appearing in 1850. Those that survived enjoyed steadily growing subscription lists. Among the newcomers to the field of religious journalism were J. I. Bonner and John Oliver Lindsay. They were able to publish the *Erskine Miscellany* (later *Due West Telescope*) as the unofficial organ of

Christian Watchman, all published in Boston, had 15,000, 10,500, and 10,200 respectively. There were many Northern religious papers with smaller circulation figures, of course, but the average greatly exceeded that of Southern papers. Western publications had about the same number of subscribers as their Southern contemporaries. See Kennedy, "Catalogue of Newspapers and Periodicals," 1850.

The average circulation of the 148 political newspapers published in the South Atlantic States in 1850 was 872. See *Seventh Census of the United States: 1850* (Washington, 1853), pp. 283, 324, 348, 384, 409.

[69] *Minutes of the General Assembly of the Presbyterian Church in the United States of America,* 1851, *passim.*

the Southern Associate Reformed Presbyterian Synod throughout the decade despite a small constituency. Three newspapers appeared in Western North Carolina at different times in support of the Western North Carolina Baptist Convention, an organization independent of the North Carolina Baptist State Convention. They were the *North Carolina Baptist,* Asheville; the *Carolina Baptist,* Hendersonville; and the *Baptist Telescope,* Hendersonville.

The General Conference of the Methodist Episcopal Church, South, in 1850 provided for the publication of a Sunday school paper as a substitute for the *Sunday School Advocate,* published in the North. The new paper was the *Sunday School Visitor,* published in Charleston from 1851 until 1855, when it was transferred to Nashville.[70] In 1851 Sidney D. Bumpass founded the *Weekly Message* in Greensboro, North Carolina, to promote piety and morality among Methodists. Although Bumpass soon died and his paper never received the official endorsement of a Methodist conference, it continued to appear, under his widow's editorship, until 1871. After the demise of the *Charleston Gospel Messenger and Protestant Episcopal Register,* G. P. Gadsden and J. H. Elliott founded the *Southern Episcopalian* as a register of ecclesiastical intelligence and defender of the Episcopal Church.[71] The *Religious Telescope,* published in Dayton, Ohio, as the official organ of the United Brethren, having offended Virginia readers by printing abolition material, W. M'K. Cain and M. Michael founded the *Virginia Telescope* at West Columbia as the unofficial organ of Virginia Brethren.[72]

Between 1856 and the Civil War four outstanding family religious weeklies were founded either as successors to older papers or as new state papers. The *Central Presbyterian* succeeded the *Watchman and Observer* at Richmond in 1856. Explaining why they were launching the paper, the editors wrote: "In the threatening aspect of political affairs, . . . it is very important that we should have an organ of communication with our people, that will be under our control, watchful of our interests, and faithful to those great *conservative* principles that underlie all our institutions." They chose the title of their paper from the fact that

[70] *Sunday School Visitor,* Charleston, Jan. 1, 1851.
[71] *Southern Episcopalian,* Charleston, I (April, 1854), 46.
[72] *Virginia Telescope,* West Columbia, Va., Jan. 25, 1855.

their "political and geographical position" was "central between the extreme North and extreme South," a fact which they felt gave them heavy responsibilities as peacemakers.[73]

Long dependent on others for religious newspapers, the North Carolina Annual Conference of the Methodist Episcopal Church, South, finally in the fifties established its own weekly. Called the *North Carolina Christian Advocate* and edited by Rufus T. Heflin, the first number was published in Raleigh on January 4, 1856. The youngest of the official Methodist newspapers, it soon equaled the others in subscribers and influence.[74] Except for a short time in the twenties, North Carolina Presbyterians published no paper of their own until George McNeill established the *North Carolina Presbyterian* at Fayetteville in 1858. This paper quickly gained a position comparable to that of the *Central Presbyterian* of Richmond and the *Southern Presbyterian* of Charleston. The last of the large ante-bellum weeklies to appear was the *Church Intelligencer,* founded March 14, 1860, in Raleigh, North Carolina, by Frederick Fitzgerald. Although privately owned, this paper became the "accredited organ" of ten Southern bishops of the Protestant Episcopal Church and the "special advocate" of the University of the South, Sewanee, Tennessee.[75]

During the late fifties Georgia Baptists were sharply divided on the question whether the use of conventions and boards instead of individual churches as agencies for missionary operations was proper. When the publishing committee of the *Christian Index,* Georgia Baptist state paper, declined to take a stand in favor of the Southern Baptist Convention's plan to use boards, Joseph L. Walker, editor of the *Christian Index,* resigned and entered religious journalism with his own publication, the *Baptist Champion.*[76] Meantime "Old Landmark" Baptists, as opponents of conventions and boards were often called, had established a powerful organ in Georgia. This was the *Landmark Banner and Cherokee Baptist,* launched by Jesse M. Wood at Rome, Georgia, as the organ of the Cherokee Baptist Convention, which was located in Northwestern Georgia and not a part of the Georgia Baptist State Convention. Moved to Atlanta, where the title was shortened to

[73] *Central Presbyterian,* Richmond, Jan. 5, 1856.

[74] *North Carolina Christian Advocate,* Raleigh, N. C., June 17, 1863.

[75] *Church Intelligencer,* Raleigh, N. C., Nov. 1, 1860.

[76] *Baptist Champion,* Macon, Ga., Aug. 15, 1859.

Banner and Baptist, this paper, with two thousand subscribers, survived until 1865.[77]

Secession

In the early thirties, when the sectional conflict over abolition began to grow bitter, writers in the Southern religious press had predicted that Northern fanaticism would eventually plunge the nation into bloody conflict. This conviction grew stronger as the decades passed and other sectional disputes developed. The thirty-one religious newspapers and magazines published in the South Atlantic States in 1860 had an average of 3,590 subscribers. The religious press was, therefore, in a position to exert considerable influence on Southern thought by the slant it gave to religious and other news. Readers of religious newspapers who depended on the general news columns and editorials of their church papers to keep them informed subscribed to no secular newspaper.

Relative to the Kansas question, some writers in the religious press wanted assurance of the extension of slavery into that area, while others were willing to leave the matter to popular sovereignty. The former included Benjamin Gildersleeve, venerable Presbyterian editor. In reply to the tirade of a Northern paper against a public meeting in Griffin, Georgia, for the purpose of encouraging Southern emigration to Kansas he asked, "Has not Georgia just as good a right to interfere with the settlement of Kansas as New York or Massachusetts? Does Kansas belong to the Northern Emigrant Aid Society?"[78] D. Francis Sprigg, an Episcopal editor, supported the proposal of William C. Rives that the question be settled by the "free and sovereign decision of the *bona fide* inhabitants of the Territory."[79] Another Presbyterian wrote regarding Henry Ward Beecher, "though all may pity, no one will take umbrage at the frothy fury of the demented Beecher, afflicted as he is with a moral leprosy which renders him at once unclean and frantic."[80]

The general reaction of the religious press to the Harper's Ferry Insurrection was calm. W. B. Wellons, a Christian editor, thought that the South should be on guard against the embryonic John Browns in its midst, but he had "no sympathy or patience with that

[77] *Banner and Baptist,* Atlanta, July 12, 1862.
[78] *Watchman and Observer,* Richmond, Oct. 11, 1855.
[79] *Southern Churchman,* Alexandria, Va., June 27, 1856.
[80] *Central Presbyterian,* Richmond, April 5, 1856.

foolish and senseless fear and fright, which rests continually on the minds of some Southerners in reference to insurrection and rebellion among the slaves."[81]

With the dawn of the election year of 1860, the *Central Presbyterian* called upon Christians of all denominations, who were said to constitute one-third of the population, to stop the insane folly which was about to loose the helldogs of war by placing the government in the "criminal hands" of the Republican party. The writer charged "every Christian man, whether lawmaker, or executor, or voter" to "carry his Christian conscience, enlightened by God's word, into his political duty."[82] Rufus T. Heflin, a Methodist editor who regretted that supporters of Breckenridge and Douglas were "wasting the strength of the South in party feuds," wanted the entire South to unite for Breckinridge.[83]

When the results of the election became known, some writers wanted an immediate dissolution of the union, some preferred to await an overt act, while others advanced additional proposals. George McNeill, for example, recommended social, commercial, and literary independence for the South, a program which would not involve the sacrifice of life or property.[84] Frederick Fitzgerald informed Northern Episcopalians that the personal liberty laws passed by the Northern states must be repealed if the South remained in the union: "We simply demand our constitutional rights, which we would prefer to keep *in peace,* but which we will have."[85] A South Carolinian, in the earliest article found in a religious publication that definitely approved secession, wrote just prior to December 17 that "disunion is the only escape from destruction."[86]

The religious press of Virginia urged readers to avoid hasty action.[87] A North Carolina editor felt that the rights of the South could be more easily maintained in the union, but "in any event we stand or fall with the honest Old North State. . . . She will

[81] *Christian Sun,* Suffolk, Va., Oct. 28, 1859.

[82] *Central Presbyterian,* Richmond, Jan. 7, 1860.

[83] *North Carolina Christian Advocate,* Raleigh, N. C., Sept. 25, 1860.

[84] *North Carolina Presbyterian,* Fayetteville, N. C., Nov. 24, 1860.

[85] *Church Intelligencer,* Raleigh, N. C., Dec. 6, 1860.

[86] *Southern Episcopalian,* Charleston, VII (Dec., 1860), 488.

[87] *Zion's Advocate,* Front Royal, Va., Dec. 15, 1860. See also *Religious Herald,* Richmond, Dec. 20, 1860.

hold to the union as long as there is hope, but when she gives it up, it will be forever!"[88]

Lincoln's inaugural removed all hope of an honorable compromise. When he called for troops, George McNeill announced dramatically that war had begun: "Our Southern brethren cannot avoid the conflict. It has been forced upon them by a fanatical and wicked government." In reply to a question regarding what North Carolina should do he wrote:

> Without assuming to speak for others, (though we doubtless reflect the opinions of 4/5 of the clergy and membership of the Southern Presbyterian church) we say that the South should unite for the sake of the South, for the sake of peace, humanity and religion, of our soil, our honor, and our slaves, and that all the Slave States should make common cause in this, the hour of their extremity.[89]

The editor of the *Southern Churchman* justified the secession of Virginia by the right of revolution.[90]

Every editor of religious periodicals in the South Atlantic States had opposed secession until it became a reality. South Carolina and Georgia editors expressed their approval either a few days before or immediately after the secession of their states; most North Carolina and Virginia editors announced approval when Lincoln called for troops; the remainder waited until after secession. Once the union had been divided, the religious press, with the exception of two border publications,[91] threw its support behind the Southern war effort. Some editors urged readers to forget their differing views on secession and follow the Scriptural injunction to submit to those actually in authority. Others wrote of the positive duty of Christians to defend their religion, homes, and institutions.

The War Years

Among the first publications to feel the impact of war was the *Christian Observer,* which had been formed by merging the *Southern Religious Telegraph,* Richmond, with the *Philadelphia Observer* and had been published in the latter place from 1839 until 1861. Amasa Converse, the editor and publisher, had re-

[88] *North Carolina Christian Advocate,* Raleigh, N. C., Jan. 8, 1861.

[89] *North Carolina Presbyterian,* Fayetteville, N. C., April 20, 1861.

[90] *Southern Churchman,* Alexandria, Va., April 26, 1861.

[91] *The Christian Banner,* Fredericksburg, Va., and the *Millennial Harbinger,* Bethany, Va.

tained his Southern views throughout the period of exile. On August 22, 1861, a United States marshal, on order of President Lincoln, closed the office of the *Christian Observer* and confiscated its property because Converse objected to the North waging war against the South. Converse fled to the Confederate States, and the United Synod of Virginia "hailed with joy" the resumption of his paper in Richmond.[92]

Other publishers encountered no difficulties of this nature. In fact, the war years saw the religious press in the South Atlantic States reach its peak both in number of publications and in total circulation. When the war began, thirty-one religious newspapers and magazines were being published in this region. Sixteen of these survived until 1865, the fifteen casualties being replaced by twenty new publications founded between 1861 and 1864.

The *Evangelical Pulpit* appeared at Forsyth, Georgia, in 1861 to publish sermons by the ablest living evangelical ministers in the Confederate States. Cut off from Northern periodicals, a group of Charleston Lutherans founded the *Southern Lutheran,* which proved to be the only journal published in the Confederacy by members of the denomination. Under the motto "Endeavoring to keep the unity of the spirit in the bond of peace," N. Aldrich and John Bachman, the principal editors, worked for a Southern Lutheran Church that would include all synods in the Confederate States whether or not they had formerly been connected with the old General Synod.[93]

Three children's papers sprang up and flourished. The war having deprived Southern Presbyterians of Sunday school papers published in the North, the Committee of Publication of the Presbyterian Church in the Confederate States in 1862 established the *Children's Friend* at Richmond. By the next year this highly successful publication had attained a circulation of ten thousand.[94] Samuel Boykin, editor of the *Christian Index,* founded the *Child's Index* at Macon, Georgia, as a substitute for Northern papers. Profusely illustrated with engravings, this Baptist publication was

[92] *Christian Observer,* Richmond, Nov. 21, 1861. The Philadelphia property was returned to Henry A. Converse, son of the editor, but he made no effort to revive the paper in Philadelphia except to issue a half-sheet on Oct. 24, 1861, explaining what had happened.

[93] *Southern Lutheran,* Charleston, Sept. 28, 1861.

[94] *Minutes of the General Assembly of the Presbyterian Church in the Confederate States of America,* 1863, p. 173.

as popular as its Presbyterian counterpart in Virginia, attaining a circulation of twelve thousand.[95] Macon, free from imminent danger of attack, was also the location of the *Children's Guide*, an illustrated Methodist Sunday school paper edited by John W. Burke.

The South Carolina Baptist state paper having expired in 1860, J. L. Reynolds and J. M. C. Breaker undertook to fill the gap by issuing a new weekly which they called the *Confederate Baptist*. Adopting a strong pro-Southern tone, they quickly attracted four thousand regular subscribers, who not only paid their subscription charges but weekly sent three thousand additional copies to the Confederate Army as gifts.[96]

During 1863 five religious newspapers designed expressly for members of the armed forces of the Confederacy were founded in the South Atlantic States. A. S. Worrell established the *Soldier's Friend*, a Baptist newspaper, in Atlanta in the intellectual, moral, and religious interest of Confederate soldiers. The Baptist family weeklies of Georgia solicited contributions with which to send the *Soldier's Friend* free to Confederate troops from "Christians, philanthropists, and patrons."[97] The *Army and Navy Messenger*, published by the Evangelical Tract Society of Petersburg, a nonsectarian organization to which General Lee contributed, enjoyed wide popularity. Ten thousand copies of the first number were sent free of charge to members of the armed forces and were reported well received.[98] The prayers, stories, military news, accounts of revivals, moral exhortations, and other items contained in this paper were addressed specifically to privates and sailors.

Two denominational papers designed for soldiers and sent to them free of charge were founded in August, 1863, at Richmond. The Soldier's Tract Association of the Methodist Episcopal Church, South, began the *Soldier's Paper* and the Committee of Publication for the Presbyterian Church in the Confederate States of America launched the *Soldier's Visitor*. Both were distributed

[95] *Child's Index*, Macon, Ga., I (Dec., 1863), 46.

[96] *Confederate Baptist*, Columbia, S. C., June 10, 1863.

[97] *Baptist Banner*, Atlanta, Jan. 31, 1863; *Christian Index*, Macon, Ga., March 18, 1864.

[98] *Army and Navy Messenger*, Petersburg, Va., May 1, 1863. The last issue of the *Army and Navy Messenger* (March 16, 1865), contained the statement that the Evangelical Tract Society had distributed to the Confederate Army 60,000,000 pages of tracts besides Bibles, hymn books, and about 350,000 copies of the *Army and Navy Messenger*.

largely by sending bundles of copies by mail or colporteur to officers and chaplains. Quotations like the Boston *Recorder's* term "punish and destroy" and Grant's order "do all the damage you can . . . let the Shenandoah valley remain a barren waste" tended to keep the Confederate soldier in a fighting frame of mind. An editorial written in February, 1865, gave "several reasons based on the ordinary administration of the divine government over the affairs of men" why the South could still expect to win the war.[99]

The fifth soldier's paper appeared at Macon, Georgia, in September, 1863, under the auspices of the Department of the South-West of the Soldiers' Tract Association of the Methodist Episcopal Church, South. Edited by Robert J. Harp and entitled the *Army and Navy Herald,* this weekly newspaper made an especially vigorous effort to keep up Southern morale.

Long cut off from Northern publications, John Bacon Crenshaw, a Quaker, founded the *Southern Friend* at Richmond, October 1, 1864, as a substitute for the Philadelphia *Friend* but not in opposition to it. Crenshaw attempted to lay before his readers accurate statements of Confederate military regulations relating to conscientious objectors.

The last new publication known to have been founded before the close of the war was the *Pacificator,* a Catholic newspaper issued in Augusta, Georgia, by Patrick Walsh and L. T. Blome. The editors first made clear the fact that they believed in secession, pledging themselves to the support of Southern independence. A statement of their basic purpose appeared in "An Address to the People of the United States" in which the continuation of the war against the South was pronounced unjust, unbecoming, and ruinous, and which closed with an appeal to Northern Catholics "to withdraw their aid and encouragement from the wicked war upon the South."[100]

Religious newspapers and magazines had survived the rigors of war surprisingly well. In 1860 newly established and old publications in the South Atlantic States had totaled thirty-one. As the year 1865 dawned twenty-eight such periodicals were being published. Of these, sixteen were well-established journals of some years standing, twelve had been founded during the war. A larger percentage of religious newspapers and magazines than of

[99] *Soldier's Visitor,* Richmond, II (Feb., 1865), 26.
[100] *Pacificator,* Augusta, Ga., Oct. 8, 1864.

other types survived the war.[101] This may be attributed to the following: since many publishers owned printing equipment, publishing costs were lower; editors worked for little or no compensation; much patriotic enthusiasm was generated by sending free copies to the armed forces of the Confederacy; and many subscribers probably felt a moral obligation to continue subscriptions to the church paper even if it meant giving up another. In view of their high rate of survival in difficult times, the conclusion that these publications satisfied the wants of readers appears justifiable.

That survival in wartime was far from easy is indicated by the descriptions of the troubles of editors and publishers which appeared in their papers. The *Southern Lutheran* of Charleston warned readers on November 2, 1861, that since most members of the staff were volunteers publication would be suspended if fighting occurred in the vicinity. Two weeks later John Bachman, an editor who was over seventy, got out a half-sheet explaining that participation by the business agent, treasurer, printers, and the other editor in the Battle of Hilton Head had interfered with regular publication. Printing paper was often obtained only with great difficulty. The editor of the *North Carolina Christian Advocate,* for instance, deeply regretted the burning in 1863 of the paper mill at Bath, North Carolina, and urged readers to sell rags to the remaining mills.[102] He complained on July 1, 1863, that paper could not be bought at any price but that he had been able to secure from private sources enough for a small half-sheet.

When in 1864 the price of the *Southern Lutheran* had to be advanced to $8 a year for a half-sheet the publisher itemized the weekly cost of getting out his 2,800 copies as follows: three reams of printing paper, $150; printing, $225; and mailing clerk, $15. This equalled 14¢ a copy or $7.28 a year, which allowed little for the editors' services and for losses from nonpaying subscribers.[103] Although the *Southern Presbyterian* had four thousand paying subscribers at the time, prices rose so rapidly in 1864 that it had

[101] Lester J. Cappon, *Virginia Newspapers, 1821-1935: A Bibliography with Historical Introduction and Notes* ("Guide to Virginia Historical Materials," Part I; New York: D. Appleton-Century Company, 1936), pp. 17-18. See also William Stanley Hoole, *A Check-List and Finding-List of Charleston Periodicals, 1732-1864* (Durham, N. C.: Duke University Press, 1936), pp. 4-5, and Mott, *American Magazines,* I, 138-139.

[102] *North Carolina Christian Advocate,* Raleigh, N. C., April 16, 1863.

[103] *Southern Lutheran,* Charleston, Aug. 25, 1864.

to be suspended for lack of cash with which to operate. At ten dollars for six months the subscription price was eight times the original charge but prices in general were twenty times as high as before the war. The editor appealed for donations.[104]

As the war drew to a close in the spring of 1865, publishers were compelled by the lack of materials, the loss of their offices by fire, the destruction of their presses by hostile armies, or the lack of mail service to suspend or abandon their publications. The general family weeklies went down last, generally as the direct result of actual devastation. Eight of the twenty-eight newspapers and magazines being published at the beginning of 1865 had breathed their last by the end of the war, but the other twenty, of which ten still survive today, were resurrected within a few months or years to form the nucleus around which the religious press of the new era developed.

[104] *Southern Presbyterian,* Augusta, Ga., Oct. 6, 1864.

Key to Symbols Used in Locating Files

Cappon	Lester J. Cappon, *Virginia Newspapers 1821-1935: A Bibliography with Historical Introduction and Notes* ("Guide to Virginia Historical Materials," Part I; New York: D. Appleton-Century Company, 1936).
DLC	Library of Congress, Washington, D. C.
GU	University of Georgia, Athens, Ga.
Hoole	William Stanley Hoole, *A Check-List and Finding-List of Charleston Periodicals 1732-1864* (Durham, N. C.: Duke University Press, 1936).
MWA	American Antiquarian Society, Worcester, Mass.
Nc	North Carolina State Library, Raleigh, N. C.
NcD	Duke University, Durham, N. C.
NcMHi	Historical Foundation of the Presbyterian and Reformed Churches, Montreat, N. C.
NcR	North Carolina Department of Archives and History, Raleigh, N. C.
NcU	University of North Carolina, Chapel Hill, N. C.
NcW	Wake Forest College, Wake Forest, N. C.
NcWiA	Archives of North Carolina Disciples of Christ, Wilson, N. C.
PCA	American Baptist Historical Society, Chester, Pa.
PCC	Crozer Theological Seminary, Chester, Pa.
PPL	Library Company of Philadelphia, Philadelphia, Pa.
PPPrHi	Presbyterian Historical Society, Philadelphia, Pa.
ScChC	Charleston Library Society, Charleston, S. C.
ScCoL	Lutheran Theological Seminary, Columbia, S. C.

ScDE	Erskine College, Due West, S. C.
ScGF	Furman University, Greenville, S. C.
ScN	Newberry College, Newberry, S. C.
ScSW	Wofford College, Spartanburg, S. C.
ScU	University of South Carolina, Columbia, S. C.
U.L.N.	Winifred Gregory, ed., *American Newspapers 1821-1936: A Union List of Files Available in the United States and Canada* (New York: The H. W. Wilson Company, 1937).
U.L.S.	Winifred Gregory, ed., *Union List of Serials in Libraries of the United States and Canada* (2nd ed.; New York: The H. W. Wilson Company, 1943).
U.L.S. (1)	Gabrielle E. Malikoff, ed., *Union List of Serials in Libraries of the United States and Canada* (2nd ed., supplement, January 1941–December 1943; New York: The H. W. Wilson Company, 1945).
V	Virginia State Library, Richmond, Va.
VRB	Virginia Baptist Historical Society, Richmond, Va.
VRC	Confederate Library and Museum, Richmond, Va.
VRF	Foreign Mission Board of the Southern Baptist Convention, Richmond, Va.
VRT	Union Theological Seminary, Richmond, Va.
VRU	University of Richmond, Richmond, Va.
VU	University of Virginia, Charlottesville, Va.

Annotated Bibliography

Advocate for the Testimony of God, as It Is Written in the Books of Nature and Revelation. *See* Apostolic Advocate.

American Baptist Memorial, a Statistical, Biographical and Historical Magazine, of the Baptist Denomination, and of the Whole Christian World

Richmond. Jan., 1855–Dec., 1856.[1] Monthly. Octavo, 32 pp. $1 a year.

Editors: John Lansing Burrows, 1855;[2] Basil Manly, Jr., 1856.[3]

Proprietors: M. Semple, 1855; Manly, 1856.

The avowed objective of the editors and proprietors was the maintenance of a medium of communication "between all sections of our land." The magazine, wrote the editor, "will not be local, sectional, or controversial." Controversy was avoided and there were subscribers in all the states of the union. In addition to features suggested by the title, there were articles on church architecture, polity, discipline, and doctrines; also sermons, book reviews, announcements, and miscellany. Burrows was especially interested in church architecture, and his articles on that subject included drawings.

U.L.S., 2nd ed., p. 117; (1), p. 49.

Other holdings: PCA 1855-1856. NcW March–Dec., 1855; 1856. VRB 1855-1856.

[1] This periodical, which had been founded in 1842 in New York, was removed at the close of 1854 from Philadelphia to Richmond, where H. K. Ellyson became the printer. At the close of 1856 Basil Manly, Jr., then the owner, transferred the unprofitable enterprise to Hiram F. Reed, who continued it from Philadelphia as the *Baptist Family Magazine*. See *American Baptist Memorial,* XV (Dec., 1856), cover.

[2] Burrows (1814-1893) was born in New York and educated at Union College and Andover Theological Seminary. In 1854 he left a Philadelphia pastorate to become pastor of the First Baptist Church, Richmond. See Cathcart,

Baptist Encyclopaedia, p. 169, and Taylor, *Virginia Baptist Ministers,* series 4, pp. 170-186.

[3] Manly, born in Charleston in 1825, was a graduate of the University of Alabama and of Princeton Theological Seminary. He preceded Burrows as pastor of the First Baptist Church, Richmond; was later principal of the Richmond Female Institute and professor in the Southern Baptist Theological Seminary. See Taylor, *Virginia Baptist Ministers,* series 4, pp. 139-150.

AMERICAN CHRISTIAN PREACHER AND DISCIPLES' MISCELLANY. *See* CHRISTIAN FRIEND

APOSTOLIC ADVOCATE

APOSTOLIC ADVOCATE, AND PROPHETIC INTERPRETER

ADVOCATE FOR THE TESTIMONY OF GOD, AS IT IS WRITTEN IN THE BOOKS OF NATURE AND REVELATION[1]

Richmond, May, 1834–Oct., 1836; Liberty, Amelia Co., Va., Nov., 1836–(April), 1839. May 1, 1834–(April), 1839.[2] Monthly. Duodecimo, 24 pp.; 36 pp. $1 a year. 1,500 subscribers.[3]

Editor and proprietor: John Thomas.[4]

This Christadelphian magazine, devoted to the "Ancient Gospel" as interpreted by Thomas, attacked the practices of other sects and attempted to launch a "Reformation." From 1837 until 1839 Thomas and Alexander Campbell, editor of the *Millennial Harbinger,* assaulted each other violently in their respective publications. Each reprinted the other's articles before attempting to disprove their validity. Although most of the space in the *Apostolic Advocate* was given to doctrinal controversy, there were several accounts of the progress of the Christadelphian "Reformation."

U.L.S., 2nd ed., p. 43; (1), p. 17, as *Advocate for the Testimony. . . .*

Other holdings: NcD June–July, 1838; vol. 5, no. 8, 1839. VRB Oct., 1834.

[1] First title used May, 1834–April, 1836; second, May, 1836–April, 1837; third, May, 1837–(April), 1839.

[2] The last issue (vol. V, no. 12), was supposed to appear in April, 1839, but was not published until July and, like several other late numbers, bore no date.

[3] *Apostolic Advocate,* I (March, 1835), 264.

[4] Thomas (1805-1871) was born in London and received the M.D. degree from St. Thomas' Hospital. He migrated to the United States in 1832, practicing medicine in New York and Philadelphia before moving to Richmond in 1834. Although Thomas began his editorial career as a follower of Alexander Campbell, the two disagreed and produced a schism among the Disciples of Christ. Those who followed Thomas adopted the name Christadelphians (Brothers of Christ). See Carroll, *Religious Forces,* p. 89, and *National Cyclopaedia of American Biography,* IV, 61. Thomas moved to Illinois after issu-

ing the last number of the *Advocate* but returned to Virginia to found the *Herald of the Future Age,* Richmond, in 1845. James C. Walker was the printer in Richmond; Thomas had his own press at Liberty.

Arminian Magazine

Rome, Ga. Jan., 1848–Aug., 1849 (?).[1] Monthly. Octavo, 32 pp., 2 cols.

Editor and publisher: Russell Reneau.

This Methodist magazine was founded "for the purpose of hurling back the assaults of the notorious *Calvinistic Magazine,*" a contemporary Presbyterian publication. When Reneau issued his prospectus he was dissatisfied with the defense made by Methodist journals against the *Calvinistic Magazine's* series of widely read articles by Frederick A. Ross entitled the "Great Iron Wheel." By the time of his first number, however, he felt that the charges had been fully met; so he only brought together the materials published by both sides and added a few remarks of his own.[2] His magazine contained, in addition to this controversial material, historical sketches of early Methodism and Methodist preachers.

U.L.S., 2nd ed., p. 328; (1), p. 133.

[1] Suspended March–Dec., 1848. In no. 9 (July, 1849) Reneau announced plans for completing vol. 1 and beginning vol. 2, but he needed more subscribers in order to avoid heavy losses and may not have issued more than the 10 nos. examined.

[2] *Arminian Magazine,* I (Jan., 1848), 18.

Army and Navy Herald

Macon, Ga. Sept. 24, 1863–April 13, 1865. Weekly. Folio, 4-8 pp., 4 cols. $20 a year; free to armed forces of the Confederate States.

Editor: Robert J. Harp.[1]

Proprietor: Department of the South-West, Soldiers' Tract Association, Methodist Episcopal Church, South.[2]

Designed expressly for the armed forces of the Confederate States and supported largely by voluntary contributions, this Methodist paper contained essays intended to boost morale, war news, poetry, selections from the Bible, and moral exhortations.

U.L.N., p. 106.

[1] Harp, a Methodist clergyman, was superintendent of the Department of the South-West of the Soldiers' Tract Association maintained by the Methodist Episcopal Church, South.

[2] John W. Burke, a Methodist minister, was treasurer of the Soldiers' Tract Association and also editor and publisher of the *Children's Guide,* Macon, Ga.

Army and Navy Messenger

Petersburg, Va.[1] May 1, 1863–March 16, 1865.[2] Semimonthly. Folio, 4 pp., 5 cols. Free to armed forces of Confederacy; $4 for 6 months. 10,000 copies.[3]

Editor: Philip Slaughter, May 1, 1863–1864; W. B. Wellons, Dec. 15, 1864–March 16, 1865.[4]

Proprietor: The Evangelical Tract Society of Petersburg.[5]

This nonsectarian newspaper, designed primarily for the use of privates in the Confederate Army, contained morale builders, prayers, military news, poetry, stories, accounts of revivals in the army, and moral exhortations.

U.L.N., p. 705. Cappon, *Virginia Newspapers,* p. 148.

Other holdings: NcD Feb. 1, 1864; Feb. 8, 1865. PCA June 15, 1863. V Jan. 1, 15, Feb. 1, Dec. 15, 1864. VU July 15, 1863.

[1] "This newspaper is printed at the Enquirer Job Office in Richmond, and is dated from Petersburg, from respect to the Evangelical Tract Society there, which endorses it. The headquarters of the editor is at Charlottesville." See *Army and Navy Messenger,* June 15, 1863.

[2] Publication had to be suspended for several months immediately preceding Dec. 15, 1864, when the first number of vol. 2 appeared.

[3] This is the number of copies printed of the first issue.

[4] After Slaughter resigned, Wellons, corresponding secretary of the Evangelical Tract Society and formerly editor of the *Christian Sun* of Petersburg, became editor.

[5] This society, representing all the evangelical denominations in Petersburg and supported by voluntary contributions, was organized July 18, 1861, to supply religious literature for the Confederate Army. General Robert E. Lee contributed $100 toward the establishment of the *Army and Navy Messenger.* See the issue for June 15, 1863, for a copy of his letter to the society.

Banner and Baptist. *See* Landmark Banner and Cherokee Baptist

Banner of the Cross

Columbia, S. C. Nov. 1, 1834–(?).[1] Monthly. Quarto, 8 pp. $1 a year.

Editors and proprietors: Students of the Southern Theological Seminary, Columbia, S. C.

The editors announced as their objectives bringing the Southern Theological Seminary more fully to the notice of the Presbyterian denomination and exciting a deeper interest in missions. Their magazine contained the history of the seminary, descriptions of mission fields, communications, and miscellaneous selections.

Not listed U.L.S.

Holdings: ScU Nov. 1, 1834.

[1] The introductory editorial declared the periodical designed for one year only. No further publication facts known.

Baptist Banner. *See* Landmark Banner and Cherokee Baptist

Baptist Champion

Macon, Ga. July 15, 1859–April 26, 1860.[1] Semimonthly, July 15, 1859–Jan. 1, 1860, $1 a year; weekly, Jan. 12, 1860–April 26, 1860, $2 a year. Quarto, 8 pp., 3 cols. 1200 subscribers.[2]

Editor and proprietor: Joseph Walker.[3]

Georgia Baptists were at this time engaged in one of their many intradenominational wars.[4] Walker, vigorous proponent of the missionary plan of the Southern Baptist Convention, resigned as editor of the *Christian Index* because the publishing committee of the Georgia Baptist State Convention, owner of the paper, refused to raise his salary of $1500. Believing that the time had come, "not simply *to bear witness* to the truth, but *to contend* for the truth," he entered the lists of religious journalism with his own publication.[5] Some months later, after an anti-Graves man had been installed as editor of the *Christian Index,* Walker closed his publication in the interest of denominational harmony.

The *Baptist Champion* was unusually well supplied with original material. Avoiding long selected articles and reviews, it contained church news, especially from Baptist associations, notices, criticisms, disquisitions on morals, and historical sketches. The names of subscribers, most of whom were Georgians, appeared in the receipts column as they paid. Advertisements received little space.

U.L.S., 2nd ed., (1), p. 163.

[1] One volume of 28 numbers completed the publication. The subscription list was sold to Samuel Boykin, who transferred it to the *Christian Index,* Macon, Ga. See *Baptist Champion,* April 26, 1860.

[2] The 1200 subscribers reported in the issue for Aug. 15, 1859, were said to pay the cost of publication but not to provide compensation for the editor.

[3] Walker (1804-1895), born in Pennsylvania, spent most of his life in Virginia, where he attended the University of Virginia and the Virginia Baptist Seminary (now University of Richmond). After the war he lived in the basement of a church and "wrote religious novels for bread and butter." See Taylor, *Virginia Baptist Ministers,* series 4, pp. 263-273.

[4] The "Graves party," named for James Robinson Graves, editor of the *Tennessee Baptist* and leader of the "Old Landmark" Baptists, opposed the use of conventions and boards as agencies for missionary operations. The *Landmark Banner and Cherokee Baptist,* Rome, was their organ in Georgia. The *Christian Index,* Macon, Georgia Baptist state paper, declined, until after the meeting of the Georgia Convention in 1860, to take a bold stand for the Southern Baptist Convention plan to use boards lest it alienate many Georgia Baptists. See *Baptist Champion,* April 19, 1860.

[5] *Baptist Champion,* July 15, 1859.

BAPTIST CHRONICLE AND MONTHLY MONITOR

Columbus, Ga. May, 1840–June, 1841.[1] Monthly. Octavo, 16 pp. $1 a year. 800 subscribers.[2]

Editor and proprietor: Joseph S. Baker.[3]

The editor proposed to impart instruction, describe the state of the church in the South and Southwest, and maintain Baptist doctrines. His special interest was church history; there was no desire to compete with general religious newspapers. The work contained doctrinal essays, historical and biographical sketches, editorials, and miscellany.

U.L.S., 2nd ed., (1), p. 163.

Other holdings: NcD Nov., 1840. NcW May–July, Oct.–Dec., 1840; Jan.–Feb., 1841. VRB May–Sept., Nov.–Dec., 1840; Jan., March–April, June, 1841.

[1] By June, 1841, this magazine was in financial distress; Baker had to announce that suspension would be necessary until he could secure 200 additional subscribers. He complained that many prospective subscribers objected to having the printing done in the North even though he had thereby saved $300 during the past year. See *Baptist Chronicle and Monthly Monitor,* I (June, 1841), 191. Before the close of the year the subscription list was "sold" to the *Baptist Memorial,* New York. See *Christian Index,* Penfield, Ga., Jan. 7, 1842.

[2] *Baptist Chronicle and Monthly Monitor,* I (June, 1841), 191.

[3] Baker (1798-1877), born in Georgia of Presbyterian parents, was graduated from Hampden-Sydney College. He later earned an M.D. degree from Columbian College (now George Washington University), but gave up the practice of medicine for the Baptist ministry. As the editor of several Georgia periodicals he wielded a "trenchant and powerful" pen. See Cathcart, *Baptist Encyclopaedia,* p. 61.

BAPTIST EXPOSITOR AND SOUTH-WESTERN INTELLIGENCER

Columbus, Ga. Oct., 1842–(?).[1] Monthly. Octavo, 32 pp. $1 a year.

Editor and proprietor: Joseph S. Baker.[2]

This magazine, directed to readers in Georgia and Alabama, was designed to contain both explanations of Baptist principles and church news. The specimen number discussed church discipline and church government.

U.L.S., 2nd ed., (1), p. 164.

Other holdings: NcD Oct., 1842.

[1] The Oct., 1842, issue was a specimen and no. 2 was to appear in Feb., 1843, if 500 subscribers had been secured by Jan., 1843. No evidence of a second issue has been found.

[2] See section on *Baptist Chronicle and Monthly Monitor* for sketch of Baker.

BAPTIST GUARDIAN

Richmond. Oct., 1847–Oct. 15, 1848 (?).[1] Semimonthly. Folio, 4 pp., 5 cols. $1 a year.

Editor: J. L. Reynolds.[2]

Publisher: H. K. Ellyson.[3]

Advertised as a religious family newspaper, not the official organ of any group, the *Baptist Guardian* contained religious and secular news, doctrinal discussions, editorials on slavery, poetry, and miscellany.

U.L.S., 2nd ed., (1), p. 164. Cappon, *Virginia Newspapers,* p. 164.

Other holdings: NcW Dec. 15, 1847.

[1] Probably founded Oct. 1, 1847 (Oct. 15, 1847, is vol. 1, no. 2), and published for one year (Oct. 15, 1848, is vol. 1, no. 24). Listed in the *Baptist Almanac and Annual Register,* 1848, p. 32, but not in *ibid.,* 1849.

[2] Reynolds (1812-1877), a Charlestonian, was graduated from the College of Charleston and Newton Theological Seminary. While editor of the *Baptist Guardian* he was pastor of the Second Baptist Church, Richmond. He later became Professor of Latin in South Carolina College. See Cathcart, *Baptist Encyclopaedia,* pp. 975-976.

[3] The Honorable Henry K. Ellyson, Richmond printer and Baptist layman, held many high offices in the city and state as well as in the denomination. He published various religious periodicals. See Cathcart, *Baptist Encyclopaedia,* p. 367.

BAPTIST MESSENGER

Elizabeth City, N. C. July, 1849–June, 1851.[1] Semimonthly. Folio, 4 pp., 6 cols. $1 a year. 650 subscribers.[2]

Editor: Charles R. Hendrickson.[3]

Publisher: W. E. Mann.

A religious family newspaper, the *Baptist Messenger* was designed to serve the Baptists of Northeastern North Carolina, where the *Biblical Recorder,* the leading Baptist paper in the state, did not circulate extensively. The *Baptist Messenger* contained secular as well as religious news, moral essays, stories, poetry, and advertisements. Hendrickson was especially interested in promoting lay and ministerial education.

U.L.S., 2nd ed., (1), p. 164.

Other holdings: NcW Sept. 5, Nov. 5, 20, Dec. 20, 1849; Feb. 5, March 20, Oct. 20, Dec. 20, 1850; March 5, 1851.

[1] The subscription list was transferred to the *Biblical Recorder,* Raleigh, N. C.

[2] Kennedy, "Catalogue of Newspapers and Periodicals" (1850).

[3] Hendrickson, born in New Jersey in 1820, began his ministerial career

as a Methodist but by 1846 was pastor of the First Baptist Church, Norfolk, Va. See Cathcart, *Baptist Encyclopaedia,* pp. 517-518.

BAPTIST PREACHER, ORIGINAL MONTHLY. *See* VIRGINIA BAPTIST PREACHER, ORIGINAL MONTHLY

BAPTIST RECORDER

Fairmont, Va. (now W. Va.). 1847 (?)–1849 (?).[1] Weekly. Folio, 4 pp., 6 cols. $1.25 a year.

Editor: Joseph L. Walker.[2]

Publisher: D. S. Morris and Co.

The *Baptist Recorder* contained both religious and general intelligence. In addition to news, there were editorials, moral exhortations, biographical sketches, and advertisements.

Not listed U.L.S.

Holdings: PCA July 13, 1848 (photostat).

[1]Few publication facts regarding this newspaper are known. The issue for July 13, 1848, is vol. 1, no. 34, and the paper is listed in the *Baptist Almanac and Annual Register,* 1850, p. 31. It was, according to the editor of the paper by which it was superseded, "literally starved to death by delinquent subscribers." See *Mountain Messenger and Baptist Recorder,* Morgantown, Va., Feb. 4, 1857.

[2] See section on *Baptist Champion* for sketch of Walker. He described his experiences with the *Baptist Recorder* as follows: "I soon saw that the paper could not live where there was no Baptist church and few Baptists; and after conducting it a year, I left it in the hands of the publishers. . . . The paper, too, had stirred up a first-class hornet's nest, which made it necessary for its editor to preach a three hours' sermon on baptism at Lumberport and to debate for four hours with the celebrated Moses Tichinell, of Palatine, on the same subject." Quoted in Taylor, *Virginia Baptist Ministers,* series 4, p. 267.

BAPTIST TELEGRAPH

Jacksonville, Fla. 1847 (?).[1] Monthly.

Editor: James McDonald.[2]

No copy known.

[1] Listed in the *Baptist Almanac and Annual Register,* 1848, p. 32.

[2] McDonald (1798-1869), a Baptist minister who had been reared in Ireland in the Catholic faith, preached in South Georgia and Florida from 1834 to 1853. His biographical sketch in the *History of the Baptist Denomination in Georgia.... Compiled for the Christian Index,* pt. 2, pp. 374-375, contains, however, no reference to the *Baptist Telegraph.*

BAPTIST TELESCOPE

Hendersonville, N. C. 1859–1860.[1] Weekly. Folio, 4 pp., 6 cols. $1.50 a year.

Editors and proprietors: W. A. G. Brown and N. Bowen.

Publisher: William Dedman.[2]

This general family religious newspaper was the unofficial organ of the Western North Carolina Baptist Convention and not a rival of the *Biblical Recorder,* Raleigh, generally regarded as the Baptist state paper.[3] Under the motto "Many Shall Run To and Fro, and Knowledge Shall be Increased," there were original articles, selections, editorials, literary notices, religious news, domestic and foreign secular news, and advertisements. A Methodist contemporary characterized the publication as "a good Baptist paper."[4]

U.L.S., 2nd ed., (1), p. 165.

[1] Founded early in 1859 (Jan. 4, 1860, is vol. 1, no. 45), the *Baptist Telescope* was published for more than a year (April 4, 1860, is vol. 2, no. 6). The editors reported in the issue for Jan. 11, 1860, that the subscription list of the *Baptist Watchman* (probably published in Knoxville, Tenn.) had been transferred to them.

[2] Although Brown and Bowen were listed as proprietors, Dedman was listed as publisher instead of printer. His duties were to set the type, print the paper, and send out the copies.

[3] An editorial in the *Baptist Telescope* (Jan. 18, 1860) pointed out that there was ample room for both papers to operate in a wide sphere of usefulness.

[4] Rufus T. Heflin in the *North Carolina Christian Advocate,* Raleigh, April 7, 1859.

BIBLICAL RECORDER

BIBLICAL RECORDER AND SOUTHERN WATCHMAN[1]

New Bern, N. C., Jan. 7, 1835–Dec., 1837; Raleigh, N. C., Jan. 13, 1838–April, 1865. Jan. 7, 1835–April, 1865.[2] Weekly. Folio, 4 pp., 5-7 cols. $2-$20 a year. 1,800 subscribers.

Editors: Thomas Meredith, Jan. 7, 1835–Nov. 13, 1850;[3] J. W. Tobey, Nov. 30, 1850–July 15, 1853;[4] Joshua John James, Jan. 13, 1854–April 17, 1861;[5] James Dunn Hufham, April 24, 1861–April, 1865.[6]

Publishers: Thomas Meredith, Jan. 7, 1835–Nov. 13, 1850; Marcus A. Meredith, Jan. 26, 1851–Oct. 5, 1854; G[eorgia] Meredith and Co., Oct. 12, 1854–Sept. 20, 1855; J. J. James and Co., Sept. 27, 1855–April 17, 1861; J. D. Hufham, April 24, 1861–April, 1865.

The *Biblical Recorder,* adopted by the North Carolina Baptist State Convention as its organ, was a family religious newspaper of wide influence. Meredith produced especially vigorous editorials in support of co-operative benevolent enterprises. This paper also contained religious essays, Biblical criticism, religious and secular news, poetry, stories, sermons, advertisements, and miscellaneous items on mercantile, agricultural, and legislative subjects.

U.L.S., 2nd ed., p. 439; (1), p. 177.

Other holdings: NcR July 29, 1863; Nov. 30, 1864. NcW [1835-1841, 1843-1846]-[1849-1856]-[1858-1861]-[1863-1864] (The volumes for the years listed here as incomplete lack only scattering numbers). ScGF Dec. 15, 1838.

[1] The second title was used from March 3, 1838, when Meredith "purchased" the subscription list of the *Southern Watchman*, Charleston, until the end of 1841.

[2] The *Biblical Recorder* superseded the *North Carolina Baptist Interpreter*, New Bern, N. C. A specimen number was issued Jan. 4, 1834, from Edenton, N. C., a year in advance of the founding. Publication was suspended throughout 1842 for lack of financial support. During this year, however, Meredith issued in Raleigh, N. C., the *Southern Christian Repository*. C. T. Bailey wrote in the *Biblical Recorder*, Aug. 16, 1876, that "During the late war the *Recorder* was the only Baptist paper within the states occupied by the hostile armies that did not suspend. The paper was made up, ready for the press, when Sherman entered Raleigh." After June, 1863, half-sheets of only two pages were issued occasionally. Despite damage done to the office by Sherman's troops, publication was resumed in Nov., 1865, and has continued to date.

[3] Meredith (1795-1850), a native Pennsylvanian, was awarded the degree of A.M. by the University of Pennsylvania. Sent about 1818 by the Baptist General Convention for Missionary Purposes as a missionary to North Carolina, he settled permanently in that state and was soon recognized as its ablest Baptist minister. See Cathcart, *Baptist Encyclopaedia*, p. 785.

[4] Tobey (1819-1885), a native of Rhode Island, was a graduate of Columbian College (now George Washington University), a former missionary to China, and pastor of the Baptist Church in Raleigh. See Tupper, *Foreign Missions of the Southern Baptist Convention*, pp. 168-170.

[5] James (1814-1892), a Virginian and a graduate of Columbian College, left a professorship in Oxford [N. C.] Baptist Female College to become editor. See *North Carolina Baptist Almanac*, 1893, p. 41. James was assisted as editor by G. W. Johnston and J. S. Walthall.

[6] Hufham (1834-1921) was a native of North Carolina, a graduate of Wake Forest College, and a prominent Baptist minister. See Cathcart, *Baptist Encyclopaedia*, p. 555.

Calvinistic Magazine

Abingdon, Va. Jan., 1846–Dec., 1850.[1] Monthly. Octavo, 32 pp. $1 a year. 1,000 subscribers.[2]

Editors and proprietors: Isaac Anderson, Frederick A. Ross, James King, and James McChain.[3]

This Presbyterian periodical, according to an editorial, was resurrected to refute the "slanders and disabuse" of Methodists, who for twelve years "had been allowed a clear field to abuse and misrepresent Presbyterians, and to decoy into their own church the members of Presbyterian churches and families." The editors feared that "the community would soon begin to take it for granted, as Presbyterians said nothing in reply to their opponents, that Calvinism was that horrible ism which, in the chaste and respectful language of one very celebrated Methodist preacher, 'came from hell and would go back to hell.' "[4] Frederick A. Ross led the assault in the widely quoted series of articles entitled "The Great Iron Wheel," a figure used to describe the machinery with which the Methodist bishop kept the wheels of itineracy constantly rolling.

The *Calvinistic Magazine* praised the doctrines, government, and discipline of the Presbyterian Church, and in strong language denounced those of their Methodist rivals. Although the editors belonged to the New School of the Presbyterian Church, they attempted to make their work acceptable to both branches.[5] The content also included missionary, literary, and political news.

U.L.S., 2nd ed., p. 590; (1), p. 234.

[1] Since five volumes of the *Calvinistic Magazine* had been published at Rogersville, Tennessee, between 1827 and 1831, the Abingdon volumes were referred to as a new series. This periodical was superseded by the *Presbyterian Witness,* Knoxville, Tennessee.

[2] Most of these resided in Eastern Tennessee and Southwestern Virginia. See *Calvinistic Magazine,* IV (Feb., 1849), 35.

[3] Anderson (1780-1857) was a native of Virginia and the chief founder of the South West Theological Seminary, Maryville, Tennessee. See Nevin, *Encyclopaedia of the Presbyterian Church,* p. 27. Ross (1796-1882) migrated from Maryland to Tennessee, where he became noted as a minister and as the author of works on theological questions and slavery. See Alexander, *History of the Synod of Tennessee,* pp. 120-121. King (1790-1867), a native Tennessean of pioneer stock, preached in the Bristol area most of his life. McChain, a Yale graduate, was pastor of the Presbyterian Church of Abingdon from 1843 until 1869. See Synod of Virginia, *Minutes,* 1867, p. 43; 1869, p. 113.

[4] *Calvinistic Magazine,* III (Jan., 1848), 1.

[5] *Calvinistic Magazine,* III (Jan., 1848), 31.

Carolina Baptist
Southern Baptist[1]

Charleston. April 1, 1846–Dec., 1860.[2] Weekly. Folio, 4 pp., 6-7 cols. $2 a year. 1,600 subscribers.[3]

Editors: T. W. Haynes (or Haines), 1846-1847;[4] "Committee of brethren of the Baptist Churches in Charleston," 1847-1848; James P. Boyce, 1848-1849;[5] "A Committee of Brethren in Charleston," 1849-1852; Edwin Theodore Winkler, 1852-1854;[6] J. P. Tustin, 1854-1859; W. B. Carson, 1859-1860.[7]

Proprietors: "Published by a Committee of Brethren in Charleston."[8]

This family religious newspaper was the most successful of the various efforts on the part of interested individuals to provide South Carolina Baptists with a paper. Recognized as the organ of the South Carolina Baptist State Convention, the *Southern Baptist* contained church proceedings, theology, foreign and domestic secular news, editorials, obituaries, markets, poetry, advertisements, and miscellany.

U.L.S., 2nd ed., (1), pp. 248, 990. Hoole, *Charleston Periodicals,* pp. 41-42.

Other holdings: NcW May 2, 1855; Oct. 27, 1860. ScGF [1848-1849, 1851-1856]. ScU March 3, 1857. VRB [1849-1857].

[1] First title used until May 29, 1847; the second thereafter.

[2] Superseded the *Carolina Baptist, A Monthly Magazine,* Charleston. Publication continued until the close of 1860 (vol. 15, no. 37), when the paper became one of the earliest victims of the coming war. The *South Carolina Baptist,* established by W. E. Walters at Anderson, April 20, 1866 (vol. 1, no. 1), had no organic connection with the *Southern Baptist.*

[3] When Haynes discontinued his monthly magazine (see p. 52), he sent the *Carolina Baptist* to its subscribers, giving the latter a list of 1,500 names. See *Carolina Baptist, A Monthly Magazine,* I (Aug., 1846), 283. Kennedy, "Catalogue of Newspapers and Periodicals" (1850), gave 1,600 subscribers. An editorial note in the *Southern Baptist,* Oct. 27, 1860, placed its subscription list at 2,880, adding that something over 500 of these copies were sent to the former subscribers of the *Telescope.* This may have been the *Baptist Telescope,* Hendersonville, N. C., which was discontinued that year.

[4] Haynes, a young Baptist minister, had recently come from the Second Baptist Church, Nashville, Tenn., to the pastorate of the Baptist Church in Greenville, S. C. After a trip to the low country he was "so delighted with Charleston" that he resigned his Greenville pastorate and moved to the larger city, changing the spelling of his name to "Haines." See *Carolina Baptist, A Monthly Magazine,* I (Sept., 1845), 19; I (Feb., 1846), 142-144.

[5] Boyce (1827-1888) was a native Charlestonian, a graduate of Brown, and a student at Princeton Theological Seminary. See Cathcart, *Baptist Encyclopaedia,* pp. 121-122, and Broadus, *Memoirs of James Petigru Boyce.*

[6] Winkler, a Georgian born in 1823, was graduated from Brown and studied at Newton Theological Seminary. He held several pastorates in Georgia and South Carolina before becoming editor of the *Alabama Baptist* in 1874. See Cathcart, *Baptist Encyclopaedia,* p. 1261.

[7] Carson (b. 1821), a native South Carolinian, was graduated from the Presbyterian Theological Seminary, Columbia, S. C., but while a student there decided to become a Baptist minister. Carson served for four years as a chaplain in the Confederate Army. See *History of the Baptist Denomination in Georgia.... Compiled for the Christian Index,* pt. 2, pp. 109-110.

[8] The men who constituted the committee or company as they were sometimes designated were preachers, lawyers, and businessmen. The publication of a weekly religious journal in Charleston cost about $100 a week, which was the equivalent of 2,500 paying subscribers at $2. The editing committee

reported to the Charleston Association in 1851 that the owners had been forced to spend several hundred dollars to keep the paper going. See *Southern Baptist,* Nov. 12, 1851; Oct. 10, 1855.

Carolina Baptist

Hendersonville, N. C. 1853–Nov. 14, 1855; 1857-1858.[1] Weekly. Folio, 4 pp., 6 cols. $2 a year.

Editors and publishers: James Blythe and N. Bowen.

"A Family Newspaper—Devoted to Religion, Religious Literature, Agriculture, and General Intelligence," the *Carolina Baptist* was the unofficial organ of the Western North Carolina Baptist Convention. It contained religious selections, politics, religious and secular news, theology, communications, marriages, obituaries, poetry, stories, advertisements, and miscellany.

Not listed U.L.S.

Holdings: NcU Feb. 7, 1855.

[1] Superseded the *North Carolina Baptist,* Asheville, the numbering of which it continued (Feb. 7, 1855, is vol. 4, no. 20). A contemporary, commenting on the suspension of the *Carolina Baptist* in 1855, stated that the expenses exceeded the receipts because of delinquent subscribers. Although, he continued, "it is a journal in which we have always found an excellent spirit, and a good measure of ability, . . . one Baptist paper is enough for any State." See *Southern Baptist,* Charleston, Nov. 26, 1855. A notice in *ibid.,* Feb. 17, 1857, stated that publication had been resumed after a prospective consolidation with the *Biblical Recorder,* Raleigh, N. C., failed to materialize. The *Biblical Recorder* announced, however, on Nov. 11, 1858, that it had purchased the subscription list of the *Carolina Baptist.*

Carolina Baptist, A Monthly Magazine

Greenville, S. C., Sept., 1845–Feb., 1846; Charleston, March–Aug., 1846. Sept., 1845–Aug., 1846.[1] Monthly. Octavo, 24 pp. $1.25 a year. 1,000 subscribers.[2]

Editor: T. W. Haynes.[3]

Publisher: O. H. Wells (Greenville); Walker and Burke (Charleston).

This magazine was lighter and of a more miscellaneous character than most monthlies. It contained church history and news, essays on morals, and sermons. There was no other Baptist periodical in South Carolina and Haynes complained bitterly that forty thousand Baptists would not adequately support his efforts: "We, in South Carolina, are asleep."[4]

U.L.S., 2nd ed., p. 617; (1), p. 248. Hoole, *Charleston Periodicals,* p. 50.

Other holdings: NcW complete file.

[1] Superseded by the *Carolina Baptist,* Charleston.

[2] *Carolina Baptist, A Monthly Magazine,* I (Feb., 1846), 143; I (April, 1846), 190.

[3] See section on the *Carolina Baptist,* Charleston, for sketch of Haynes.

[4] *Carolina Baptist, A Monthly Magazine,* I (April, 1846), 190.

CAROLINA CHRISTIAN MONTHLY. *See* CHRISTIAN FRIEND

CAROLINA INTELLIGENCER

Shelby, N. C. 1853 (?) -1855.[1] Weekly.

Editor and proprietor: Alexander J. Cansler.

No copy known.

[1] The earliest reference noted to this newspaper edited by a Baptist minister appeared in the *Biblical Recorder,* Raleigh, N. C., May 13, 1853. At the close of 1855 the editor transferred his subscription list to the *Biblical Recorder* for stock in the *Biblical Recorder* Company. See *Biblical Recorder,* Jan. 5, 1856. Kenny, *American Newspaper Directory* (1860), p. 55, lists an *Intelligencer* published at Shelby. This either refers to a different paper or is an error regarding the closing date.

CAROLINA PROGRESSIONIST
PROGRESSIONIST[1]

Cross Anchor, S. C. 1859 (?)-1860 (?). Weekly. No copy known.

[1] Listed by the first title in *American Christian Record,* p. 692, as a Spiritualist weekly and by the second title in Kenny, *American Newspaper Directory,* 1860, p. 67, as a religious weekly.

CENTRAL PRESBYTERIAN

Richmond. Jan. 5, 1856–March 16, 1865.[1] Weekly. Folio, 4 pp., 6-7 cols. $2.50 a year.

Editors: Thomas Verner Moore, Moses Drury Hoge, and Benjamin Gildersleeve, Jan. 5, 1856–Dec. 29, 1860;[2] William Brown, Jan. 5, 1861–March 16, 1865.[3]

Proprietors: An association of gentlemen in Virginia and North Carolina.[4]

The editors explained in the following selection from their opening number why they were launching this newspaper, which became the major Presbyterian publication of the upper South: "In the threatening aspect of political affairs, and the peril, . . . that now menaces the permanence of our Federal Union, it is very important that we should have an organ of communication with our people, that will be under our control, watchful of our interests, and faithful to those great *conservative* principles that underlie all our institutions. Our political and geographical position, central between the extreme North and extreme South, creates peculiar responsibilities and duties. . . . We have in our colored population an interest that God has trusted specially to our charge." Published during a momentous decade by alert editors, this weekly devoted considerable space to public affairs as well as to church and secular news, sermons, and essays. Stories, poems, market prices, advertisements, marriages, and obituaries also appeared.

U.L.S., 2nd ed., p. 632. Cappon, *Virginia Newspapers,* pp. 165-166.

Other holdings: NcU March 8, 1856; Jan. 15, 1859; Jan. 2, 1861; July 23, 1863; June 30, Sept. 15, 29, 1864.

[1] Superseded the *Watchman and Observer,* Richmond. Although the office burned April 3, 1865, Brown resumed publication July 20, 1865, and the paper still exists as one of several publications forming the *Presbyterian of the South.*

[2] Moore (1818-1871), a native of Pennsylvania, graduated from Dickinson College and Princeton Seminary. From 1847 until 1868 he served as pastor of the First Presbyterian Church, Richmond. See *National Cyclopaedia of American Biography,* XIX, 362. Hoge (1818-1899), a native Virginian, graduated from Hampden-Sydney College before becoming pastor of the Second Presbyterian Church, Richmond, a position he held for more than half a century. See *Dictionary of American Biography,* IX, 121-122. Gildersleeve (1791-1875), a native of Connecticut and a graduate of Princeton Theological Seminary, had a long career as a religious journalist in the South. He also preached and taught and was the father of Basil L. Gildersleeve, the noted professor. See Nevin, *Encyclopaedia of the Presbyterian Church,* p. 266.

[3] Brown, born in Virginia in 1811, graduated from Washington College and Princeton Seminary. He preached in Augusta County, Virginia, for twenty-five years before becoming editor of the *Central Presbyterian,* to which he then devoted all his time. See Presbyterian Synod of Virginia, *Minutes,* 1894, pp. 333-335.

[4] The paper was listed as edited and published by Moore, Hoge and Company (later by Brown) for an "association of gentlemen in Virginia and North Carolina" who owned the stock. The paper maintained an office on Main Street, five doors below the Exchange Bank.

CHARLESTON CATHOLIC MISCELLANY. *See* UNITED STATES CATHOLIC MISCELLANY

CHARLESTON GOSPEL MESSENGER, AND PROTESTANT EPISCOPAL REGISTER. *See* GOSPEL MESSENGER, AND SOUTHERN CHRISTIAN REGISTER

CHARLESTON OBSERVER

Charleston. Jan. 6, 1827–Aug. 9, 1845.[1] Weekly. Folio, 4 pp., 5-6 cols. $3.50 a year.

Editor and proprietor: Benjamin Gildersleeve.[2]

When the *Southern Intelligencer,* a Presbyterian newspaper published in Charleston, was suspended, Gildersleeve accepted overtures from Presbyterian friends in Charleston to give up his *Georgia Reporter and Christian Gazette* and undertake publication of a religious newspaper in that city.[3] The Synod of South Carolina and Georgia recommended the new paper as devoted to the best interests of the denomination. Some Congregationalist patronage also developed.[4] Although it lacked variety at first, the *Charleston Observer* soon came to have editorials, essays, church proceedings, religious and secular news, communications, prices current, advertisements, and poetry.

U.L.S., 2nd ed., p. 644. Hoole, *Charleston Periodicals,* pp. 28-29.

Other holdings: NcU April 11, 1835; Nov. 26, 1836.

[1] Formed by combining the subscription lists of the *Southern Intelligencer,* Charleston, and the *Georgia Reporter and Christian Gazette,* Sparta, Ga. Suspended Dec. 28, 1839–Feb. 22, 1840, except for an extra, because of the destruction of the printing office by fire. Merged Aug. 21, 1845, with the *Watchman of the South,* Richmond, to form the *Watchman and Observer.*

[2] See section on *Central Presbyterian* for sketch of Gildersleeve.

[3] *Georgia Reporter and Christian Gazette,* Sept. 25, 1826; *Watchman and Observer,* Richmond, Aug. 7, 1851.

[4] *Charleston Observer,* Sept. 27, 1828.

Children's Friend

Richmond. Aug., 1862–Feb. 1, 1865.[1] Monthly, Aug., 1862–Dec., 1863; semimonthly, Jan., 1864–Feb. 1, 1865. Folio, 4 pp., 3 cols. 50¢-$2 a year. 10,000 subscribers.[2]

Editor: William Brown.[3]

Publisher: The Presbyterian Church in the Confederate States.[4]

Established as a replacement for the *Sabbath-School Visitor* of Philadelphia, this paper contained stories, letters, poetry, engravings, and songs with the music.

U.L.S., 2nd ed., p. 666.

Other holdings: NcMHi June, Nov.–Dec., 1863; Feb. 1, 15, March 15, July 1, Nov. 1, 15, Dec. 1, 1864; Jan. 15, Feb. 1, 1865. VRC July 1, 1864.

[1] Resumed in 1866 with a new series and published until 1915.

[2] Presbyterian Church in the Confederate States of America, *Minutes of the General Assembly,* 1863, p. 173.

[3] Brown edited the *Central Presbyterian,* Richmond, at this time.

[4] Published by the Committee of Publication (William D. Cooke, publishing agent) of the Presbyterian Church in the Confederate States of America.

Children's Guide

Macon, Ga. 1863–April, 1865, or later.[1] Monthly. Folio, 4 pp., 3 cols.

Editor and publisher: John W. Burke.[2]

This illustrated Methodist Sunday School paper was published as a substitute for the "variety of books" no longer available. With the motto, "To Guide our Feet into the Way of Peace," the content was divided between religious and literary subjects. There were stories, poems, travel accounts, obituaries of children, puzzles, riddles, enigmas, and religious exhortations. An unusually large amount of the material was original.

U.L.S., 2nd ed., p. 666.

Other holdings: NcU April, 1865.

[1] Dec., 1863, is vol. 1, no. 6. April, 1865, probably the last issue, is vol. 2, no. 10. Burke declared toward the close of the war that he intended to continue the paper for the children's benefit as long as he could, "whether it pays us any money or not." Quoted in *Southern Christian Advocate,* Augusta, Ga., April 13, 1865.

[2] See section on *Army and Navy Herald* for sketch of Burke.

Child's Index[1]

Macon, Ga. Sept., 1862–April, 1865.[2] Monthly. Folio, 4 pp., 4 cols. 50¢-$4 a year. 12,000 subscribers.[3]

Editor and publisher: Samuel Boykin.[4]

The editor's salutatory, addressed to children, stated that "Since we have been engaged in repelling our wicked invaders, you have been deprived of the neat and interesting papers you used to get from the North," and declared his purpose of supplying the need with a periodical designed for Southern children. Profusely illustrated with engravings, the *Child's Index* specialized in stories, anecdotes, poetry, letters, and music.

U.L.S., 2nd ed., p. 667; (1), p. 270.

Other holdings: VRC Jan., 1865.

[1] The name was drawn from the *Christian Index,* organ of the Georgia Baptist State Convention.

[2] A specimen appeared Sept., 1862; no. 2, Feb., 1863. Superseded after the war by *Child's Delight* (June, 1866, is vol. 1, no. 5), which was later merged into *Kind Words,* founded by the Sunday School Board of the Southern Baptist Convention in Jan., 1866. Brantley, *Georgia Journalism,* p. 53, says *Kind Words* was "a small Baptist Sunday School sheet founded in 1863, as a weekly." The *Child's Index,* which he does not list, is probably the paper meant.

[3] *Child's Index,* I (Dec., 1863), 46.

[4] Boykin, born in Georgia in 1829, graduated from the University of Georgia and traveled a year in Europe before entering the Baptist ministry. See Cathcart, *Baptist Encyclopaedia,* pp. 123-124.

CHRISTIAN BANNER

Fredericksburg, Va. 1848–May 9, 1861; May 9, 1862–Aug. 13, 1862, or later. Weekly; semiweekly after May 9, 1862. Folio, 4 pp., 5 cols. 700 subscribers.

Editor: James W. Hunnicutt.[1]

Proprietors: Hunnicutt, Magrath, and Taliaferro.[2]

The editor, a Free Will Baptist minister, was more concerned with slavery and secession than with church affairs. In sharp language he urged the South not to submit to the "intrigues of secessionists." He stated in 1862 that he would continue "to write just as nearly what we please as circumstances will allow. . . . We shall exert our undivided and untiring influence and efforts to get our fellow citizens to become reconciled and return to the union."[3]

U.L.N., p. 699. Cappon, *Virginia Newspapers,* p. 90.

Other holdings: NcD June 14, 18, 26, 1862.

[1] Hunnicutt, an anti-Negro and antisecessionist South Carolinian, was forced to suspend publication May 9, 1861. Under protection of the U. S. Army he resumed publication May 9, 1862. See Cappon, *Virginia Newspapers,* p. 90. For a contemporary Southerner's dislike of Hunnicutt, see *Christian Sun,* Suffolk, Va., Aug. 26, 1859.

[2] In 1862 Hunnicutt was sole owner and also the printer, using brown paper and a worn press. See *Christian Banner,* July 14, 1862.

[3] The editorial from which the above is quoted first appeared May 9, 1862, and was repeated in each issue until June 14, 1862. This paper followed the unusual practice of presenting the same material, even to news in some cases, for weeks at a time. On June 18, 1862, for example, there were only two and one-half columns not found verbatim in the issue for June 14.

CHRISTIAN BAPTIST

Buffaloe Creek, Brooke County, Va. (now W. Va.).[1] Aug., 1823–July, 1830.[2] Monthly. Duodecimo, 24 pp. $1 a year. 7,000 subscribers.

Editor and publisher: Alexander Campbell.[3]

The editor's prospectus set forth the principles he intended to follow: "The *Christian Baptist* shall espouse the cause of no religious sect. . . . Its sole object shall be the eviction of truth, and the exposure of error in doctrine and practice." But this periodical and its successor, the *Millennial Harbinger,* actually became the strongest forces in the founding of a new denomination, the Disciples of Christ.[4] Lacking variety, the *Christian Baptist* contained little besides Campbell's essays on doctrines and his letters to or from correspondents.

U.L.S., 2nd ed., p. 675; (1), p. 274.

Other holdings: NcW Aug., 1826–July, 1827. VRB Aug., 1823–July, 1826; Aug., 1828–July, 1829.

[1] This was the location of Campbell's farm, the actual place of publication. Later Bethany post office was established here.

[2] Superseded by the *Millennial Harbinger*, Bethany, Va.

[3] Campbell (1788-1866), a Scotch-Irish preacher who came to the United States in 1809 and later founded the Disciples of Christ, was the most successful editor and publisher of religious periodicals in the South Atlantic States and ranks high among the important religious leaders of the century. See *Dictionary of American Biography,* III, 446-448, and Richardson, *Alexander Campbell.* Solomon Sala was Campbell's first printer.

[4] Willard A. Fortune, *The Disciples in Kentucky,* p. 103.

CHRISTIAN BAPTIST. *See* CHRISTIAN FRIEND

CHRISTIAN FRIEND, 1853-1854
CHRISTIAN FRIEND AND BIBLE UNIONIST, 1854-1855
AMERICAN CHRISTIAN PREACHER AND DISCIPLES' MISCELLANY, 1855-1856
CHRISTIAN PREACHER, 1857
DISCIPLES' ADVOCATE, 1857-1858
CHRISTIAN BAPTIST, 1859
CAROLINA CHRISTIAN MONTHLY, 1860[1]

Wilson, N. C., 1853; Goldsboro, N. C., 1853-1854; Hookerton, N. C., 1854-1855; Kinston, N. C., 1855-1860. 1853-1860.[2] Monthly. Octavo, 16-32 pp. $1-$2 a year.

Editor and proprietor: John T. Walsh.[3]

This magazine, bearing the motto "Ye are my friends if ye do whatsoever I command you," was the unofficial organ of the Disciples of Christ in North Carolina. The editor sought to maintain a publication devoted to the advancement of "Primitive Christianity," a new version of the Bible, temperance, letters, and denominational news.

Not listed U.L.S.

Holdings: NcWiA [1853-1860]. PCA Jan., 1859.

[1] Although the title was changed almost every year, the annual volumes were numbered consecutively (*Carolina Christian Monthly,* March, 1860, is vol. 8, no. 3), edited by the same man, and constitute a single publication.

[2] Notice that the first number had been published appeared in the *Spirit of the Age,* Raleigh, N. C., May 25, 1853. A contemporary editor stated that in June, 1860, Walsh had announced the transfer of his subscription list to the *Family Visitor* (no place given). "We regret," wrote the contemporary, "that this valuable adjunct of the cause in the 'old North state,' could not be sustained. It deserved a better fate." See *Christian Intelligencer,* Richmond, July 10, 1860.

[3] Walsh (1816-1886), a Virginian with the M.D. degree from the Eclectic

Medical College of Pennsylvania, began his public career as a Methodist preacher, changed to the Baptist ministry, then came under the influence of Alexander Campbell. In 1852 Walsh moved from Richmond to North Carolina, where he soon became the leader of the Disciples of Christ. See Ware, *Disciples of Christ in North Carolina,* pp. 203-214, 347.

CHRISTIAN INDEX AND BAPTIST MISCELLANY

CHRISTIAN INDEX

Washington, Ga., Sept. 14, 1833–1840; Penfield, Ga., 1841-1856; Macon, Ga., 1857–April 13, 1865. Sept. 14, 1833–April 13, 1865.[1] Weekly. Folio,[2] 4 pp., 6 cols. $2-$20 a year. 3,000 subscribers.[3]

Editors: Jesse Mercer and William H. Stokes, 1833-1840;[4] Stokes, 1840-1842; Joseph S. Baker, 1843-1848;[5] Billington M. Saunders, 1849; John Francis Dagg, 1850-1855;[6] T. D. Martin, 1856; Joseph L. Walker, 1857-1859;[7] Ebenezer W. Warren, 1859-1860; Samuel Boykin, 1860-1865.[8]

Publishers: Mercer, 1833-1840; Baptist Convention of the State of Georgia, 1840-1861; Boykin, 1861-1865.

While published in Philadelphia by William T. Brantly, a native of North Carolina, the *Christian Index* became noticeably pro-Southern and lost many of its Northern subscribers. Mercer, favorably impressed by Brantly's proposal to transfer the paper to the South, in 1833 purchased the subscription list, name, and good will. As the organ of the Baptist Convention of the State of Georgia, the *Christian Index* ably supported its program of benevolent projects. The content included church and secular news, editorials, sermons, essays on morals and benevolence, poetry, advertisements, and miscellany.

U.L.S., 2nd ed., three entries: p. 678 as *Christian Index* and as *Christian Index and Baptist Miscellany;* p. 739 as *Columbian Star*. U.L.S., 2nd ed., (1), p. 275.

Other holdings: NcW [1830-1833]. ScGF Nov. 15, 1855.

[1] Superseded the *Columbian Star,* which was first issued in Washington, D. C., Feb. 2, 1822. In 1827 the name *Columbian Star and Christian Index* was adopted and the place of publication changed to Philadelphia. The first part of the name was dropped Jan. 1, 1831. Suspended at the close of the Civil War, publication was resumed in Atlanta Nov. 9, 1865, and has continued to date.

[2] The format between 1833 and 1865 was successively folio, octavo, folio, quarto, and folio. After 1863 only a half-sheet of 2 pages appeared much of the time.

[3] This is an average for the entire period. In 1860 there were 5,000 subscribers (United States Census, Manuscript Returns, 1860: Georgia, Social Statistics, Bibb County), and the *Christian Index* for March 4, 1864, placed

the circulation at 6,000, besides a "large number" of copies that were sent to soldiers.

[4] Mercer (1769-1841) was a North Carolinian by birth but spent most of his life in Georgia. Lacking formal learning, he became, nevertheless, an important figure in the councils of American Baptists. His leadership has been attributed to "his frank democracy, modesty, and devotion to the support of benevolent enterprises, especially foreign missions and higher education." After marrying a wealthy widow he was able to engage in considerable philanthropy. See *Dictionary of American Biography,* XII, 542-543.

Stokes, a native of South Carolina, had devoted the preceding decade to teaching and preaching. By self-application he had secured a fair education and was a better writer than Mercer, doing most of the editorial work. See *History of the Baptist Denomination in Georgia. . . . Compiled for the Christian Index,* p. 507.

[5] See section on *Baptist Chronicle and Monthly Monitor* for sketch of Baker.

[6] Dagg, a graduate of the University of Alabama and of the Theological School of Mercer University, was the son of the eminent Georgia Baptist leader, John L. Dagg. See *History of the Baptist Denomination in Georgia.... Compiled for the Christian Index,* p. 231. A recent writer for the *Christian Index,* Sept. 14, 1933, incorrectly listed John L. Dagg as editor. The special Baptist World Alliance issue of the *Christian Index,* June 15, 1939, indulged in similar errors, and the Hundredth Anniversary number, because of the belief that the *Columbian Star* was founded in 1821, appeared Dec. 25, 1920, more than a year too early.

[7] See section on *Baptist Champion* for sketch of Walker.

[8] See section on *Child's Index* for sketch of Boykin.

Christian Intelligencer
Union Christian Intelligencer[1]

Charlottesville, Va., Jan. (?), 1844–Sept. 7, 1846; Scottsville, Va., Sept. 21, 1846–1850, or later; Richmond, 1855; Charlottesville, Va., April, 1857, or earlier–March 20, 1860; Richmond, April 3, 1860–Jan. 25, 1862, or later. Jan. (?), 1844–Jan. 25, 1862, or later.[2] Semimonthly. Folio, 4 pp., 6 cols. $2 a year.

Editors: James W. Goss, 1844–Dec. 15, 1845; R. L. Coleman, Jan. 5, 1846–Dec., 1853;[3] A. B. Walthall and Coleman, Jan., 1854–Dec. 15, 1859; John G. Parrish, Jan. 11, 1860–Jan. 25, 1862, or later.

Proprietors: Goss, 1844-1845; S. W. Thacker, Jan. 5–Aug. 3, 1846; Coleman, Aug., 1846– (?).[4]

The *Christian Intelligencer,* organ of the Disciples of Christ in Virginia and a general family religious newspaper, was more moderate in its attitude toward other denominations than earlier Disciples periodicals had been. It contained religious news, theology, letters, poetry, literary notices, agriculture, markets, and advertisements.

U.L.S., 2nd ed., p. 678. Cappon, *Virginia Newspapers,* p. 66.

Other holdings: NcD March 24, April 21, Dec. 15, 1845; [1846]; Aug. 1, 1857.

[1] Second title used 1858-1859.

[2] Superseded the *Christian Publisher,* Charlottesville, Va.

[3] Coleman (1807-1880), the principal editor, was a Virginian who began his ministerial career as a Baptist but after hearing Alexander Campbell preach in 1830 became one of his outstanding co-workers. See Power, *Sketches of Our Pioneers,* pp. 136-139.

[4] Shortly after the death of Thacker in 1846 the Convention of Disciples in Virginia became proprietor. The editors, now named by the Convention, had charge of business matters. See *Union Christian Intelligencer,* Dec. 15, 1859.

Christian Journal (proposed)

Richmond. 1825.[1] Weekly. $3 a year.

Editor and proprietor: David Roper.

The prospectus contained the following evaluation of the significance of early religious journalism: "The press is now generally admitted to be one of the most efficient instruments of supporting any cause to which it may be enlisted. In Politics, Science and the Arts, its power is felt and acknowledged. Nor have Christians neglected to avail themselves of its influence. A thirst for newspaper reading prevails among all ranks of society throughout our country, and therefore opens an easy medium of access to many whose reading is almost exclusively confined to these fugitive productions. . . . It will, therefore, be our great object to collect and present to our readers the most interesting accounts of the advancement of vital godliness among all denominations of Christians. . . . The *Christian Journal* will not, however, be exclusively devoted to religious intelligence."

No copy known.

[1] The prospectus declared that publication would begin as soon as justified by the number of subscribers, but there is no evidence that the first issue ever appeared. See *Family Visitor,* Richmond, Oct. 8, 1825, for a copy of the proposals.

Christian Magazine of the South

Columbia, S. C., Jan., 1843–June, 1849; Winnsboro, S. C., July, 1849–Dec., 1851. Jan., 1843–Dec., 1851.[1] Monthly. Octavo, 32 pp. $1 a year. 1,000 subscribers.[2]

Editor and proprietor: James Boyce.[3]

As the organ of the Associate Reformed Presbyterian Synod of the South, this periodical consisted largely of church proceedings, moral and religious essays, communications to the editor, and sermons. In the announcement of reasons for founding the magazine Boyce pointed out that the widely dispersed character of the three thousand members of the Southern Synod of the denomination made such a publication imperative as a means of fostering a "public spirit" and of improving "our ministers and correspondents as to their writing talents."[4]

U.L.S., 2nd ed., p. 679.

Other holdings: ScDE complete file.

[1] Superseded by the *Erskine Miscellany,* Due West, S. C.

[2] This was the average for the nine years. See *Christian Magazine of the South,* IX (Dec., 1851), 379.

[3] Boyce, born in North Carolina in 1808, became, after his graduation from Jefferson College, a leader among the ministers of the Associate Reformed Presbyterian Church. See *Due West* (S. C.) *Telescope,* Sept. 3, 1852, and the *Autobiography of Rev. James Boyce, D. D.* The printers were I. C. Morgan in Columbia and E. H. Britton in Winnsboro.

[4] *Christian Magazine of the South,* I (Jan., 1843), 27.

Christian Mirror

Charleston. Jan. 22–April 16, 1814, or later. Weekly. Octavo, 16 pp. $2.25 for 6 months.

Editor: Andrew P. Gready.[1]

This early nonsectarian newspaper contained accounts of activities among several Protestant denominations. There were also religious essays, biographical sketches, poems, selections from classical literature, philosophical essays, and letters.

U.L.S., 2nd ed., p. 679.

[1] No editor is named in the files of the *Christian Mirror,* but Gready is mentioned as editor in several notices which appeared in the Charleston *Courier* between Oct. 25, 1813, and Jan. 16, 1814. See Hoole, *Charleston Periodicals,* p. 22.

Christian Monitor

Richmond. July 8, 1815–Aug. 30, 1817.[1] Weekly, July 8, 1815–June 22, 1816; semimonthly, Sept. 14, 1816–Aug. 30, 1817. Octavo, 8-16 pp. $2 a year.

Editor and proprietor: John Holt Rice.[2]

The communication of religious news being the principal purpose of this Presbyterian editor, the *Christian Monitor* contained accounts of revivals, proceedings of benevolent societies, stories about missionaries, and anecdotes.

U.L.S., 2nd ed., p. 680; (1), p. 275.

[1] Superseded by the *Virginia Evangelical and Literary Magazine,* Richmond.

[2] Rice (1777-1831) was a native Virginian and a graduate of Hampden-

Sydney. One of the foremost writers, educators, and clergymen of his time, he organized several educational and benevolent societies, preached in various places, and in 1824 became Professor of Theology in the Seminary at Hampden-Sydney. See *Dictionary of American Biography,* XV, 541-542.

CHRISTIAN OBSERVER

Philadelphia and Richmond, Jan. 3–July 25, 1861; Philadelphia, Aug. 1–[Oct. 24, 1861];[1] Richmond, Sept. 19, 1861–April 7, 1865. Sept. 19, 1861–April 7, 1865.[2] Weekly. Folio, 4 pp., 6-7 cols. $2.50 a year. 3,000 free copies to the Confederate Army weekly.[3]

Editor and proprietor: Amasa Converse.[4]

The *Christian Observer,* a Presbyterian paper now published in Louisville, Kentucky, and still owned by the the Converse family, traces its descent from the *Religious Remembrancer,* established in Philadelphia September 4, 1813. On this basis it claims to be "the oldest religious weekly and the oldest journal with a continuous publication" in the United States. This claim is disputed by the *Herald of Gospel Liberty,* a Christian publication founded at Portsmouth, New Hampshire, September 1, 1808, which asserts that it is the "oldest religious newspaper." The controversy revolves around the question of what constitutes continuous publication and legitimate descent.[5]

The content of the *Christian Observer* during the war years reflects the editor's strong pro-Southern views. In addition to the usual church and military news, communications, obituaries, poetry, and advertisements, there were editorial denunciations of the North and essays designed to boost Southern morale.

U.L.S., 2nd ed., p. 680; (1), p. 275. Cappon, *Virginia Newspapers,* pp. 166-167.

[1] Although printed in Philadelphia as formerly, the *Christian Observer* was dated at Philadelphia and Richmond for seven months in 1861 to show its Southern leanings. Since there had been no mail service to the South for two months, Richmond, where F. Bartlett Converse, associate editor and son of the editor, resided, was omitted from the date line during August. On Oct. 24, 1861, Henry A. Converse, acting proprietor and also son of the editor, issued a half-sheet in Philadelphia explaining that on Aug. 22, 1861, a United States marshal, on order of President Lincoln, had closed the office of the *Christian Observer* and confiscated its property because of its opposition to the war. The suit instituted against the paper was later withdrawn, but the acting proprietor, to whom the property had been returned, declined to resume publication in Philadelphia.

[2] In the first number published in Richmond (Sept. 19, 1861), Amasa Converse gave a full account of the suppression of his paper in Philadelphia and of his flight to the Confederate States. The military situation prevented pub-

lication March 23, 1865, but the *Christian Observer* office escaped the fire which destroyed the offices of four other religious weeklies on April 3. Suspended after the April 7 issue (vol. 44, no. 13), regular publication was resumed June 1, 1865.

[3] *Confederate Baptist,* Columbia, S. C., June 17, 1863.

[4] Converse (1795-1872), born in New Hampshire and a graduate of Dartmouth College, taught school and studied at Princeton Theological Seminary before entering the Presbyterian ministry. Editor for nearly half a century (he became co-editor of the *Visitor and Telegraph,* Richmond, 1827), he achieved prominence as a New School leader. See Nevin, *Encyclopaedia of the Presbyterian Church,* p. 155, and the *Christian Observer,* Oct. 15, 1873.

[5] For the arguments on each side see "Keeping the Record Straight, Religious Journalism in America" in *Christian Observer,* Feb. 19, 1936, and Barrett, *Religious Journalism, passim.*

Christian Preacher. *See* Christian Friend

Christian Publisher

Charlottesville, Va., Oct., 1836–Oct., 1838; Richmond, Jan.-Dec., 1839; Charlottesville, Va., Jan., 1840–Aug., 1843. Oct., 1836–Aug., 1843.[1] Monthly, duodecimo, 24 pp., $1 a year, Oct., 1836–Dec., 1840; semimonthly, folio, 4 pp., 5 cols., $2 a year, Jan. 19–Dec. 17, 1841; monthly, folio, 8 pp., 3 cols., $1 a year, Jan., 1842–Aug., 1843.

Editors and proprietors: Reuben Lindsay Coleman, Oct., 1836–Oct., 1838; James Henshall, Jan.-Dec., 1839; Coleman and James W. Goss, Jan., 1840–Aug., 1843.[2]

This Disciples of Christ publication, of which the avowed objective was "to unmask error and expose its deformity," was established in opposition to John Thomas, editor of the *Apostolic Advocate.*[3] Accordingly, the content was largely theological and controversial. The semimonthly numbers added variety—book reviews, dialogues, church history, communications, and poetry.

U.L.S., 2nd ed., p. 680.

Other holdings: VRB Dec., 1840.

[1] Aug. 7, 1843 (vol. 2, no. 11), is the last number seen; one more may have appeared. Superseded in 1844 by the *Christian Intelligencer,* Charlottesville, Va.

[2] See section on *Christian Intelligencer* for sketch of Coleman.

[3] *Christian Publisher,* II (July, 1843), 66.

Christian Repository

Atlanta. 1852 (?).[1] Monthly.

Editors: Joseph L. Walker and C. D. Kirk.[2]

No copy known.

[1] Listed in the *Baptist Almanac,* 1853, p. 42, as appearing currently.

[2] See section on *Baptist Champion* for sketch of Walker.

CHRISTIAN SENTINEL
METHODIST CHRISTIAN SENTINEL
VIRGINIA AND NORTH CAROLINA CONFERENCE JOURNAL
RICHMOND CHRISTIAN ADVOCATE[1]

Richmond. June 8, 1832–March 30, 1865.[2] Weekly. Folio, 4 pp., 6-7 cols. $1.50-$2.50 a year. 4,000 subscribers.[3]

Editors: Ethelbert Drake, June 8, 1832–Feb. 26, 1836; "Bro. Smith," 1838;[4] Leroy M. Lee, 1839–Sept. 30, 1858, or later;[5] Leonidas Rosser, Feb. 10, 1859 (?)–Sept. 20, 1860 (?);[6] James A. Duncan, April 11, 1861 (?)–March 30, 1865.[7]

Proprietors: Robert Nesbitt and James C. Walker, June 8, 1832–May, 1834; Drake, June 6, 1834–Feb. 26, 1836; Virginia Methodist Episcopal Conference, 1836-1839; Virginia and North Carolina Conferences, 1839; General Conference of the Methodist Episcopal Church, 1840-1845; General Conference of the Methodist Episcopal Church, South, 1845–March 30, 1865.[8]

This outstanding Methodist weekly, the official organ of the General Conference of the Methodist Episcopal Church, South, contained church proceedings, essays on benevolent projects, letters, church history, religious and secular news, and items under the following standing captions: Married, Died, Poetry, Biography, Agricultural, Advertisements, Temperance, and Miscellaneous.

U.L.S., 2nd ed., p. 390, as *Baltimore and Richmond Christian Advocate;* p. 682 as *Christian Sentinel;* p. 2418 as *Richmond Christian Advocate.*

Other holdings: GEU vols. [13, 15-17]. NcR April 26, 1833. NcU [1845, 1847-1848, 1850, 1856, 1860, 1864]. VU Dec. 22, 1859; March 6, 1860.

[1] The prospectus stated that the name would be *Richmond Evangelist,* but the first title listed above was adopted before publication began and used until May, 1833. See *Religious Herald,* Richmond, Dec. 9, 1831, for the original prospectus. Second title used June 6, 1834–Feb. 26, 1836, or later; third title, sometimes shortened to *Conference Journal,* in use in 1839 and 1840; fourth title adopted just prior to July 10, 1840, and used thereafter. See *Southern Christian Advocate,* Charleston, July 10, 1840.

[2] Publication had to be suspended because of war conditions. The paper reappeared, however, Sept. 7, 1865, and continued publication until combined with the *Baltimore Christian Advocate* on Dec. 20, 1900, to form the *Baltimore and Richmond Christian Advocate.*

[3] This is an average. The *Methodist Christian Sentinel,* Nov. 7, 1834, placed its circulation at 2,000; the *Richmond Christian Advocate,* Feb. 9, 1854, gave 6,000, and on May 21, 1863, reported "several thousand" free copies being sent weekly to the army.

[4] A notice in the *Southern Christian Advocate,* Charleston, Dec. 21, 1838, stated that "Bro. Smith" was retiring from the editorship. This may have been W. A. Smith, a member of the publishing committee at that time.

[5] Lee (1808-1882), the principal editor, was a native Virginian and a prominent Methodist preacher. See "Pen and Ink Sketch of Rev. Leroy M. Lee, D.D.," *Southern Methodist Pulpit,* Richmond, II (1849), 50-55.

[6] Rosser (1815-1892), a Virginian and a graduate of Wesleyan University, was outstanding as a minister and author. See Simpson, *Cyclopaedia of Methodism,* 4th rev. ed., p. 767.

[7] Duncan (1830-1877), a Virginian, later became president of Randolph-Macon College.

[8] Drake stated in the *Methodist Christian Sentinel,* Feb. 26, 1836, that the paper had been purchased from him by the Virginia Conference. The *Conference Journal,* Oct. 31, 1839, was published by a committee for the Virginia and North Carolina Annual Conferences. The *Richmond Christian Advocate* was published Sept. 10, 1840, and thereafter by a committee for the General Conference or (after 1845) the General Conference, South. After 1836 the editors and publishing committees were selected by these ecclesiastical bodies.

Christian Spiritualist
Spiritualist[1]

Macon, Ga. 1859 (?)-1860 (?). Weekly.

No copy known.

[1] Listed by the first title in *American Christian Record,* p. 693, and by the second in Kenny, *American Newspaper Directory,* 1860, p. 13.

Christian Sun

Hillsboro, N. C., 1844-1849; Pittsboro, N. C., 1849-1850 (?);[1] Raleigh, N. C., 1853 (?) -1854;[2] Suffolk, Va., 1855–May 16, 1862 (?);[3] Petersburg, Va., April (?)–Nov. 11, 1864, or later. Jan., 1844–Nov. 11, 1864, or later.[4] Monthly, 1844-1846 (?); semimonthly, 1850; weekly, 1853 (?)-1864 (?). Octavo, 16 pp., 1844-1850 (?); folio, 4 pp., 6 cols., 1853 (?)-1864 (?). $1-$10 a year. 1,200 subscribers.

Editors: Daniel Wilson Kerr, Jan., 1844–March, 1850;[5] Mrs. Daniel Wilson Kerr and W. S. Gunter, March, 1850-(?); H. B. Hayes, W. B. Wellons, J. R. Holt, April 20, 1853, or earlier–Dec. 26, 1854; W. B. Wellons, 1855-1864 (?).

Proprietors: North Carolina and Virginia Christian Conference, 1844-1847; Southern Christian Association (known later as Southern Christian Convention), 1847-1864 (?).[6]

The *Christian Sun,* the only periodical known to have been

published by members of the Christian Church in the South Atlantic States before the Civil War, was the official organ of the Southern Christian Convention. This body maintained an editorial council which chose the editors and exercised general supervision over the paper. The *Christian Sun* contained sermons, essays, church proceedings, secular and religious news, discourses on temperance, poetry, and advertisements.

U.L.S., 2nd ed., p. 682; (1), p. 276.

Other holdings: Nc April 20, 1853. NcD [April 8, 1859–Oct. 18, 1861]; Nov. 11, 1864. NcR vol. 3, nos. 1-12, 1846. NcU Dec. 2, 9, 16, 23, 1859; Jan. 6, 1860.

[1] The founding of the *Christian Sun* in Hillsboro and its removal to Pittsboro are described in Barrett, *Religious Journalism,* pp. 366, 370. Kennedy, "Catalogue of Newspapers and Periodicals," 1850, lists Pittsboro as the place but how long the paper was published there has not been determined.

[2] The issue for April 20, 1853, is the earliest examined that was published in Raleigh.

[3] Coggeshall, *The Newspaper Record,* pp. 43, 64, listed a *Christian Sun* at Raleigh and another at Suffolk but was confused by the change. Kenny, *American Newspaper Directory,* 1860, pp. 54, 73, likewise confused, listed *Christian Suns* at Hillsboro and Suffolk.

[4] Publication was suspended for some months immediately after the issue for Dec. 26, 1854. W. B. Wellons revived the *Christian Sun* and moved it to Suffolk in 1855. Forced to suspend near the close of the war, publication was not resumed until Feb., 1867. Now published in Richmond.

[5] Kerr (1796-1850), a Virginian, spent his life teaching, writing, and preaching in Virginia and North Carolina. He was associated for a time with James O'Kelly, one of the founders of the Christian Church, and later became the recognized leader of the North Carolina and Virginia Christian Conference. See Barrett, *Religious Journalism,* p. 357, and Neese, "The First Half Century of the Christian Denomination in the South," pp. 50-52.

[6] These bodies determined policies and named the editors, who served as "publishing agents." See *Christian Sun,* April 20, 1853. Before the Convention acquired its own printing press the paper was printed by Dennis Heartt (Hillsboro) and Alexander Dismarks (Pittsboro).

Christian Telescope

Montpelier, N. C. 1835 (?), 1850 (?).[1] Semimonthly. Octavo, 8 pp. 50¢ a year.

Editor and proprietor: John Monroe.[2]

This Baptist editor favored Bible, missionary, and tract societies, and included news of revivals, biographical sketches, obituaries, and original communications. He stated that the profits from the publication would be applied to the printing of the Bible in Burmese.

No copy known.

[1] Receipt of the first issue was acknowledged and its contents described by the *Southern Baptist and General Intelligencer,* Charleston, Aug. 14, 1835. The *Religious and General Intelligencer,* Wilmington, N. C., June 27, 1850, invited attention to a recent issue of Monroe's paper, describing it as a new publication.

[2] Monroe was born in Richmond County, N. C., in 1804 and preached in that area most of his life. Cathcart, *Baptist Encyclopaedia,* p. 809.

Christian Union

Augusta, Ga. Jan., 1856–1858 or later.[1] Monthly. Octavo, 32-48 pp. $1.50-$2 a year.

Editors: J. S. Lamar and A. G. Thomas.[2]

Proprietors: The Disciples of Christ.[3]

This Disciples of Christ publication worked for the conversion of the world and the union of all Christians around the principles set forth in the Bible. The editors rejected the creeds of the various churches, "because," they wrote, "upon no one of them however much of truth it may contain, is it possible for all Christians to be united." The periodical was addressed to persons of all denominations, who were invited to accept either the name Disciples or the name Christians.[4] The content, made up of letters, essays, and sermons, was almost entirely religious in character.

U.L.S., 2nd ed., p. 683.

Other holdings: NcD March, 1856.

[1] Although no copy is known of later date than Dec., 1856, receipt of the issue for Jan., 1857 (vol. 2, no. 1), was acknowledged by the *Millennial Harbinger,* Bethany, Va., VII (Feb., 1857), 113, and an agent of the *Christian Union* was permitted to address the State Convention of the Baptist Denomination in South Carolina (see *Minutes,* 1858, p. 5) a year later in the interest of his publication.

[2] Only Lamar resided in Augusta. Thomas was from Griffin, Ga., and there were two associate editors: D. Hook and P. F. Lamar of Atlanta. The work was printed by F. H. Singer. By the close of 1856 J. S. Lamar had become sole editor, but he was determined to continue and enlarge the magazine. Alexander Campbell referred to him as "our estimable brother," declaring his publication "in accordance with our highest approbation." See *Millennial Harbinger,* VII (Feb., 1857), 113.

[3] Editors, who served without pay, were elected by an "annual meeting" of Disciples of Christ in Georgia. Business matters were handled by J. S. Lamar. See *Christian Union,* I (Dec., 1856), 377.

[4] *Christian Union,* I (Jan., 1856), 1.

Christian Union and Religious Review

King William Court House, Va. 1856 (?).[1] Monthly.

Editor and proprietor: E. Orvis.

A Disciples of Christ magazine published in the interest of Christian union.

No copy known.

[1] Listed in *Christian Union,* Augusta, Ga., I (May, 1856), 159, as appearing currently.

Christian Union Magazine

Virginia. 1855-(?). Monthly.

Editor and proprietor: Potter.[1]

Nonsectarian.

No copy known.

[1] The only available information about this periodical appeared in the *Southern Episcopalian,* Charleston, II (Sept., 1855), 274-275. Recognizing the July issue as the third number of a new periodical published in Virginia, the Charleston editor wrote as follows: "It professes to be anti-sectarian, and coupling this with its title, we are led to conclude, that its intention is, to present itself to the several denominations of evangelical Christians as a common organ. The design is good, but will demand for its successful execution a large share both of the charity and wisdom of the gospel. . . . We wish Mr. Potter all success in his Christian undertaking."

Christian Warrior

Richmond. April (?), 1842 (May 28, 1842, is vol. 1, no. 7)–1845. Weekly. Folio, 4 pp., 4 cols. $1.50 a year.

Editor: Daniel D. Smith.[1]

Publishers: Henry C. Toler and Company.

The *Christian Warrior,* a champion of Universalism, defied the religious press of Richmond to prove the validity of the doctrine of never-ending punishment. It heaped pungent invectives on the "proselyting" leaders of the sects of the city, accusing them of attempting to prevent persons from attending Universalist meetings. In addition to controversial discussions of doctrines there were articles in support of temperance and on Universalist history.

Not listed U.L.S.

Holdings: NcD May 28, 1842.

[1] An "Association of Gentlemen" assisted Smith. R. T. Wicker and Jacob Frieze, former editor of the *Liberalist,* Wilmington, N. C., edited vol. 3. See Eddy, *Universalism in America,* II, 595.

Church Intelligencer

Raleigh, N. C., March 14, 1860–April 8, 1864; Charlotte, N. C., Sept. 14, 1864–May 4, 1865. March 14, 1860–May 4, 1865.[1] Weekly. Folio, 8 pp. (4 pp. or less after Nov., 1861), 4-5 cols. $2.50-$60 a year. 2,000 subscribers.

Editors: Frederick Fitzgerald, March 14, 1860–June, 1861; T. S. W. Mott, July, 1861–April 8, 1864;[2] F. M. Hubbard and George M. Everhart, Sept. 14, 1864–May 4, 1865.

Proprietors: Mott, March 14, 1860–April 8, 1864; Protestant Episcopal Church Publishing Association, Sept. 14, 1864–May 4, 1865.

Although privately owned until 1864, the *Church Intelligencer* was the accredited organ of ten Southern bishops of the Protestant Episcopal Church and the special advocate of the University of the South, Sewanee, Tennessee. Editors were chosen by the bishops, who exercised "more or less supervisory care" and "greatly directed the tone," which was pro-Southern.[3] The *Church Intelligencer* professed to be, "not a religious journal exclusively, but a scientific and literary one" as well. The content included church news, poetry, letters, book reviews, selections, secular news, editorials, and stories.

U.L.S., 2nd ed., p. 688.

Other holdings: DLC May 1, 1863; Jan. 8, Feb. 12, 19, March 4, 26, April 8, 1864. Nc March 14, Aug. 30, Sept. 20, Dec. 13, 1860; Jan. 24, June 6, July 18, Aug. 2, Oct. 4, 11, Nov. 29, 1861; Jan. 24, 31, 1862; Oct. 23, 30, 1863; Nov. 23, 1864. NcR [March 14, 1860–April 6, 1865]. NcU [March 14, 1860–April 20, 1865]. ScU Oct. 5, 1864–Feb. 9, 1865.

[1] No issue appeared Nov. 15, 1861, because of the lack of paper. After the fall of several Confederate States had greatly reduced his list of subscribers, the proprietor suspended publication April 8, 1864, and turned the paper over to the Council of Bishops. No further issues appeared until the bishops brought about a resumption of publication in Charlotte, Sept. 14, 1864. Publication had to be suspended from Feb. 23 until March 16, 1865, because Charlotte was threatened by hostile armies. See *Church Intelligencer*, Feb. 23, 1865. The editors got out a paper April 20, 1865, even though they knew it could not be mailed. Apparently the last issue during the closing weeks of the war appeared May 4, 1865. The suspension which followed lasted until Aug. 31, 1865, when regular publication was resumed. The last issue examined is vol. 6, no. 3, dated Feb. 1, 1866. U.L.S., 2nd ed., p. 688, errs in closing the publication in 1865.

[2] The original prospectus announced that Henry F. Greene would be editor, but he died, Feb. 28, 1860, before the first number appeared. The bishops of ten Southern dioceses in session at Sewanee, Tennessee, later named George F. Cashman editor and Mott associate editor. When the former declined the appointment, the bishops chose Fitzgerald, who had actually edited the paper from the beginning, permanent editor. See *Church Intelligencer*, Nov. 1, 1860; May 9, 1861. Fitzgerald, already engaged in preaching and teaching (Saint Mary's School) in Raleigh, soon left Mott, an equally able Episcopal clergyman and writer, in complete charge of the paper.

[3] *Church Intelligencer*, Nov. 1, 1860.

COMMISSION

Richmond. Jan., 1849–June, 1851.[1] Monthly. Folio, 4 pp., 4 cols. 25¢ a year. 8,000 subscribers.[2]

Editor: James B. Taylor.[3]

Proprietor: Board of Foreign Missions of the Southern Baptist Convention.

With the motto "Go ye into all the world and preach the gospel to every creature," the *Commission* was devoted exclusively to foreign missions. It contained descriptions of mission fields, arguments in support of missions, letters from missionaries, requests for funds, and a children's department.

U.L.S., 2nd ed., (1), p. 302.

Other holdings: PCA April, 1850. VRB April, 1851.

[1] An account of the founding of the *Commission* appeared in Southern Baptist Convention, *Proceedings,* 1849, pp. 16-18. The *Commission* was superseded in 1851 by the *Home and Foreign Journal,* Richmond.

[2] Kennedy, "Catalogue of Newspapers and Periodicals" (1850).

[3] Taylor (1804-1871), an Englishman who migrated to Richmond, was Corresponding Secretary of the Board of Foreign Missions of the Southern Baptist Convention from its formation until his death. See Cathcart, *Baptist Encyclopaedia,* p. 1134.

COMMISSION; OR, SOUTHERN BAPTIST MISSIONARY MAGAZINE

Richmond. July, 1856–Sept., 1861. Monthly. Octavo, 32 pp. $1 a year. 1,700 subscribers.

Editor and proprietor: Board of Foreign Missions of the Southern Baptist Convention.[1]

Like the *Commission,* published from 1849 until 1851, this periodical was devoted entirely to informing Southern Baptists about their foreign-mission projects. It was founded because the *Home and Foreign Journal* was not large enough to serve all of the Baptist Boards.[2] The content included editorials, journals of missionaries, letters, church proceedings, selections, and book notices.

U.L.S., 2nd ed., p. 746; (1), p. 302.

Other holdings: NcW [1856-1861]. ScGF Sept., 1856. VRB complete file. VRC [1856-1861]. VRF complete file. VU Nov., 1860.

[1] Abram Maer Poindexter (1809-1872), one of the secretaries of the Board, was the principal editor. A North Carolinian, he attended Columbian College, now George Washington University. See Taylor, *Virginia Baptist Ministers,* series 3, pp. 146-164.

[2] *Commission; Or, Southern Baptist Missionary Magazine,* I (July, 1856), 1-2.

CONFEDERATE BAPTIST

Columbia, S. C. Oct. 1, 1862–Jan. 25, 1865, or later. Weekly. Folio, 4 pp., 5 cols. $2 a year. 4,000 subscribers.[1]

Editors: J. L. Reynolds and J. M. C. Breaker.[2]

Proprietors: S. W. Bookhart and A. K. Durham.[3]

This wartime publication was intensely patriotic and unusually prosperous for a young newspaper. Although designed to be acceptable to the entire South, it was offered in particular to South Carolina Baptists, whose unofficial organ, the *Southern Baptist*, Charleston, had been discontinued. The *Confederate Baptist* contained letters from soldiers, editorials, church and secular news, obituaries, poetry, stories, and advertisements.

U.L.S., 2nd ed., p. 756; (1), p. 307. The PCA file, listed as complete, lacks many issues.

Other holdings: ScGF Dec. 17, 1862; April 29, June 10, 17, 1863.

[1] *Confederate Baptist*, June 10, 1863. About 3,000 additional copies were sent weekly to the Confederate Army as gifts from readers of the *Confederate Baptist* who contributed to a fund established for that purpose.

[2] See section on *Baptist Guardian* for sketch of Reynolds. Breaker, born in South Carolina in 1824, was graduated from Furman and after holding several pastorates in his native state removed to Texas. The *Confederate Baptist*, Jan. 7, 1863, contained a notice that Breaker had severed his connections, leaving Reynolds sole editor.

[3] Bookhart was later replaced by Mason and the title of the owners changed from proprietors to publishers. See *Confederate Baptist*, June 29, 1864.

CONFEDERATE BAPTIST REVIEW (proposed)

Columbia, S. C. 1863 (?).[1] Monthly. Octavo, 36 pp. $5 a year.

Editor: J. L. Reynolds.[2]

Proprietors: I. D. Durham and G. T. Mason.

No copy known.

[1] The first number was to be published as soon as merited by the subscription list. See *Baptist Banner*, Atlanta, Aug. 22, 1863. There is no evidence that it ever appeared.

[2] Reynolds was editor of the *Confederate Baptist*, Columbia, S. C.

DISCIPLES' ADVOCATE. *See* CHRISTIAN FRIEND

DUE WEST TELESCOPE. *See* ERSKINE MISCELLANY

EPISCOPAL PROTESTANT

Charleston. Nov. (?), 1843–July (?), 1845.[1] Weekly. $3 a year.

Editor and proprietor: William H. Barnwell.[2]

The editor's aim, as stated in the prospectus, was to set forth, "in distinctive contrast with Romanism, Oxfordism, and a questionable orthodoxy, the doctrines of Grace, as they are declared in the Holy Scriptures, and were held and taught at the Reformation." Barnwell intended to make this Episcopal newspaper "decidedly Evangelical and Protestant" in tone.[3]

No copy known.[4]

[1] Receipt of first number acknowledged by *Charleston Observer,* Dec. 2, 1843. The editor of the *Charleston Observer* stated Aug. 2, 1845, that the current issue of the *Episcopal Protestant* announced its discontinuance because of the ill health of the editor. The editor of the *Watchman of the South,* Richmond, noted Aug. 7, 1845, that the *Episcopal Protestant* had united its subscription list with the *Episcopal Recorder,* Philadelphia. This he deemed a wise move: "There are too many mills and too few grists to grind in these days. We speak figuratively and of newspapers."

[2] Barnwell, an Episcopal clergyman, was rector of St. Peter's Church, Charleston.

[3] Prospectus quoted in *Christian Magazine of the South,* Columbia, S. C., II (March, 1844), 89.

[4] Hoole, *Charleston Periodicals,* p. 47, lists the *Episcopal Protestant* but mistakenly "believes that this proposed magazine never reached the first issue."

Erskine Miscellany
Due West Telescope[1]

Due West, S. C. Feb. (?), 1850 (June 22, 1850, is vol. 1, no. 19)–Aug. 29, 1862, or later.[2] Weekly. Folio, 4 pp., 6-7 cols. $2 a year.

Editors and publishers: J. I. Bonner and John Oliver Lindsay, 1850-1851;[3] Lindsay, 1851-1852; Bonner, 1852-1862, or later.

As successor to the *Christian Magazine of the South,* the *Erskine Miscellany* was adopted as the organ of the Southern Associate Reformed Presbyterian Synod. The prospectus declared that "especial attention" would be given to literature, and poetry, essays, and notices of new books did appear in large numbers. "With Politics," wrote the editors, "we will not meddle, except to give a brief summary of Political occurrences, without comment."[4] Although never widely patronized because the denomination remained small, this weekly was a successful effort to maintain a paper devoted to religion, literature, and general intelligence.

U.L.N., p. 643. U.L.S., 2nd ed., p. 346, as *Associate Reformed Presbyterian.*

Other holdings: NcD June 22, 1850; Feb. 7, June 27, 1851; July 13, 1860; Feb. 28, 1862. NcU April 29, 1853. ScDE Sept. 3, 1852; June 18, 1858.

[1] First title used until 1851, the second thereafter.

[2] Superseded the *Christian Magazine of the South,* Winnsboro, S. C.; published without interruption "until the blast of war struck down its staff." See Agnew, "History of Town of Due West," p. 14. It reappeared after the war as the *Associate Reformed Presbyterian,* which is still published. See *Christian Index,* Atlanta, Feb. 14, 1867, for notice of the first number of a new series.

[3] Bonner and Lindsay, both Associate Reformed Presbyterian ministers, founded the paper and printed it on their own press. About 1852 Lindsay transferred his ecclesiastical relations to the Presbyterian Church and left Bonner as sole editor and proprietor. See Presbyterian Synod of South Carolina, *Minutes,* 1901, pp. 58-61. W. R. Hemphill, J. A. Sloan, and James Boyce assisted Bonner.

[4] *Christian Magazine of the South,* VII (Dec. 1849), 374.

Evangelical and Literary Magazine, and Missionary Chronicle.

See Virginia Evangelical and Literary Magazine

Evangelical Inquirer

Richmond. Oct., 1826–Sept., 1827.[1] Monthly. Octavo, 32 pp. $2 a year.

Editor and proprietor: Henry Keeling.[2]

The demise of the *Latter Day Luminary,* Washington, District of Columbia, left Virginia Baptists without a periodical. Keeling pointed out that continued "dependence on our northern brethren for literary and religious periodical publications . . . certainly could bring no honor to ourselves."[3] He determined, therefore, to establish a monthly magazine and was so successful that in 1828 he enlarged the project with the issuing of a weekly newspaper, the *Religious Herald.*[4] The *Evangelical Inquirer* contained essays on doctrines and morals, church news, and biographical, literary, and political sketches.

U.L.S., 2nd ed., p. 975.

Other holdings: VRB complete file.

[1] Superseded by the *Religious Herald,* Richmond.

[2] Keeling (1795-1870) was a native Virginian and a graduate of the Theological Institution of the Baptist General Convention, Philadelphia. Although never an outstanding preacher, he became a successful editor and teacher. Thomas W. White printed his magazine. See Taylor, *Virginia Baptist Ministers,* series 5, pp. 504-507.

[3] *Evangelical Inquirer,* I (Jan., 1827), 128.

[4] Keeling's success in making "several hundred" dollars on the *Evangelical*

Inquirer was most unusual in the field of religious journalism. See *Virginia Baptist Preacher,* Richmond, I (Jan., 1842), Preface.

EVANGELICAL LUTHERAN PREACHER, AND PASTORAL MESSENGER

Winchester, Va. May, 1833–April, 1835.[1] Monthly. Octavo, 16 pp. 1,100 subscribers.[2]

Editor and proprietor: Lewis Eichelberger.[3]

The editor declared that he founded this religious magazine because of a keen sense of his responsibility as a preacher: "Men must believe or perish, . . . the day cometh that shall burn as an oven." The publication consisted of sermons and articles explaining Lutheran principles. With the motto "Go ye into all the world and preach the Gospel to every creature," Eichelberger's periodical was decidedly evangelical in tone and designed to reach the rapidly growing English-speaking portion of the denomination.[4]

U.L.S., 2nd ed., p. 975.

Other holdings: ScCoL complete file.

[1] Superseded by the *Lutheran Observer,* Baltimore.

[2] *Evangelical Lutheran Preacher, and Pastoral Messenger,* I, vi.

[3] Eichelberger was a Lutheran pastor in Winchester, Va.

[4] *Evangelical Lutheran Preacher and Pastoral Messenger,* I, iii.

EVANGELICAL MISCELLANY AND ECCLESIASTICAL REVIEW (proposed)

Petersburg, Va. 1840. Monthly. Octavo, 24 pp. $1.50 a year.

Editor and proprietor: William Southward.[1]

No copy known.

[1] Southward (1785-1850) was born in England and attended Cambridge. He came to the United States when middle-aged and in 1840 was pastor of the Petersburg, Va., Baptist Church. See Taylor, *Virginia Baptist Ministers,* series 2, pp. 76-80. According to his prospectus (*Watchman of the South,* Richmond, Jan. 9, 1840), Southward intended to begin publication when 800 subscribers had been secured. The first number probably never appeared.

EVANGELICAL MUSEUM

Fayetteville, N. C. Jan.–Nov., 1828, or later. Monthly. Octavo, 48 pp. $3 a year.

Editor and publisher: Colin McIver.[1]

The last issue of the *North Carolina Telegraph* contained notice that Colin McIver, who had purchased its printing establishment, would issue two new periodicals as soon as he received sufficient subscribers. A year's efforts secured only limited patronage, but having, as he said, "embarked in this undertaking from a sense of duty," McIver launched the *Evangelical Museum* and the *Virginia and North Carolina Presbyterian Preacher* in January, 1828. The *Evangelical Museum,* despite the periodicity and format, was much like a newspaper and contained secular news along with discussions of theology, arguments for temperance, biographical sketches, church histories, book notices, and religious news. The editor proposed to adhere to the Confession of Faith of the Presbyterian Church of America.[2]

U.L.S., 2nd ed., p. 975; (1), p. 391.

Other holdings: NcD Jan., 1828.

[1] McIver, a native of Scotland, came to Fayetteville in 1809 to teach school. Though never pastor in Fayetteville, he became a leader in the religious and literary life of the community. See Oates, *Story of Fayetteville,* p. 850.

[2] *Evangelical Museum,* I (Jan., 1828), 3.

EVANGELICAL PORT-FOLIO (proposed)

Fayetteville, N. C. 1829 (?).[1] Weekly. Folio. $1.50 a year.

Editor and publisher: Colin McIver.[2]

No copy known.

[1] The prospectus appeared in the *Virginia and North Carolina Presbyterian Preacher,* Fayetteville, N. C., Oct., 1828, and ran until July, 1829. There is no evidence that the first number of the *Evangelical Port-Folio* ever appeared.

[2] McIver was editor and publisher of the *Evangelical Museum,* Fayetteville, N. C., and the *Virginia and North Carolina Presbyterian Preacher.*

EVANGELICAL PULPIT

Forsyth, Ga. Sept., 1861–June, 1862, or later. Monthly. Octavo, 16 pp. $1 a year.

Publishers: Wilkes and Marshall.[1]

The subtitle announced that the periodical would contain sermons of the ablest living ministers of the various evangelical denominations in the Confederate States of America. No editorial material appeared and most of the sermons were by Baptists.

U.L.S., 2nd ed., p. 975.

[1] No editor was named; the publishers operated a printing office.

EVANGELICAL UNIVERSALIST

Macon, Ga. April 7, 1838–1840 (?).[1] Weekly. Quarto, 8 pp., 3 cols., April 7, 1838–April 17, 1839; folio, after April 17, 1839. $3 a year.

Editors: John Gregory and L. F. W. Andrews.[2]

Proprietors: Gregory, Andrews, and [C. A.] Hall.[3]

As the unofficial organ of Southern Universalists this newspaper printed the appointments of ministers, theological discussions, stories, advertisements, and selections from other periodicals. The current controversy between Universalist ministers and Alexander Campbell received considerable attention. The editors emphasized that they were the uncompromising opponents of "all Heresy, delusion and error, especially the God-dishonoring and blasphemous sentiment of endless misery."[4]

U.L.S., 2nd ed., p. 975.

Other holdings: NcD April 7, 1838–April 17, 1839.

[1] Formed by consolidating the *Southern Evangelist,* Charleston, with the *Southern Universalist,* Macon.

[2] Philo Brownson, Jerome Harris, S. J. McMorris, H. F. Stearns, and Allen Fuller were associate editors. All the editors were Universalist ministers, most of them from the North. See Eddy, *Universalism in America,* II, 594.

[3] Hall, a printer, formed with the editors the firm named above. The *Evangelical Universalist* announced on July 21, 1838, that Gregory had sold his interest to Jerome Harris and on Feb. 6, 1839, that Harris had become sole proprietor.

[4] *Evangelical Universalist,* April 7, 1838.

Family Christian Album

Richmond. Jan.–Dec., 1855, or later.[1] Monthly. Octavo, 32 pp. $1.50 a year.

Editress and proprietress: Mrs. E. P. Elam.

Under the motto, "Attend to the morals of your child," the *Family Christian Album* bore a special dedication to mothers who were concerned about the moral and religious training of their children. As much literary as religious in character, it contained stories, poems, anecdotes, and miscellaneous selections. Most of the articles were written by women and were nonsectarian.

U.L.S., 2nd ed., p. 990.

Other holdings: VRB Sept.–Oct., 1855.

[1] Although no notice of plans to discontinue appeared, publication probably ceased with the issue for Dec., 1855.

Family Visitor

North Carolina. 1860.[1]

No copy known.

[1] In June, 1860, John T. Walsh, editor of the *Carolina Christian Monthly,* a Disciples of Christ magazine, announced the transfer of his subscription list to the *Family Visitor,* no place given. See *Christian Intelligencer,* Richmond, July 10, 1860. On Nov. 13, 1860, the editor of the *Christian Intelligencer* remarked concerning his exchanges that "The Family Visitor, N. C., is passing into the fourth week of his absence."

FAMILY VISITOR

RICHMOND FAMILY VISITOR[1]

Richmond. April 6, 1822–Dec. 30, 1826.[2] Weekly. Folio, 4 pp., 4-5 cols. $1.50-$3 a year.

Editors and proprietors: Nathan Pollard, April 6, 1822–Dec. 11, 1824; Pollard and Charles Goddard, Dec. 18, 1824–Oct. 22, 1825; Pollard, Oct. 29, 1825–Dec. 30, 1826.[3]

Pollard's prospectus stated that his aim would be to supply readers with accounts of the "progress of religion among all denominations" and "to exclude every thing of a sectarian controversial character." Most of the material was gleaned from the twenty religious and ten political newspapers Pollard received. There were letters from missionaries, descriptions of mission fields, foreign and domestic secular news, church proceedings, accounts of revivals, anecdotes, and poetry, with Presbyterian items more numerous than those of other denominations.

U.L.N., p. 710, as *Southern Religious Telegraph.* Cappon, *Virginia Newspapers,* p. 175.

Other holdings: NcMHi April 5, 1823; [June 18, 1825–Dec. 30, 1826].

[1] Second title used after April 8, 1826.

[2] Superseded by the *Visitor and Telegraph,* Richmond.

[3] Pollard, a layman, was proprietor of the Franklin Press, Richmond.

FLORIDA BAPTIST UNION

Thomasville, Ga. 1856 (?) -1857 (?).[1] Weekly.

Editors: Baker and Fleming.[2]

No copy known.

[1] Listed in the *American Baptist Almanac,* 1857, p. 29; 1858, p. 31, as appearing currently.

[2] Joseph S. Baker, then preaching in Southern Georgia and Northern Florida, was probably one of the editors. See section on *Baptist Chronicle and Monthly Monitor* for sketch of Baker.

GEORGIA ANALYTICAL REPOSITORY

Savannah, Ga. May/June, 1802–March/April, 1803. Bimonthly. Duodecimo, 48 pp.

Editor and proprietor: Henry Holcombe.[1]

The *Georgia Analytical Repository* was the first religious periodical published in the South Atlantic States. In the preface Holcombe explained that he was establishing the magazine because of the irreligious conditions of Georgia society and the prevalence of crime, adding, "in a land mourning on account of such sins, and pained with the irremediable inefficacy of *human laws,* some have asked if these, and other existing means of order and happiness, might not be aided, at this time, by a *periodical publication.*" The editor launched the "adventurous enterprize" only because he felt keenly the necessity of so doing. In an effort to secure popular approval, Holcombe dedicated his magazine to Josiah Tattnall, Junior, Governor of Georgia, and solicited the aid of several "worthy persons" as contributors.

Although Baptists have long claimed the *Georgia Analytical Repository,* Holcombe adhered rather carefully to his prefatory statement that on his publication "the spirit of a *party* shall *never breathe.* Controversy will be carefully avoided, and the strictest impartiality observed toward all denominations." Despite an appeal to the religious and literary interests of persons of all denominations, Holcombe had to discontinue his magazine after one year because there was not, wrote a Baptist historian, enough "literary spirit" in the people to sustain it.[2]

Holcombe's six numbers contained historical sketches of all the churches in Savannah, proceedings of benevolent and religious associations, accounts of revivals, essays on civil government, and biographical notes. Especially significant were an account of the proceedings which led to the organization of the General Committee of the Georgia Baptists (later Georgia Baptist State Convention), a description of the first efforts to mitigate the severity of the penal code of Georgia, the story of the Savannah Female Orphan Asylum established by Holcombe, and the several descriptions of camp meetings.

U.L.S., 2nd ed., p. 1107.

[1] Holcombe (1762-1824) was a native of Virginia and a captain in the Revolutionary Army. He had little formal schooling but the College of Rhode Island (now Brown University) conferred upon him the degree of D.D. From 1800 until 1812 he was pastor of the Savannah Baptist Church and, from the latter date until his death, of the First Baptist Church, Philadelphia. See *Dictionary of American Biography,* IX, 133-134, and Holcombe's autobiographical work entitled *The First Fruits.*

[2] *History of the Baptist Denomination in Georgia. . . . Compiled for the Christian Index,* pt. 2, p. 274.

GEORGIA CHRISTIAN REPERTORY

Macon, Ga. Jan. (?), 1831 (Dec. 15, 1831, is vol. 1, no. 47)–Sept. 12, 1832, or later.[1] Weekly. Folio, 4 pp., 4-5 cols. $3 a year.

Editor and proprietor: G. Capers.

Devoted to religion, literature, science, general intelligence, and the defense of the doctrines and discipline of the Methodist Church, this general family weekly contained religious selections, poetry, editorials, foreign and domestic news, church proceedings, and advertisements.

Not listed U.L.S.

Holdings: NcD Dec. 15, 1831; March 7, Sept. 12, 1832.

[1] Notice that Capers had discontinued his paper and intended moving to Alabama appeared in the *Christian Sentinel,* Richmond, Feb. 22, 1833.

GEORGIA CHRISTIAN SENTINEL

Covington, Ga. 1837-(?).

Editor and proprietor: William B. Harrison.

This was a privately owned Methodist publication, not the organ of any annual conference. A contemporary editor, acknowledging receipt of the second number, said its character was decidedly religious. Regarding Harrison, a Methodist minister, the contemporary wrote: "Success to him in his attempts to do good, and a safe conduct through the pecuniary dangers which surround religious newspapers."[1]

No copy known.

[1] William Capers in *Southern Christian Advocate,* Charleston, Oct. 28, 1837.

(GEORGIA EXPRESS) [1]

Athens, Ga. 1807 (?).

No copy known.

[1] The following is the only information available concerning an unclassified religious publication which preceded the *Georgia Express:* "The first newspaper ever published in Athens, was established by Rev. John Hodge, and the press and type were brought from Philadelphia in a road wagon by Mr. John Espey, about 1807. The name I do not recollect, but it was designed for a religious and literary paper. It was short-lived. Mr. Hodge from ill health was obliged to abandon the tripod and sold out to Alexander McDonnell, a practical printer who had been imported with the press from Philadelphia. McDonnell changed the name of the paper as well as its character and called it *The Georgia Express.*" See Hull, *Sketches from the Early History of Athens,* p. 36.

GEORGIA REPORTER AND CHRISTIAN GAZETTE

Sparta, Ga. April (?)–Oct. 2, 1826.[1] Weekly. Folio, 4 pp. $3 a year.

Editors and proprietors: B. Gildersleeve and Co.[2]

The mottoes of this Presbyterian paper were the same as those of the *Missionary,* which it superseded. Gildersleeve was censured by the *Wesleyan Journal* for advertising in a religious newspaper for a runaway slave. He replied with a criticism of the *Wesleyan Journal* for "hanging out a sectarian title" in order to "secure a more certain patronage." The Methodist editor then stated that everybody knew Gildersleeve's publication was Presbyterian.[3]

U.L.N., p. 110.

[1] Superseded the *Missionary,* Mount Zion, Ga., and began a new numbering (April 10, 1826, is vol. 1, no. 2). Gildersleeve moved to Charleston late in 1826, and early in the next year founded the *Charleston Observer,* which superseded the *Georgia Reporter and Christian Gazette.* Jacob P. Norton, one of Gildersleeve's partners in Sparta, announced that he would begin the *Hancock Advertiser* on Oct. 13, 1826, and continue in it the advertisements begun in the religious newspaper. See *Georgia Reporter and Christian Gazette,* Oct. 2, 1826.

[2] See section on *Central Presbyterian* for sketch of Gildersleeve.

[3] *Wesleyan Journal,* Charleston, May 6, 27, June 17, 1826.

GOSPEL MESSENGER, AND SOUTHERN CHRISTIAN REGISTER

CHARLESTON GOSPEL MESSENGER, AND PROTESTANT EPISCOPAL REGISTER[1]

Charleston. Jan., 1824–March, 1853.[2] Monthly. Octavo, 32 pp. $3 a year. 300 subscribers.[3]

Editors: "A Society of Gentlemen, Members of the Protestant Episcopal Church," Jan., 1824–Dec., 1826; "Members of the Protestant Episcopal Church," Jan., 1827–Dec., 1835; "Editorial Board," March, 1836–March, 1853.[4]

Proprietors: Members of the Diocese of South Carolina.[5]

This magazine was the official organ of the Bishop of the Episcopal Diocese of South Carolina. It contained sermons, church proceedings, episcopal addresses, book reviews, poetry, religious news, and proceedings of various Charleston benevolent societies.

U.L.S., 2nd ed., p. 644; (1), p. 259.

[1] The first title, sometimes written *Gospel Messenger and Southern Episcopal Register,* was used through Feb., 1836. The second title, with "Charleston" sometimes omitted, was used thereafter.

[2] The suspension of publication during Jan. and Feb., 1835, caused vol. 13 to begin in March. There was no issue for March, 1840; so vol. 17 began in April. Superseded by the *Southern Episcopalian,* Charleston.

[3] Kennedy, "Catalogue of Newspapers and Periodicals" (1850).

[4] The prospectus was written by Bishop Nathaniel Bowen and signed by E. Thayer, whose address was The Theological Bookstore, Charleston. For twelve years immediately prior to his death in June, 1852, the magazine was under the "sole control" of Bishop C. E. Gadsden, a native of Charleston and a graduate of Yale. He was followed as editor by Thomas J. Young, who died in Oct., 1852. The remaining numbers were edited by C. Wallace. "The

Gospel Messenger," wrote the editor in Sept., 1852 (XXIX, 161), "has always been under the immediate control and direction of the Bishop of the Diocese."

[5] All financial affairs were handled by the printers (C. C. Sebring, Jan., 1824–Dec., 1826; A. E. Miller, Jan., 1827–March, 1853), who were listed as publishers. On several occasions Gadsden advanced cash with which to sustain the work. (See covers of vols. for 1846-1849). Miller discontinued the magazine on his own authority because the support was inadequate and he could "retain" no "suitable" editor. See issue for March, 1853 (XXIX, fly leaf). Had there been profits they would have gone to the Protestant Episcopal Society for the advancement of Christianity in South Carolina.

Herald of the Future Age

Richmond. 1845-1847.[1] Monthly.[2] Octavo, 24 pp.

Editor and proprietor: John Thomas.[3]

Issued by the founder of the Christadelphians, this magazine was filled with his calculations of the date for the imminent second coming of Christ to Jerusalem and the beginning of the millennium. Under the motto "If ye be Christ's, then are ye Abraham's Seed, and Heirs according to the promise," Thomas contended that the "Son of Man will return to the wedding in power and great glory A.D. 1866-7," and that the "restitution of all things" would occur forty years later, giving "A.D. 1906 for the reunion of the Twelve Tribes into one nation and kingdom." There were also accounts of the activities of Thomas' followers.

Not listed U.L.S.

Holdings: MWA vol. 2, nos. 1-12. V vol. 3, no. 5.

[1] This magazine is undated. "We do not," wrote Thomas, "put the name of the month to our numbers, because perverse circumstances retard their periodicity." See *Herald of the Future Age,* III, 120. The publication is, however, referred to in the *Christian Intelligencer,* Charlottesville, Va., June 30, 1845; an editorial in vol. 3, no. 5, is dated June 10, 1847; and the dates 1845-1847 are given in the *National Cyclopaedia of American Biography,* IV, 61.

[2] Listed incorrectly in Cappon, *Virginia Newspapers,* p. 175, as a daily.

[3] See section on *Apostolic Advocate* for sketch of Thomas. His teachings are explained in Hastings, *Encyclopaedia of Religion and Ethics,* III, 569-571.

Herald of Truth

Hendersonville, N. C. 1855-1856 or later.[1] $1.50 a year.

Editor and proprietor: William Hicks.[2]

This publication was an individual enterprise devoted to the interests of Methodism.

No copy known.

[1] The *Nashville Christian Advocate,* Feb. 8, 1855, contained notice of the receipt of the first number. The publication is listed in Coggeshall, *The Newspaper Record,* p. 43, and Deems, *Annals of Southern Methodism for 1857,*

p. 270, and quoted in the *Southern Christian Advocate,* Charleston, Sept. 11, 1856.

[2] Hicks, a Methodist clergyman, belonged to the Holston Conference. See *Nashville Christian Advocate,* Feb. 8, 1855.

Herald of Truth (proposed)

Newton, N. C. 1861. Weekly. $1 a year.

Editor: R. L. Abernethy.

The prospectus stated that the publication would be devoted to the interests of Christianity in general, without respect to sects or denominations, and would sustain all institutions and enterprises "that look to the moral and civil interests of our country."[1]

No copy known.

[1] *Southern Lutheran,* Charleston, Oct. 12, 1861. Dated Sept., 1861, the prospectus declared publication would begin in Oct. Although Abernethy's proposals ran for three months in the *Southern Lutheran,* there is no evidence that his first issue ever appeared.

Home and Foreign Journal

Richmond. July, 1851–Sept., 1861.[1] Monthly. Folio, 4 pp., 4 cols. 25¢ a year. 14,000 subscribers.[2]

Editors and proprietors: Boards of the Southern Baptist Convention.[3]

The prospectus of the *Home and Foreign Journal* declared that the high subscription price and postage rate of the *Southern Baptist Missionary Journal,* Richmond, had so restricted its circulation that the claims of the boards were not adequately placed before the public. Accordingly, this more popular publication was to be issued. The space was divided among the boards and contained their proceedings, letters from missionaries, lists of donors, miscellany, youth's department, and appeals for funds.

U.L.S., 2nd ed., p. 1038, as *Foreign Mission Journal.*

Other holdings: PCA Oct., 1852; Jan., 1853; May, 1855; Feb., 1858; Jan., March, 1860. VRB July, 1851–June, Aug., 1855–April, July–Oct., Dec., 1860–Sept., 1861.

[1] Superseded the *Southern Baptist Missionary Journal* and the *Commission.* Suspended from Sept., 1861, until May, 1868, when publication was resumed in Richmond.

[2] *Home and Foreign Journal,* X (Aug., 1860), 7.

[3] From 1851 until 1856 the paper was issued by the Domestic Mission Board and the Foreign Mission Board. In July of the latter year the Bible Board was added. After Aug., 1857, the publication was dated from Richmond, Marion, Ala., and Nashville, where the Foreign, Domestic, and Bible Boards respectively were located. The Secretaries of the Boards—James B. Taylor and A. M. Poindexter of the Foreign, Russell Holman and Joseph

Walker of the Domestic, and William C. Buck of the Bible—sent editorial matter to the printer, H. K. Ellyson, in Richmond.

LANDMARK BANNER AND CHEROKEE BAPTIST
BANNER AND BAPTIST
BAPTIST BANNER[1]

Rome, Ga., Oct. 5, 1859–June 7, 1860; Atlanta, June 14, 1860–June 25, 1864; Augusta, Ga., July 23, 1864–April 22, 1865. Oct. 5, 1859–April 22, 1865.[2] Weekly.[3] Folio, 4 pp., 7-5 cols. $2-$20 a year. 2,000 subscribers.[4]

Editors and proprietors: Jesse M. Wood, Oct. 5–Dec., 1859; Wood and John H. Rice, Jan. 5–Sept. 6, 1860;[5] Wood and H. C. Hornady, Sept. 13, 1860–June, 1862; Hornady, June–Sept., 1862; Hornady and James N. Ells, Sept.–Dec., 1862;[6] Ells, Jan.–Aug., 1863; Ells and A. C. Dayton, July 25, 1863–Sept., 1864;[7] Ells, Sept., 1864–April 22, 1865.

This privately owned newspaper was the organ of the Cherokee Baptist Convention, located in Northwestern Georgia and not a part of the Georgia Baptist State Convention. It advocated the principles of "Old Landmarkism," which included, according to Wood, the belief that Baptist churches could not invite ministers of other denominations into their pulpits because such ministers lacked a valid claim to the true "apostolic pattern."[8] The *Christian Index,* organ of the Georgia Baptist State Convention, and the *Baptist Champion,* privately owned paper, opposed Wood's old landmarkism and his "anti-board" policy.[9] Edited with considerable zeal and ability, the *Landmark Banner and Cherokee Baptist* had exceptionally good coverage of religious news. It also contained secular news, military operations included, advertisements, and miscellany.

U.L.S., 2nd ed., p. 1538, as *Landmark Banner and Cherokee Baptist;* p. 396, as *Baptist Banner;* (1), p. 396.

Other holdings: PCA [1862-1865]. ScGF Oct. 15, 1864.

[1] The first title was used until July 13, 1861, after which (July 20) a reduction in size made necessary a shortening of the name and the second title was adopted. With the beginning of vol. 4 late in 1862 the still shorter third title appeared.

[2] Since the editors were usually owners or part owners of an established printing house, this paper appeared with remarkable regularity and with few reductions in size throughout the war. Ells's effort to get his steam press out of Atlanta before the city fell having failed, he engaged J. T. Paterson and Co. to print the paper for him in Augusta. Ells and E. T. Winkler began a new series Sept. 9, 1865, but continued it only until Nov. 25, 1865.

[3] Brantly, *Georgia Journalism*, p. 30, lists a monthly entitled *Baptist Banner* but locates no file. Probably the weekly *Baptist Banner,* which he does not list, is meant.

[4] Wood wrote in the issue for Oct. 6, 1860, that he had launched the paper with only 900 subscribers. By 1860, however, the number had reached 2,000. See United States Census, Manuscript Returns, 1860: Georgia, Social Statistics, Fulton County. Large sums of money were contributed to send additional copies to Confederate soldiers.

[5] The paper was founded by Wood, a farmer and Baptist minister residing near Rome, and printed at first in Rome by Mason's Job Office. On Nov. 9, 1859, Wood, with the help of a hired printer, began printing the paper on his own press in Rome. At the beginning of 1860 he moved into town, forming a partnership with Rice. Later that year the partners moved to Atlanta, where they formed the company of Wood, Rice, and [C. R.] Hanleiter and opened the Franklin Printing House.

[6] On July 9, 1862, J. J. Toon and Company, which included Hornady, bought the Franklin Printing House. A few weeks later, Ells, a printer and layman formerly associated with the *Southern Field and Fireside,* Augusta, bought half interest in the paper from Hornady. See *Banner and Baptist,* July 12, Sept. 27, 1862.

[7] Dayton (1813-1865), born in New Jersey, received the M.D. degree from the Medical College of New York City. In 1852 he left the Presbyterian Church to become a Baptist minister, but after one sermon never again entered a pulpit. Dayton wrote *Cornelia Birdmore,* which ran in the *Baptist Banner, Theodosia, Infidel's Daughter,* and other popular religious novels. See Cathcart, *Baptist Encyclopaedia,* pp. 319-320.

Dayton, Ells, and Josephus Camp were listed as editors from April 16, 1864, until May 28, 1864, when Camp was replaced by S. D. Niles.

[8] *Landmark Banner and Cherokee Baptist,* Oct. 5, 1859.

[9] *Baptist Champion,* Macon, Ga., Jan. 19, 1860. Opposing the activities of the missionary boards of the Southern Baptist Convention, the *Landmark Banner and Cherokee Baptist* contended that a church or a small group of churches of like order should send out all missionaries. See *Baptist Banner,* Aug. 20, 1864.

Lay-Man's Magazine

Martinsburg, Va. (now W. Va.). Nov. 16, 1815–Nov. 7, 1816, or later.[1] Weekly. Octavo, 8 pp. $1.50 a year.

Printer: John Alburtis.

The editor, who carefully concealed his identity, proposed to follow in this early Episcopal publication events in the spiritual war being waged by the benevolent societies of his day. "In the name of the Lord," he wrote, "lift we up our banner and commence a crusade against pride, profligacy, lukewarmness and ignorance."[2] The content included stories, hymns, poetry, essays on morals, church proceedings, missionary intelligence, and sermons.

U.L.S., 2nd ed., p. 1550.

[1] The last known issue (vol. 1, no. 51) did not contain the usual notice of plans to discontinue.

[2] *Lay-Man's Magazine,* Nov. 16, 1815.

LIBERALIST

Wilmington, N. C. 1826-1828 (?). Semimonthly, octavo, 1826; weekly, folio, 1827-1828 (?).

Editor: Jacob Frieze.[1]

No copy known. U.L.N., p. 510, lists the *Liberalist and Wilmington Reporter* as a secular newspaper probably founded in 1827. Likely the *Liberalist* was merged with a secular paper to form this publication.

[1] Frieze, a Universalist minister from Rhode Island, organized a Universalist State Convention in North Carolina. See Eddy, *Universalism in America,* II, 391-392.

LITERARY AND EVANGELICAL MAGAZINE. *See* VIRGINIA EVANGELICAL AND LITERARY MAGAZINE

LONE BAPTIST AND CHRISTIAN INVESTIGATOR (proposed)

In 1860 Joseph S. Baker issued from Jacksonville, Florida, proposals for a periodical of this title designed to promote Christian unity throughout the nation. The form was to be royal octavo, there would be no charge, and publication would begin when 30,000 names had been secured.[1]

No copy known.

[1] Although the prospectus ran for some time in several papers, publication probably never began. See *Zion's Advocate,* Front Royal, Va., May 5, 1860, and *Landmark Banner and Cherokee Baptist,* Rome, Ga., March 1, 22, 1860.

LYNCHBURG EVANGELICAL MAGAZINE

Lynchburg, Va. Jan., 1810–Jan., 1811 (?).[1] Monthly. Octavo, 32 pp. $1.50 a year. 300 subscribers.[2]

Editor: Samuel K. Jennings.

Printer: William W. Gray, Jan.–Nov., 1810; Jacob Haas, Dec., 1810– (?).

The editor of this early religious magazine intended to maintain a "catholic spirit as far as consistent with sound doctrine." He regarded the statement "God willeth every man to be saved" as a summary of evangelical doctrine and a suitable polar star for his journalistic career.[3] Although meant to be nonsectarian, the periodical exhibited a preference for the teachings of John Wesley and selections from the *London Methodist Magazine.* Presenting little editorial material, the *Lynchburg Evangelical Maga-*

zine leaned heavily toward articles and letters on prayer, death, and hell. "Captain Bligh's Narrative," which ran serially, added variety.

U.L.S., 2nd ed., (1), p. 622.

Other holdings: NcD Jan., 1810–Jan., 1811. NcU Jan.–Dec., 1810.

[1] NcD lists vol. 2, 1811, no. 1, but the file could not be located for examination. Other files close with Dec., 1810, though there was no editorial indication that this would be the last issue.

[2] The issue for Dec., 1810, contained the names of the 300 subscribers, most of them grouped by circuits.

[3] *Lynchburg Evangelical Magazine,* I (Jan., 1810), 3.

MESSENGER OF PEACE, AND NORTH CAROLINA EVANGELICAL HERALD (proposed)

Raleigh, N. C.[1] 1832. Monthly. Quarto. $1 a year.

No copy known.

[1] An unsigned prospectus announced plans for "publishing in the City of Raleigh, pursuant to the wishes of a great portion of the Baptist Church throughout this State, under the management of an association of gentlemen of that denomination, a religious newspaper" of the above title. Publication was to begin Jan. 1, 1832. See *Religious Herald,* Richmond, Nov. 18, 1831. This proposed periodical probably never reached the first issue.

METHODIST CHRISTIAN SENTINEL. *See* CHRISTIAN SENTINEL

METHODIST PROTESTANT BANNER

Charleston. 1840 (?).[1] Monthly.

No copy known.

[1] William Capers, Methodist Episcopal editor, commented as follows: "THE METHODIST PROTESTANT BANNER is the name of a small sheet published monthly in this city 'under the direction of a Committee of the South Carolina Conference.' We notice its publication without the least intention of controverting its contents, (for which we are in no respect answerable), but to give information of the fact that a paper avowedly hostile to our church is published as above. . . . The title of 'The South Carolina Annual Conference' has so long been the designation of the body to which we belong, . . . that the assumption of it by another for the publication of such matter as we see before us looks like it was meant to deceive." See *Southern Christian Advocate,* Charleston, Jan. 24, 1840.

METHODIST SUNDAY-SCHOOL RECORDER[1]

Richmond. 1834.[2]

Editor and proprietor: Ethelbert Drake.[3]

This Sunday school publication was designed to "maintain the truths of the Gospel as taught and believed in the Methodist E. Church, and by her standard writers." Planned for both teachers and scholars, it proposed "to mingle amusement with instruction" and defend the "principles of religion and morality."[4]

No copy known.

[1] In the original proposal the name was to be *Methodist Sunday-School Journal,* but this was changed because of the similarity to the *Sunday School Journal* of Philadelphia. See *Christian Sentinel,* Richmond, June 7, 28, 1833.

[2] The *Methodist Christian Sentinel,* Richmond, reported Sept. 5, 1834, that the first or specimen number had appeared. Regular publication, scheduled for Oct. 11, 1834, had to be postponed for lack of subscribers. Drake wrote in the *Methodist Christian Sentinel,* April 3, 1835, that 500 names had been secured but that 1,000 were needed to pay the expenses of publication. The second number probably never appeared.

[3] Drake was also editor and proprietor of the *Christian Sentinel.*

[4] *Methodist Christian Sentinel,* Sept. 5, 1834.

Millennial Harbinger

Bethany, Va. (now W. Va.). 1830-1865.[1] Monthly.[2] Duodecimo, 1830-1847; Octavo, 1848-1865; 48-60 pp. $2 a year. 8,000 subscribers.

Editor and publisher: Alexander Campbell.[3]

The *Millennial Harbinger* continued with great success the evangelical program of the Disciples of Christ launched by the *Christian Baptist.* Its object was to introduce "that political and religious order of society called THE MILLENNIUM, which will be the consumation of that ultimate amelioration of society proposed in the Christian Scriptures."[4] More than half the space was filled with letters to and from Campbell's followers; the remainder with essays, sermons, and sketches on church history.

U.L.S., 2nd ed., p. 1747; (1), p. 665.

Other holdings: NcW complete file. VRB [1830-1865].

[1] Superseded the *Christian Baptist,* Buffaloe Creek, Va. The Civil War brought no interruption and publication continued until 1870.

[2] In addition to the regular numbers there were numerous extras on special subjects. In numbering the annual volumes a new series was begun every seven years.

[3] See section on *Christian Baptist,* Buffaloe Creek, Va., for sketch of Campbell. He was assisted during the later years by W. K. Pendleton and Robert Richardson, teachers in Bethany College, Archibald W. Campbell, and others.

[4] *Millennial Harbinger,* I (Jan., 1830), 1.

Missionary

Mount Zion, Hancock Co., Ga. May (?), 1819–Oct. 10, 1825, or later.[1] Weekly. Folio, 4 pp. $3 a year.

Editors and proprietors: Nathan S. S. Beman, Benjamin Gildersleeve, and Isaac Wales, May, 1819–May 30, 1821; Beman, Jacob P. Norton, and Gildersleeve, May 30, 1821–Oct. 10, 1825, or later.[2]

The prospectus stated that the *Missionary* would be principally though not exclusively a vehicle of religious news. Avoiding strict sectarianism, the Presbyterian editors wrote that "reports of various charitable societies; the interesting transactions of Baptist Associations, Methodist Conferences and Presbyterian Synods; revivals of religion . . . and Essays, Moral and Religious," would constitute the material.[3] This journal may be regarded as a "religious and miscellaneous" newspaper, with the emphasis on news of foreign missions. The two mottoes were "Go ye into all the world and preach the Gospel to every creature," and George Washington's "Of all the dispositions which lead to political prosperity, Religion and Morality are indispensable supports."

U.L.N., p. 108.

[1] The earliest issue examined is vol. 1, no. 36 (Jan. 28, 1820). Superseded in 1826 by the *Georgia Reporter and Christian Gazette.*

[2] During the first two years the *Missionary* was "Edited and Published by N. S. S. Beman and Co.," which included the persons named above, but a notice in the issue for May 30, 1821, told of the dissolution of the firm, with Norton replacing Wales. After June, 1822, the paper was "Edited and Published by B. Gildersleeve and Co." Gildersleeve had been the principal editor from the first. See *Watchman and Observer,* Richmond, Aug. 7, 1851. See section on *Central Presbyterian* for sketch of Gildersleeve.

[3] *Southern Evangelical Intelligencer,* Charleston, June 5, 1819.

MONTHLY MISCELLANY; A RELIGIOUS AND LITERARY REVIEW, AND MONTHLY REGISTER OF DISCOVERIES AND IMPROVEMENTS IN THE ARTS AND SCIENCES

"Issued simultaneously at Richmond, Atlanta, and New Orleans."[1] Jan.–July, 1849, or later.[2] Monthly. Octavo, 32 pp. $2 a year.[3]

Editor and proprietor: Joseph S. Baker.[4]

The editor's purpose in issuing this unique Baptist magazine was to avoid the "great danger that, amid the rage for inventions and improvements to facilitate and expedite mechanical labor, the intellectual and moral culture of the public mind will be overlooked and neglected."[5] The content included essays on education and systematic theology, church history, missionary intelligence, book reviews, cuts and engravings of mechanical inventions, and agricultural and political news.

U.L.S., 2nd ed., p. 1806.

Other holdings: PCA March, 1849. VRB Jan., March, May–July, 1849.

[1] The content of all copies of each number was identical but the place of publication given on each copy was either Atlanta, Richmond, or New Orleans. The proprietor had all the printing done in Philadelphia because the cost there was lower. See *Monthly Miscellany,* I (Jan., 1849), cover.

[2] The last number examined is dated July, 1849, but the magazine is listed in the *Baptist Almanac and Annual Register* for 1850, p. 31, and for 1852, p. 44. It is not, however, listed in *ibid.* for 1851.

[3] This publication was conducted on the joint-stock principle, with every subscriber a stockholder. All profits were to be divided among the subscribers and credited to them on subscriptions for the next year. See *Monthly Miscellany,* I (Jan., 1849), cover.

[4] See section on *Baptist Chronicle and Monthly Monitor* for sketch of Baker.

[5] *Monthly Miscellany,* I (Jan., 1849), 1.

MONTHLY VISITANT; OR, SOMETHING OLD

Alexandria, Va. July–Dec., 1816. Monthly. Octavo, 40 pp.

Editor and proprietor not given. Printed by S. Snowden.

Under the motto "No man having drunk old wine, straightway desireth new; for he saith, the old is better," the editor announced his determination to disregard all modern sects and advocate a simple form of religion based directly on the Holy Scriptures. "The design of the present publication will be gained," he wrote, "if it fix the attention of any to the doings of the Lord."[1] Sermons, religious essays and exhortations, and news of the operations of benevolent societies filled the pages of this nonsectarian periodical.

U.L.S., 2nd ed., p. 1807.

Other holdings: PPPrHi complete file.

[1] *Monthly Visitant; Or, Something Old,* I (July, 1816), 2.

MORNING WATCH

Evergreen, Anderson District, S. C. Nov., 1837–Aug., 1840.[1] Monthly. Octavo, 32 pp. $2 a year. 550 subscribers.[2]

Editors and proprietors: John M. Barnes and Charles F. R. Shehane.[3]

This Disciples of Christ magazine, "Devoted to Religious Reformation and the Millennial Reign of Christ," sought to exhibit "that class of Scripture Prophecy which proves the SPEEDY PERSONAL RETURN of the MESSIAH, . . . to take vengeance on them that know not God." Containing no secular material, the *Morning Watch* was filled with sermons, exhortations, letters, descriptions of the editors' travels, and church histories. In style and content it resembled Alexander Campbell's periodicals.

U.L.S., 2nd ed., p. 1816.

[1] Superseded the *Disciple,* Tuscaloosa, Ala.

[2] *Morning Watch,* I (Feb., 1838), 128.

[3] Barnes had recently been "cast off" by the Woodward (S.C.) Baptist Church on the charge of having "embraced the heretical doctrines of Alexander Campbell." See *Morning Watch,* I (Nov., 1837), 30. Shehane became sole editor and proprietor in 1839.

MOUNTAIN MESSENGER AND BAPTIST RECORDER[1]

Morgantown, Va. (now W. Va.). 1850 (?)–1859 (?).[2] Weekly. Folio, 4 pp., 7 cols. $1.50 a year. 400 subscribers.[3]

Editor and proprietor: Simeon Siegfried.[4]

A contemporary editor who noted the existence of the *Western Virginia Baptist,* Buchanan, and the *Mountain Messenger and Baptist Recorder* regretted these diversions from the "legitimate patronage" of the *Religious Herald,* Richmond, pointing out that Virginia Baptists could properly support only one paper.[5] Under the motto "Primitive Christianity, Literature, Science, Agriculture and News," Siegfried included items of interest to all members of a family. This publication, with its columns of general news, was designed to make it unnecessary for a reader to subscribe to a secular newspaper.

U.L.S., 2nd ed., (1), p. 692.

Other holdings: PCA Dec. 17, 24, 1856; Feb. 4, Aug. 19, Oct. 14, Nov. 4, 1857.

[1] Various running titles were used. Listed in the *Baptist Almanac* from 1851 to 1854 as *Messenger and Recorder;* in *ibid.* from 1855 to 1858 as *Mountain Messenger;* in Coggeshall, *The Newspaper Record* (1856), p. 63, as *Messenger and Baptist Recorder,* and in Kenny, *American Newspaper Directory* (1860), p. 72, as *Baptist Recorder.*

[2] Superseded the *Baptist Recorder,* Fairmont, Va. Cited in the *Baptist Memorial and Monthly Record,* New York, IX (1850), 369, as a "new paper."

[3] Kennedy, "Catalogue of Newspapers and Periodicals" (1850).

[4] William D. Siegfried was assistant editor.

[5] J. P. Tustin in *Southern Baptist,* Charleston, Jan. 27, 1857.

NAZARENE BANNER

Atlanta. May 20, 1863–1864. Monthly. Folio, 4 pp., 5 cols. $8 for 100 copies; free to armed forces of the Confederacy.

Editor and publisher: James N. Ells.[1]

Published by a Baptist editor and supported by contributions from the Christian public, this newspaper was "devoted to the interests of Army Colportage and General Missions." It received the endorsement of secular as well as religious newspapers.[2]

No copy known.

[1] Ells was editor and publisher of the *Baptist Banner,* Atlanta.

[2] The *Southern Confederacy,* May 24, 1863, contained a notice with this comment: "We ask every patriot to give it a hearty support and contribute liberally towards its regular issue, with an edition large enough to send to every department of the army. We know not how a little money spent could do as much good as in the circulation of this paper." Quoted in Brantley, *Georgia Journalism,* p. 53. See also *Baptist Banner,* May 9, 30, 1863.

North Carolina Baptist

Asheville, N. C. 1851 (?) –1853.[1] Weekly.

Editors and proprietors: W. C. Berry, James Blythe, and J. M. Bryan.[2]

This privately owned religious newspaper was the unofficial organ of the Western North Carolina Baptist Convention.

No copy known.

[1] Referred to in the *Biblical Recorder,* Raleigh, N. C., Feb. 27, 1852, and the *Southern Baptist,* Charleston, Aug. 17, 1853. The *Biblical Recorder,* Oct. 7, 1853, stated that it had been replaced by the *Carolina Baptist,* Hendersonville, N. C.

[2] *Baptist Almanac,* 1853, p. 42.

North Carolina Baptist Interpreter

Edenton, N. C., Jan., 1833–June, 1834; New Bern, N. C., July–Dec., 1834. Jan., 1833–Dec., 1834.[1] Monthly; semimonthly.[2] Octavo, 24 pp. $1 a year.

Editor and publisher: Thomas Meredith.[3]

Meredith's principal objective in establishing this magazine was to promote the objects of the recently founded North Carolina Baptist State Convention, which were the education of young ministers and the employment of missionaries. Accordingly, it contained, in addition to theological discussions and religious news, articles in support of missions, education, and Sunday schools.

U.L.S., 2nd ed., p. 2026.

Other holdings: NcW complete file.

[1] Superseded by the *Biblical Recorder,* New Bern, N. C.

[2] Monthly throughout 1833; issued semimonthly and monthly in alternate months during 1834 making an annual volume of eighteen numbers.

[3] See section on *Biblical Recorder* for sketch of Meredith.

North Carolina Christian Advocate

Raleigh, N. C. Jan. 4, 1856–May (?), 1861; April 2, 1863–March 28, 1865.[1] Weekly. Folio, 4 pp., 6-8 cols. $2-$10 a year. 5,000 subscribers.[2]

Editors: Rufus T. Heflin, Jan. 4, 1856–May (?), 1861;[3] William E. Pell, April 2, 1863–March 28, 1865.[4]

Proprietors: North Carolina Annual Conference of the Methodist Episcopal Church, South, Jan. 4, 1856–May (?), 1861; "A Joint Stock Company Under the Patronage of the North Carolina Conference," April 2, 1863–March 28, 1865.

This general family religious newspaper was the official medium of communication between Methodist leaders in North Carolina and their constituents. Widely supported and well edited, it contained church news, selections, editorials, letters, proceedings of church bodies, poetry, general news, advertisements, miscellany, and essays on moral and public issues.

U.L.S., 2nd ed., p. 2027.

Other holdings: Nc April 9, 23, June 10, July 1, 22, Sept. 16, Oct. 28, Dec. 9, 1863. NcD [1856-1857, 1863-1865]. NcR Nov. 7, 1856; Feb. 4, 1858; Sept. 29, 1859; Sept. 23, Dec. 2, 1863; April 30, May 7, Sept. 2, 9, 1864. NcU [1856-1861, 1863-1865].

[1] U.L.S., 2nd ed., p. 2027, erroneously gives 1855 as the date of the first number. Johnson, *Ante-Bellum North Carolina,* p. 802, also gives 1855 and cites Greensboro, N. C., as the original place of publication. The 1861-1863 suspension was due to wartime conditions. After a long suspension at the close of the war, the paper was re-established in 1867 by H. T. Hudson and renamed first the *Episcopal Methodist* then the *Raleigh Christian Advocate.* The periodical was later transferred to Greensboro, where it is now published under the original name, *North Carolina Christian Advocate.*

[2] This was approximately the number of copies printed weekly during the war. Regular subscribers received 3,000, soldiers in the Confederate Army the remaining 2,000. See *North Carolina Christian Advocate,* June 17, 1863.

[3] The first publishing committee appointed by the North Carolina Conference to establish a newspaper consisted of William E. Pell, William Carter, R. T. Heflin, N. H. D. Wilson, and William Barringer. See *Weekly Message,* Greensboro, N. C., Sept. 18, 1855, for the prospectus they issued. Upon the recommendation of this committee, the bishop appointed Heflin, North Carolinian and Methodist clergyman, first editor.

[4] Pell, native North Carolinian, Methodist minister and experienced newspaperman, was elected editor by the North Carolina Conference. See *North Carolina Christian Advocate,* Jan. 8, 1861; April 9, 1863.

North Carolina Presbyterian

Fayetteville, N. C. Jan. 1, 1858–March 8, 1865.[1] Weekly. Folio, 4 pp., 7 cols. $2 a year. 4,600 subscribers.[2]

Editors: George McNeill, Jan. 1, 1858–Aug., 1861;[3] James H. McNeill, Aug. 24, 1861–March 8, 1865.[4]

Proprietors: The North Carolina Presbyterian Publishing Company.[5]

Convinced that the religious newspapers published in Virginia and South Carolina did not meet the needs of North Carolina Old School Presbyterians, George McNeill founded the *North Carolina Presbyterian* as the organ of that group. Under his vigorous leadership it became the largest Presbyterian paper in the South. It contained church proceedings, editorials on moral and public issues, religious and general news, obituaries, advertisements, poetry, stories, and miscellany.

U.L.S., 2nd ed., p. 2257, lists the *Presbyterian Standard,* Charlotte, N. C., and dates it back to 1858 without a reference to the *North Carolina Presbyterian.*

Other holdings: Nc May 28, 1859; June 9, 16, 30, 1860; Feb. 2, July 13, 1861; May 10, 1862; Jan. 31, 1863. NcD [Jan. 1, 1858–March 8, 1865]. NcMHi [1858-1864]. NcR Jan. 8, Feb. 12, March 5, June 26, Aug. 21, Sept. 11, 25, Nov. 6, 1858; Jan. 1, 1859; July 6, Aug. 24, 1861; May 24, Nov. 29, 1862; Jan. 17, Aug. 8, 22, 29, 1863; Dec. 7, 1864. PPPrHi Jan. 1, 1858–May 18, 1861. VRT [June 4, 1858–Oct. 10, 1863].

[1] Sherman's troops destroyed the printing office and equipment March 12, 1865. Being unable to restore the damaged property after the war, the old stock company bestowed its subscription books and good will upon William McKay, who, with Bartholomew Fuller as editor, resurrected the journal Jan. 10, 1866. Known for a time as the *Presbyterian Standard,* it is still published as one of several papers which were merged to form the *Presbyterian of the South,* Richmond.

[2] An editorial in the *North Carolina Presbyterian,* Oct. 27, 1860, listed the number of subscribers at 3,000, of whom 800 were "Macs." This number remained relatively unchanged during the war and about 1,600 additional copies were sent to Confederate troops weekly. The editor pointed out on Jan. 7, 1860, that at the close of 1859 his "list of subscribers was larger than that of any paper in North Carolina, or any Presbyterian paper south of Mason's and Dixon's line. . . ."

[3] McNeill (1827-1861) was a native North Carolinian and a graduate of both Delaware College and Princeton Seminary. See Nevin, *Encyclopaedia of the Presbyterian Church,* pp. 508-509. His assistant editors included Bartholomew Fuller, W. L. Miller, John M. Sherwood, and James H. McNeill.

[4] James H. McNeill, brother of the former editor and likewise a Presbyterian minister, spent much of his time with the Confederate Army as Colonel of the Fifth Regiment of North Carolina Cavalry. In his absence some of the ministers who had assisted George McNeill got out the paper. James H. McNeill was killed before Petersburg March 31, 1865.

[5] This joint stock company consisted originally of forty-eight members who subscribed one hundred dollars each to provide a printing establishment. See *North Carolina Presbyterian,* Jan. 7, 1860.

NORTH CAROLINA TELEGRAPH

Fayetteville, N. C. Jan. 27–Dec. 29, 1826.[1] Weekly. Octavo, 16 pp. $2.50 a year.

Editor and proprietor: Robert Hall Morrison.[2]

Although a small octavo, this Presbyterian publication contained the type of material usually found in the large religious folios of the day. The departments were entitled "Religious," "Miscellany," "Religious Intelligence," "Foreign Intelligence," "Poetical," "Fayetteville Prices," and "Political Intelligence."

U.L.S., 2nd ed., (1), p. 768.

[1] Before the close of 1826 Morrison sold his subscription list to the proprietor of the *Richmond Family Visitor,* who merged the two papers to form the *Visitor and Telegraph,* Richmond. See *North Carolina Telegraph,* Dec. 29, 1826.

[2] Morrison, a native North Carolinian, was a graduate of the University of North Carolina and in 1826 pastor of the Presbyterian Church in Fayetteville. At the close of his editorship he moved to Mecklenburg County, North Carolina, where he later became the first president of Davidson College. See Shaw, *Davidson College,* pp. 26-28. Since the press Morrison had ordered from Philadelphia before launching his paper did not arrive on time, the first issues were printed for him on the press of the Fayetteville *Sentinel* by Hunter and McDonald. See *North Carolina Telegraph,* Jan. 27, 1826.

NORTH WESTERN VIRGINIA BAPTIST
NORTHWESTERN VIRGINIA BAPTIST

Grafton, Taylor Co., Va. (now W. Va.). 1859-1861 (?).[1] Folio. $2 a year.

Editor: D. B. Purington.

Publisher: S. Siegfried.

No copy known.

[1] Hailed in 1859 as a new paper, the *North Western Virginia Baptist* was said to occupy the former field of the *Baptist Recorder and Messenger,* Morgantown, Va. See *Baptist Champion,* Macon, Ga., Dec. 15, 1859. Purington's views on the board question in the Southern Baptist Convention were orthodox. See *Landmark Banner and Cherokee Baptist,* Atlanta, Jan. 19, 1861.

PACIFICATOR

Augusta, Ga. Oct. 8, 1864–March (?), 1865.[1] Weekly. Folio, 4 pp. 5 cols. $15 a year.

Editors and proprietors: Patrick Walsh and L. T. Blome.

Under the motto "Put up thy sword into its sheath, and the God of Peace will be with thee," the editors of this Catholic newspaper sought "to aid, by every honorable means . . . , in restoring to our Confederacy an early, honorable, and lasting peace." They hoped to convince Catholics in the North that the continuation of the war against the South was "unjust, unbecoming and ruinous." In addition to addresses on the above subject, the content included church news, stories, letters, war news, and communications from the hierarchy.

U.L.N., p. 102.

Other holdings: NcD June 24, 1865.

[1] Suspended briefly near the close of the war; resumed in May, 1865, and published apparently for only a few weeks thereafter. The last issue examined is vol. 1, no. 35, dated June 24, 1865.

PARISH VISITOR

Richmond. Jan., 1851-1856 (?).[1] Monthly.

Episcopal.

No copy known.

[1] Listed in McLean, "Periodicals Published in the South before 1880" and in Gilmer, *Checklist of Southern Periodicals to 1861,* p. 46, as founded in Richmond, Jan., 1851. The following contemporary notices appeared but it is not certain that they refer to the Richmond publication: "The Parish Visitor for April [1855], is filled with valuable matter, suitable for family reading, and calculated to promote vital piety." In acknowledging the July, 1856, issue the same writer remarked that the *Parish Visitor* was not a newspaper, "nor does it take a controversial position." See *Southern Episcopalian,* Charleston, II (May, 1855), 86; III (Aug., 1856), 265.

PASTOR'S AND PEOPLE'S JOURNAL

Macon, Ga. April, 1857–March, 1858. Monthly. Octavo, 32 pp. $1 a year. 1,000 subscribers.[1]

Editors and proprietors: R. L. Breck and William Flinn.[2]

This Presbyterian publication combined the features of newspapers and magazines. Evangelical in character and designed to increase personal piety, it contained discussions of doctrines, missions, and education, editorials, secular and religious news, obituaries, advertisements, and miscellaneous literature. The editors denied any desire to conflict with the *Southern Presbyterian,* acknowledged organ of the Synod, and appealed to Presbyterians to support both publications.[3]

Not listed U.L.S.

Holdings: NcD April, 1857–Jan., March, 1858.

[1] This was the number of copies mailed of the first issue, many to nonsubscribers.

[2] The editors, who were Presbyterian ministers, discontinued the publica-

tion after the twelfth number. Their printing was done by the *Georgia Telegraph* Power Press.

[3] *Pastor's and People's Journal,* I (Jan., 1858), 317.

PERIODICAL LIBRARY

Penfield, Ga. 1847-(?).[1] Quarterly.

Editor: Joseph S. Baker.[2]

This Baptist periodical served as a companion publication to the *Christian Index,* Baptist weekly which Baker also edited.

No copy known.

[1] Announcements appeared that the fourth number would be published in Dec., 1847. See *Baptist Guardian,* Richmond, Dec. 15, 1847. Listed in *Baptist Almanac,* 1848, p. 32.

[2] See section on *Baptist Chronicle and Monthly Monitor* for sketch of Baker.

PRESBYTERIAN PREACHER. *See* VIRGINIA AND NORTH CAROLINA PRESBYTERIAN PREACHER

PRIMITIVE BAPTIST

Tarboro, N. C., Jan. 9, 1836–Dec. 4, 1847; Raleigh, N. C., Jan., 1848–Sept. 24, 1864 (?).[1] Jan. 9, 1836–Sept. 24, 1864, or later.[2] Semimonthly, Jan. 9, 1836–Dec., 1845; monthly, Jan. 3, 1846–Dec. 4, 1847 (1 vol. in 2 yrs.); semimonthly, Jan., 1848–Sept. 24, 1864 (?). Octavo, 16 pp. $1 a year. 1,500 subscribers.

Editors: Mark Bennett, Jan. 9, 1836–Dec. 22, 1838;[3] "Primitive (or Old School) Baptists," Jan. 12, 1839–Dec. 4, 1847;[4] Burwell Temple, Jan., 1848–Sept. 24, 1864 (?).[5]

Publishers: George Howard, Jan. 9, 1836–Dec. 4, 1847; Burwell Temple, Jan., 1848–Sept. 24, 1864 (?).

Joshua Lawrence, aggressive but unlearned Primitive Baptist leader, was largely responsible for establishing this publication, to which he contributed widely. His principles are embodied in the following from the specimen number: "Believing that Theological Schools, Bible, Missionary, Tract, and Sunday School Union Societies, are the same in principle—unscriptural—savor more of 'lucre' than of 'good-will towards men,' we are opposed to them." Letters, articles on controversial doctrines, sermons, church news, and denunciations of benevolent projects filled the *Primitive Baptist.*

U.L.S., 2nd ed., p. 2260; (1), p. 855.

Other holdings: NcD [1844-1848]. NcR Sept. 25, 1858; March

12, 1859; Oct. 24, 1863. NcU [1860-1864]. NcW [1836-1841]-[1843, 1849-1864].

[1] After Jan., 1848, this periodical was printed at the "Office of the *Primitive Baptist,*" located nine miles east of Raleigh, and dated from the nearest post office. These were, in the order used, Raleigh, Eagle-Rock, Milburnie, and Raleigh.

[2] A specimen number appeared Oct. 3, 1835. Publication was suspended after the issue dated Oct. 12, 1861, for about one year because the printers had volunteered for the Confederate Army. Once resumed, publication continued until near the close of the war, when another suspension occurred (Sept. 24, 1864, is vol. 26, no. 11; Jan. 26, 1870, is vol. 27, no. 1). Publication ceased in 1879.

[3] Bennett, a North Carolinian, combined preaching and farming. He resigned the editorship in 1838 because he no longer accepted Primitive Baptist tenets. "I yielded," he wrote, "my hearty assent to missions as heaven's instruments, and ceased my opposition." See *Christian Index,* Penfield, Ga., April 12, 1844.

[4] Although the publisher directed correspondents "to consider themselves collectively as the Editors," he had complete charge of getting out the paper and did the small amount of editing that the publication received.

[5] Temple, an outstanding editor and publisher in both the ante-bellum and postwar periods, was an Old School minister from Johnston County, North Carolina. See Pittman, *Biographical History of Primitive or Old School Baptist Ministers,* p. 263.

PROGRESSIONIST. *See* CAROLINA PROGRESSIONIST

RELIGIOUS AND GENERAL INTELLIGENCER

Wilmington, N. C. 1849-1850.[1] Weekly. Folio, 4 pp., 6 cols. $2 a year. 650 subscribers.[2]

Editor and proprietor: James McDaniel.[3]

Publishers: W. J. Yopp and W. P. Smith.

Established to supply Baptists in the Wilmington area with a newspaper, the *Religious and General Intelligencer* made no effort to undermine the *Biblical Recorder,* Baptist state paper published in Raleigh. McDaniel expressed special interest in promoting a general revival of religion, attacking those who opposed revivals on the ground that they produced spurious religion.[4] The content embraced religious and secular news, editorials, correspondence, advertisements, selections, poems, and miscellany.

U.L.S., 2nd ed., (1), p. 888.

[1] The prospectus bore the date Nov. 22, 1849, and April 4, 1850, is vol. 1, no. 19, indicating that publication began before the close of 1849. Toward the close of 1850 (Nov. 7, 1850, is vol. 1, no. 50) the subscription list was transferred to the *Biblical Recorder* as a friendly gesture to Thomas Meredith's widow, who was continuing that publication and needed the income. See *Biblical Recorder,* Jan. 25, 1851.

[2] Kennedy, "Catalogue of Newspapers and Periodicals" (1850).

[3] McDaniel, native North Carolinian, was one of the founders of the North Carolina Baptist State Convention and a prominent pastor of the Fayetteville and Wilmington Baptist Churches in that state. See Cathcart, *Baptist Encyclopaedia,* p. 768.

[4] *Religious and General Intelligencer,* April 25, 1850. A contemporary comment on McDaniel's paper read as follows: "It is not so exclusively religious, as most religious papers; but, to many, will not be less acceptable on that account. The editor has not, as is customary, given any reasons, for engaging in his enterprize. In this respect he is certainly original." Editorial in *Baptist Messenger,* Elizabeth City, N. C., Dec. 20, 1849.

Religious Herald

Richmond. Jan. 11, 1828–March 30, 1865.[1] Weekly. Folio, 4 pp., 5-7 cols.[2] $2.50-$10 a year. 2,756 subscribers.[3]

Editors: Henry Keeling, Jan. 11, 1828–Feb. 11, 1831;[4] William Sands, Feb. 18–April 15, 1831;[5] Eli Ball, April 29–Dec., 1831;[6] Ball and Sands, Jan. 13, 1832–May 31, 1833; Sands, June 7, 1833–Jan. 1, 1857; Sands and David Shaver, Jan. 8, 1857–March 30, 1865.[7]

Publishers: Sands, Jan. 11, 1828–April 15, 1831; Ball and Sands, April 29, 1831–May 31, 1833; Sands, June 7, 1833–Jan. 1, 1857;[8] Sands and Shaver, Jan. 8, 1857–March 30, 1865.

Sands made the *Religious Herald,* which was adopted as the organ of the Baptist General Association of Virginia, a leading family religious newspaper. With a run of thirty-seven years before suspension at the close of the war, it was published longer in the ante-bellum South than any other Baptist paper.[9] The content included essays on doctrines and practices, church proceedings, news of revivals and missionary activities, foreign and domestic secular news, editorials, poetry, stories, advertisements, discussions of slavery and other public questions, and miscellany.

U.L.S., 2nd ed., p. 2342; (1), p. 889. Cappon, *Virginia Newspapers,* p. 182.

Other holdings: PCA [1855-1859, 1862-1865]. NcW [1851-1856, 1858-1859, 1863].

[1] Superseded the *Evangelical Inquirer,* Richmond, the name of which was changed to avoid confusion with the *Richmond Enquirer.* See *Religious Herald,* Jan. 11, 1828. Publication was suspended July 18–Aug. 15, 1861, because of the lack of paper. Issues were frequently omitted toward the close of the war, when the printers were required to perform militia duty every other day. See issue for July 21, 1864. The printing office was destroyed by fire April 3, 1865. On Oct. 19, 1865, J. B. Jeter and A. E. Dickinson resumed publication of the *Religious Herald* and it has appeared continuously since that date.

[2] Reduced because of wartime shortages to a half-sheet of two pages Aug. 15, 1861–March 30, 1865.

[3] This was the circulation in 1850. The *Religious Herald,* Sept. 8, 1864,

stated that the publishers were sending 3,200 copies to the Confederate Army weekly.

[4] See section on *Evangelical Inquirer* for sketch of Keeling.

[5] Sands (1793-1868), an Englishman and a printer by trade, came to the United States in 1818. William Crane persuaded him to come to Richmond to publish a Baptist paper, supplying $677 with which to purchase a press and type from Fielding Lucas. Sands became a successful publisher and, as a layman, one of the most influential Baptists in Virginia. See Taylor, *Virginia Baptist Ministers,* series 5, p. 506.

[6] Ball (1786-1853) was born in Vermont and preached in New England until 1823. Removing then to Virginia, he became an active preacher, teacher, and editor. See Cathcart's *Baptist Encyclopaedia,* pp. 64-65.

[7] Shaver (1820-1902) was a native Virginian and a trained Baptist preacher. A contemporary editor wrote regarding the *Religious Herald* as follows: "Bro. Shaver, its principal editor, is almost unsurpassed as such, and as a scholar and writer has no superior in all the religious press South." See *Christian Index,* Macon, Ga., Oct. 21, 1864.

[8] From Jan. 17 until Sept. 19, 1834, the *Religious Herald* was "Printed and Published by William Sands, for the Virginia Baptist Book and Tract Society," whose property it had become, but on Sept. 26, 1834, Sands again appeared as proprietor.

[9] The *Christian Index,* founded in 1822, was published in the North until 1833.

Religious Magazine[1]

No copy known.

[1] Ethelbert Drake acknowledged receipt of the first number in the *Methodist Christian Sentinel,* Richmond, Feb. 20, 1835. Origin [*sic*] Batcheler was the editor and R. I. Smith of Richmond one of the publishers. No further information available.

Richmond Christian Advocate. *See* Christian Sentinel

Richmond Family Visitor. *See* Family Visitor

Roanoke Religious Correspondent; Or, Monthly Evangelical Visitant

Danville, Va., Aug., 1821–May, 1823; Milton, N. C., June–Dec., 1823. Aug., 1821–Dec., 1823.[1] Monthly. Octavo, 16 pp. $1.25 a year.

Editor and proprietor: John Jenkins.[2]

This early Baptist periodical contained church proceedings, accounts of revivals, letters to the editor, missionary journals, sermons, and two long continued articles entitled "Letters to a Young Minister of the Gospel" and "The Virginia Baptist Chronicle."

U.L.S., 2nd ed., p. 2429.

Other holdings: NcW Aug., 1821–July, 1822; Jan.–May, July, Sept., Nov., 1823. VRB April–Dec., 1823.

[1] Suspended Aug.–Dec. 1822. Discontinued after the completion of 2 vols. of 12 nos. each.

[2] Jenkins (1758-1824), a native of Virginia, taught school and was pastor of several small Baptist churches. He did not own a printing press (his periodical was printed at the office of the *Roanoke Sentinel*), and was unable to secure enough subscribers to make his editorial venture financially successful. See Taylor, *Virginia Baptist Ministers,* series 2, pp. 349-353.

SEMI-MONTHLY PROGRESSIONIST

Newnan, Ga.[1] 1856-1859.[2]

Editor: C. F. R. Shehane, 1856–May, 1857; J. M. H. Smith, June, 1857–1859.

A Universalist periodical.

No copy known.

[1] Eddy, *Universalism in America,* II, 598, gives the place incorrectly as Newman, Ga.

[2] Superseded by the *Universalist Herald,* Montgomery, Ala.

SIGNS OF THE TIMES

Alexandria, D. C. (now Va.). Nov., 1836–April, 1840.[1] Semimonthly.[2] Folio, 8 pp., 3 cols. $1 a year. 3,000 subscribers.[3]

Editor and proprietor: Gilbert Beebe.[4]

This was the first Old School Baptist periodical issued in the United States. The prospectus stated that it would be "decidedly opposed to Bible, Tract and Missionary Societies, Theological Seminaries, Sabbath School Unions, etc. etc. waging war with the mother Arminianism, and her entire brood of institutions."[5] Although welcomed by the *Primitive Baptist,* Tarboro, North Carolina, when first transferred to the South, Beebe's publication soon became unpopular with many Old School Baptists in that area and *Zion's Advocate,* Front Royal, Virginia, was established specifically to oppose his alleged errors. The content, consisting largely of letters, editorials, and theological essays, was highly controversial.

Not listed U.L.S.

Cappon, *Virginia Newspapers,* p. 45.

Other holdings: NcD [1838]. NcU 1840.

[1] Founded Nov. 28, 1832, in New Vernon, Orange Co., N. Y., the *Signs of the Times* was transferred to Alexandria, D. C., in Nov., 1836, published there until April 1, 1840, then returned to New Vernon for a long run.

[2] Cappon, *Virginia Newspapers,* p. 45, incorrectly lists this publication as a weekly.

[3] *Signs of the Times,* Nov. 30, 1838.

[4] Beebe (1800-1881), a scholarly writer, was born in Connecticut but spent a large part of his career preaching and writing in New York. See Pittman, *Biographical History of Primitive or Old School Baptist Ministers,* pp. 29-30. One reason for his return to New Vernon in 1840 was the offer of an attractive pastorate there. See Beebe, *Editorial Articles Copied from the Signs of the Times,* p. 601.

[5] Quoted in *Christian Index,* Philadelphia, Sept. 29, 1832.

Soldier's Friend

Atlanta. Jan. 10, 1863–March, 1864, or later. Weekly. Folio, 4 pp., 5 cols. Free to Confederate troops.

Editor and proprietor: A. S. Worrell.

Devoted to the intellectual, moral, and religious interests of Confederate soldiers, this Baptist newspaper sought to prepare them "for the greatest of emergencies, *death*."[1] Secular news, including the latest telegraphic reports, added variety to its pages. Baptist family weeklies solicited contributions for the *Soldier's Friend* from "Christians, philanthropists, and patriots."[2]

U.L.N., p. 101.

Other holdings: PCA July 23, 30, 1863.

[1] *Soldier's Friend,* Jan. 10, 1863.

[2] *Baptist Banner,* Atlanta, Jan. 31, 1863; *Christian Index,* Macon, Ga., March 18, 1864.

Soldier's Paper

Richmond. Aug. 1, 1863–April 1, 1865. Semimonthly. Folio, 4 pp., 3 cols. Free to soldiers.

Editor: William M. Bennett.[1]

Publisher: Soldier's Tract Association, Methodist Episcopal Church, South.

Sustained entirely by voluntary contributions from civilians and soldiers, the *Soldier's Paper* was sent in large quantities to commanding officers of regiments, brigades, and divisions for distribution. It contained stories, essays, editorials, letters, secular and religious news, obituaries, poetry, and miscellany. Most of the material, especially the original portion, was addressed to Confederate soldiers and designed to raise their morale.

U.L.N., p. 709. Cappon, *Virginia Newspapers,* pp. 183-184.

[1] No editor was named in the first numbers. Communications were to be addressed to Reverend William M. Bennett, Superintendent and General Agent of the Soldier's Tract Association. On April 1, 1865, Bennett was listed as "editor protem" and a notice stated that the editor, whose name was not given, had successfully run the blockade from Charleston to Nassau on his way to England.

SOLDIER'S VISITOR

Richmond. Aug., 1863–Feb., 1865, or later. Monthly. Folio, 4 pp., 4 cols. Free to soldiers; $1.50 a year to others. 8,000 circulation.

Edited and published by the Committee of Publication for the Presbyterian Church in the Confederate States of America.

Sustained largely by gratuitous contributions, the *Soldier's Visitor* was sent to any chaplain, officer, or private who requested copies. Soldiers usually preferred religious newspapers to tracts or books. Prayers, editorials, essays, selections, secular news, and other material "suitable for our soldiers" filled the pages of the *Soldier's Visitor.* Denunciations of "Our Enemy's Evil Deeds" were much in evidence.

U.L.N., p. 709. U.L.S., 2nd ed., p. 2635.

Other holdings: NcD Jan.–Feb., 1865.

SOUTHERN ADVOCATE

Raleigh, N. C. 1850 (?).[1] Semimonthly. 450 subscribers.

No copy known.

[1] Listed in Kennedy, "Catalogue of Newspapers and Periodicals" (1850), and Roorbach, *Bibliotheca Americana,* p. 650, as a religious publication having 450 subscribers.

SOUTHERN BAPTIST. *See* CAROLINA BAPTIST, Charleston

SOUTHERN BAPTIST ADVOCATE

Charleston. Feb., 1843–Jan. 27, 1844.[1] Weekly. Folio, 4 pp., 5 cols. $2 a year. 700 subscribers.[2]

Editor: Thomas Curtis.[3]

Proprietors: A Baptist Society Formed by Delegates of the South Carolina Convention.

After the Baptist State Convention of South Carolina had failed to carry out a resolution to establish a newspaper, several delegates privately organized a society for the purpose. The prospectus they issued stated that the publication would "exhibit a Southern warmth and earnestness of purpose" as it formed an organ of correspondence and co-operation among Baptists. The paper contained Biblical criticism, editorials, church news and proceedings, secular news, market prices, obituaries, book reviews, and miscellany.

U.L.S., 2nd ed., (1), p. 990. Hoole, *Charleston Periodicals,* p. 46.

Other holdings: ScGF Feb. 11, 1843.

[1] Suspended at the close of vol. 1 for lack of adequate patronage. See *Southern Baptist Advocate,* Jan. 27, 1844, and *Christian Index,* Penfield, Ga., Feb. 9, 1844. The Baptist State Convention of South Carolina had promised co-operation in 1843 but was forced to admit a year later that all efforts to establish a Baptist paper in that state had failed. The Convention recommended the *Biblical Recorder,* Raleigh, N. C. See State Convention of the Baptist Denomination in South Carolina, *Minutes,* 1843, p. 5; 1844, p. 5.

[2] *Carolina Baptist, A Monthly Magazine,* Charleston, I (April, 1846), 190.

[3] Curtis (*ca.* 1790-1858), a native of England and well-known Baptist minister, founded Limestone College in South Carolina. See Cathcart, *Baptist Encyclopaedia,* p. 302.

Southern Baptist and General Intelligencer
Southern Watchman and General Intelligencer[1]

Charleston. Jan. 3, 1835–Feb. 15, 1838.[2] Weekly. Octavo, 16 pp.; folio, 4 pp., 5 cols. $3 a year.

Editors and proprietors: William Henry Brisbane, 1835-1836;[3] Basil Manly, 1836-1837;[4] William T. Brantly, 1838.[5]

Brisbane, the founder of this Baptist paper, proposed to fulfil the need for a denominational organ in South Carolina. He supplied the publication with an unusually large amount of editorial matter on church discipline, moral issues, education, and projects of Christian benevolence. In addition to the usual church news, correspondence, theological discussions, and poetry, the paper contained secular news, domestic and foreign, market prices, and general miscellany. Despite a hearty recommendation from the South Carolina Baptist State Convention, the inclusion of secular news, and distinguished editors, this paper failed to prosper.[6]

U.L.S., 2nd ed., p. 2645; (1), pp. 990, 994. Hoole, *Charleston Periodicals,* p. 36.

Other holdings: PCA June 2, 1837. ScGF Jan. 3–Dec. 25, 1835; Oct. 6, Nov. 3, 1837.

[1] First title used until 1836, the second thereafter.

[2] Early in 1838 James S. Burges, who was listed as publisher, "sold" the subscription list to Thomas Meredith, publisher of the *Biblical Recorder,* Raleigh, N. C., and the two papers were merged under the title *Biblical Recorder and Southern Watchman.* The first number under the new arrangement appeared in Raleigh March 3, 1838, but bore the names of both Raleigh and Charleston on the date line. Meredith had to suspend publication for a time after Dec., 1841, and the "Southern Watchman" part of the title was not revived.

[3] Brisbane (1803-1878), born in Charleston of aristocratic parentage, studied

under Catholic Bishop John England and in a military school in Middletown, Connecticut. Although a popular Baptist minister in South Carolina, he migrated to Ohio in order to free his large holding of slaves. See Cathcart, *Baptist Encyclopaedia,* p. 135.

[4] Manly (1798-1868) was a native of North Carolina and a Graduate of the College of South Carolina. From 1826 until 1837 he served as pastor of the First Baptist Church, Charleston, accepting in the latter year the presidency of the University of Alabama. See *Dictionary of American Biography,* XII, 237.

[5] Brantly (1787-1845), a North Carolinian, was graduated from the College of South Carolina. After a pastorate at the First Baptist Church of Philadelphia, where he also edited the *Christian Index,* he succeeded Manly as pastor of the First Baptist Church of Charleston and became in addition president of the College of Charleston. See Cathcart, *Baptist Encyclopaedia,* pp. 128-129. From the beginning the *Southern Baptist and General Intelligencer* had been printed by James S. Burges. When Brantly accepted the presidency mentioned above he relinquished the editorship, and Burges, unable to find a suitable editor, sold the subscription list. See *Southern Christian Herald,* Cheraw, S. C., March 8, 1838.

[6] State Convention of the Baptist Denomination in South Carolina, *Minutes,* 1835, p. 7. The *Triennial Baptist Register, 1836,* p. 177, sketches the early history of this weekly.

Southern Baptist Messenger

Lexington, Ga., 1851-1852; Covington, Ga., 1853-1861. Jan., 1851–June 15, 1861, or later.[1] Semimonthly. Quarto, 8 pp. $1 a year. 2,000 subscribers.[2]

Editor and publisher: William L. Beebe.[3]

With about three hundred agents and two thousand subscribers scattered widely over the South, this aggressive Northern editor, who carefully avoided discussions of politics and slavery until after secession, when he came out for the South, ruined the prosperity of the *Primitive Baptist* of North Carolina, the other outstanding Old School Baptist publication in the South.[4] He claimed, however, that delinquent subscribers made his paper a constant liability.[5] The *Southern Baptist Messenger's* motto read: "One Lord, One Faith, and One Baptism." Its content, like that of most periodicals of minority groups and sects, was highly controversial on religious subjects. There were communications, proceedings, editorials, marriages, deaths, and receipts for subscription payments.

U.L.S., 2nd ed., p. 2645; (1), p. 990.

[1] There were suspensions and delays in 1861, when the printers were called into the Confederate Army. See *Southern Baptist Messenger,* May 1, 1861. Publication probably ceased entirely early in the war.

[2] This is an average. The editor claimed 2,800 on Dec. 1, 1857. There

were 2,500 in 1860. See United States Census, Manuscript Returns, 1860: Georgia, Social Statistics, Newton County.

[3] J. L. Purington was co-editor in 1859. Beebe (1829-1901), son of the eminent Gilbert Beebe, was born and educated in the North, to which he returned at the close of his editorial career in Georgia. See Pittman, *Biographical History of Primitive or Old School Baptist Ministers,* p. 30.

[4] *Zion's Advocate,* Front Royal, Va., Oct. 16, 1858.

[5] *Southern Baptist Messenger,* Dec. 1, 1860.

Southern Baptist Missionary Journal

Richmond. June, 1846–May, 1851.[1] Monthly. Octavo, 24 pp. $1 a year. 1,700 subscribers.[2]

Editor: James B. Taylor.[3]

Publisher: H. K. Ellyson.[4]

The founding of this periodical was a direct outgrowth of the establishment in 1845 of the Southern Baptist Convention, which needed a vehicle for direct communication between its newly constituted boards and the denomination. The *Southern Baptist Missionary Journal,* the official organ of the Foreign and Domestic Mission Boards, was entirely missionary in character. Its pages were filled with letters and journals of missionaries, sermons and essays on missions, news of missionary activities, and appeals for financial contributions for missions.

U.L.S., 2nd ed., p. 2645; (1), p. 990.

Other holdings: NcD Aug., 1846. NcW June, 1846–May, 1847; July, 1849. VRB complete file. VRF complete file.

[1] Superseded by the *Home and Foreign Journal,* Richmond. U.L.S., 2nd ed., p. 2645, states that the *Southern Baptist Missionary Journal* was merged into the *Commission; Or, Southern Baptist Missionary Magazine,* but actually the latter was not founded until five years later. The *Southern Baptist Missionary Journal* and the *Commission,* also discontinued in 1851, were combined to form the *Home and Foreign Journal,* Richmond.

[2] The 1,639 subscribers to vol. 1 were distributed by states as follows: Va., 406; Ga., 401; Ala., 233; S. C., 171; Miss., 142; N. C., 135; and the remainder in small groups in 16 states. See "Report of H. K. Ellyson to the Foreign Mission Board of the Southern Baptist Convention, April 30, 1847" (MS now in possession of the Foreign Mission Board of the Southern Baptist Convention, Richmond). The Southern Baptist Convention (*Proceedings,* 1849, p. 17) stated regarding missions that the largest donations came from those sections of the country in which Baptist periodicals had the widest circulation.

[3] Taylor, corresponding secretary of the Board of Foreign Missions of the Southern Baptist Convention, was listed as editor June–Sept., 1846. Afterwards, the publication was listed as edited by Taylor and the Corresponding Secretaries of the Board of Domestic Missions of the Southern Baptist Convention. See section on *Commission* for sketch of Taylor.

[4] Published by Ellyson for the Board of Foreign Missions of the Southern Baptist Convention, June–Sept., 1846; by Ellyson for the Boards of Missions of the Southern Baptist Convention after Sept., 1846. The contract between

Ellyson and the Board of Foreign Missions made him responsible for the "entire control of the business and pecuniary department," and the Board could "not in any manner be held or deemed liable for any of the expenses." Ellyson was to pay the Board $150 when the receipts amounted to $1,000; $400 when $2,000; etc., for the sole right to publish the periodical. See "Articles of agreement between H. K. Ellyson and the Board of Managers for Foreign Missions of the Southern Baptist Convention" (MS now in possession of the Foreign Mission Board of the Southern Baptist Convention, Richmond). The Southern Baptist Convention (*Proceedings,* 1851, p. 21), reported a total net revenue from the first four volumes of the magazine of $536.86.

SOUTHERN BAPTIST PREACHER, OR, SERMONS BY LIVING BAPTIST MINISTERS IN THE SOUTH

Washington, Ga., Nov., 1839–July, 1840; Penfield, Ga., Jan.–Nov., 1841. Nov., 1839–Nov., 1841. Monthly.[1] Octavo, 16 pp. $1 a year.

Editor and proprietor: William H. Stokes.[2]

The founder's purpose was "to stir up our Brethren, if possible, to an effort to contribute something towards a Southern Baptist Literature," but it was only with great difficulty that he secured the twelve sermons which constituted the volume. Publication ceased for lack of contributors and subscribers.[3]

U.L.S., 2nd ed., (1), p. 990.

Other holdings: VRB Nov., 1839.

[1] Announced as a monthly, this periodical was published at irregular intervals, twenty-five months being required for the completion of one volume of twelve numbers.

[2] Stokes was at the same time editor of the *Christian Index,* Washington, Ga.

[3] See issues for Nov., 1839; July, 1840; and Nov., 1841.

SOUTHERN BAPTIST PULPIT OR MONTHLY SERMONS
SOUTHERN BAPTIST PULPIT AND MONTHLY RECORD[1]

Fayetteville, N. C., Nov., 1839–April, 1840; Cheraw, S. C., May–Oct., 1840 (?).[2] Nov., 1839–Oct., 1840 (?). Octavo, 16 pp. $1.50 a year.

Editor and proprietor: William Potter.

Each issue contained a sermon by a well-known Southern Baptist minister. Some issues also included church news.

Not listed U.L.S.

Holdings: NcD Dec., 1839; Jan., April–May, 1840. NcU Nov., 1839. NcW March, 1840.

[1] Titles used interchangeably depending on whether or not a particular issue contained anything more than a sermon.

[2] On the cover of the issue for April, 1840, the proprietor stated that

he had lost money on the periodical but would complete at least one volume of twelve numbers.

SOUTHERN BAPTIST REVIEW

Raleigh, N. C. Jan.–Dec., 1849. Monthly; bimonthly.[1] Octavo, 40 pp. $1 a year.

Editor and proprietor: Thomas Meredith.[2]

In launching the magazine Meredith declared that "something of the kind is indispensable to the cultivation and preservation of a creditable literature among our ministers and people in the Southern States."[3] It contained essays, sermons, addresses, editorials, book reviews, and notes.

U.L.S., 2nd ed., (1), p. 990.

Other holdings: NcD Dec., 1849. VRB complete file.

[1] The first two numbers appeared monthly, the remaining five bimonthly.
[2] See section on *Biblical Recorder* for sketch of Meredith.
[3] *Southern Baptist Review,* I (Jan., 1848), 5.

SOUTHERN CHRISTIAN ADVOCATE

Charleston, June 24, 1837–March 27, 1862; Augusta, Ga., April 10, 1862–April 13, 1865. June 24, 1837–April 13, 1865.[1] Weekly.[2] Folio, 4 pp., 5-7 cols.[3] $2-$20 a year. 4,000 subscribers.[4]

Editors: William Capers, June 24, 1837–June 12, 1840;[5] William May Wightman, June 19, 1840–June 9, 1854;[6] E. H. Myers, June 16, 1854–April 13, 1865.

Proprietors: General Conference of the Methodist Episcopal Church, 1837-1845; General Conference of the Methodist Episcopal Church, South, 1845-1865.[7]

The *Southern Christian Advocate* was established by the General Conference of the Methodist Episcopal Church at the request of Southern delegates, who, "in view of the peculiar political aspect of the times," wanted a weekly newspaper of their own.[8] Adopted as their official organ by several Southern annual conferences, the *Southern Christian Advocate* contained church news and proceedings from all the Southeastern States. There were also editorials, biographical sketches, essays, obituaries, secular news, market prices, poetry, miscellany, and several departments such as Sunday schools, parents, youth, and temperance. Advertisements, barred entirely at first, were never admitted in large quantities.

U.L.S., 2nd ed., p. 2646; (1), p. 991. Hoole, *Charleston Periodicals,* pp. 38-41.

Other holdings: GU [1862-1863]. NcD May 24, 1860; Jan. 14, 1864. ScSW [June 24, 1837–April 13, 1865] (lacks only scattering numbers).

[1] After a brief suspension at the close of the war, publication was resumed in Macon, Ga., June 29, 1865, and has been continued in various places since that time. See Crum, *History of the Southern Christian Advocate, passim.*

[2] Brantley, *Georgia Journalism,* p. 34, incorrectly lists this publication as a monthly.

[3] Although reduced to 5 columns, a full sheet of 4 pages appeared until the last months of the war.

[4] This was the average circulation. The 3,840 subscribers reported in the issue for March 26, 1841, were distributed as follows: 1,850 in South Carolina and states north; 1,990 in Georgia and states southwest.

[5] Capers (1790-1855), an able leader and the most popular Methodist preacher in the South, was born in Charleston and attended South Carolina College. See *Dictionary of American Biography,* III, 483-484. A contemporary secular editor regarded Capers as "among the first preachers in the *Southern Country,*" Northern clergymen being considered unworthy of inclusion in the comparison. See Charleston *Mercury,* Jan. 31, 1855. Capers is remembered for his special efforts to Christianize the slaves of S. C. and Ga. See Crum, *History of the Southern Christian Advocate,* p. 8.

[6] Wightman (1808-1882), a native of Charleston, was graduated from Charleston College and became a successful Methodist preacher. He resigned the editorship to become president of Wofford College. See Charleston *Mercury,* July 24, 1854; *Southern Methodist Pulpit,* Richmond, III (1850), 14-20; and Shipp, *Methodism in South Carolina,* p. 648.

[7] Resolutions passed by the General Conference in May, 1836, authorized the publication of weekly religious papers at Richmond, Nashville, and Charleston. This body named a publishing committee, which chose the editors and printers and fixed the subscription prices and advertising rates. In the *Southern Christian Advocate,* March 17, 1843, the committee announced that it had purchased a power press and set up its own printing office. This office, located in the Southern Methodist Book Store, 100 Hayne Street, published its first number May 5, 1843. The General Conference, South, took over in 1845 without confusion and managed the paper in the same way as had the former body.

[8] *Southern Christian Advocate,* June 24, 1837.

SOUTHERN CHRISTIAN HERALD

Columbia, S. C., March 18, 1834–March 30, 1836; Cheraw, S. C., April 8, 1836–Dec. 14, 1838. March 18, 1834–Dec. 14, 1838.[1] Weekly. Folio, 4 pp., 6 cols. $3 a year.

Editors and proprietors: Richard S. Gladney, March 18, 1834–March 30, 1836; M. McLean, April 8, 1836–Dec. 14, 1838.[2]

The *Southern Christian Herald* appeared as a result of the controversy in the Presbyterian Church that culminated in the schism of 1837. Devoted to the Old School, it was established to aid in "the restoration of the Presbyterian church to gospel order and sound doctrine; and especially the bringing over of Southern Presbyterian Institutions, and a large portion of Southern Presbyterians to co-operate in this great work." The editor declared in the last issue that this objective had been achieved. During the trial of the Albert Barnes case before the General Assembly and other crises full reports appeared weekly. In addition to religious and moral essays, editorials, poetry, stories, and religious miscellany, there was considerable material of a secular nature. This was one of the few religious newspapers that advertised sales of slaves and for runaways.

U.L.S., 2nd ed., p. 2646.

Other holdings: NcD Nov. 11, 1836; Oct. 27, 1837; April 6, 1838. NcM [Jan. 27, 1836–Dec. 14, 1838]. NcU [Dec. 9, 1834–Aug. 11, 1837]. ScN March 18, 1834–March 24, 1837.

[1] Superseded by the *Watchman of the South,* Richmond. For notice of the transfer of the subscription list see *Watchman of the South,* Dec. 20, 1838.

[2] Gladney, a Presbyterian minister, founded the paper. In Columbia, before the paper had its own office, Samuel Weir was listed as publisher. When Gladney had to sever connections with the paper, McLean, a physician, accepted responsibility for its control and moved it to Cheraw, where he also published the *Gazette.* McLean's printers included G. H. Taylor and T. A. Pettegrew.

Southern Christian Repository

Raleigh, N. C. May–Oct., 1842. Monthly. Octavo, 32 pp. $2 a year. 500 subscribers.[1]

Editor and publisher: Thomas Meredith.[2]

"The present Periodical," wrote Meredith, "is offered to the [Baptist] denomination, partly as a substitute for the *Recorder and Watchman,* and partly as a Repository of Literature and Theology, adapted generally to the wants of the South." He had attempted unsuccessfully to transfer the subscription list of his *Biblical Recorder and Southern Watchman,* then suspended, to some suitable religious newspaper.[3] This monthly contained religious news and other features of weeklies as well as essays, sermons, speeches, and church history.

Not listed U.L.S.

Holdings: NcW May–June, 1842.

[1] *Southern Christian Repository,* I (May, 1842), 2.

[2] See section on *Biblical Recorder* for sketch of Meredith.

[3] *Southern Christian Repository,* I (May, 1842), 1.

SOUTHERN CHRISTIAN SENTINEL

Charleston. March 2, 1839–Dec., 1841. Weekly, March 2, 1839–April (?), 1841; monthly, May–Dec., 1841. Folio, 4 pp., 5 cols., as weekly; octavo, 32 pp., as monthly. $3 a year.

Editor and proprietor: Thomas Magruder.[1]

Founded after the division of the Presbyterian Church in 1837, this newspaper advocated a Southern Presbyterian organization based on the principles of the plan proposed by Archibald Alexander in 1832. The Alexander plan would have vested ecclesiastical authority in the presbyteries and synods instead of in the General Assembly.[2] Although Magruder declared that he would advocate "no *new Divinity;* no doctrine or measure which has any affinity to *New Schoolism,*" he opposed the Old School and contemporaries regarded him as of the New School.[3] Disliking the term "New School," Magruder, whose paper was the organ of the Charleston Union Presbytery, claimed devotion only to "Constitutional Presbyterianism." The *Southern Christian Sentinel* contained church proceedings, essays, editorials, sermons, church history, communications, market prices, and advertisements.

U.L.S., 2nd ed., p. 2646.

Other holdings: NcMHi Oct.–Nov., 1841. ScU Sept. 26, 1840.

[1] Magruder, a Presbyterian minister, was listed as editor and proprietor of the weekly only. The monthly was said to be "Conducted by Members of the Charleston Union Presbytery," but communications were still to be addressed to Magruder. B. B. Hussey, 36 and 48 Broad Street, printed both the weekly and the monthly.

[2] *Southern Christian Sentinel,* March 2, 1839.

[3] *Christian Index,* Penfield, Ga., Oct. 15, 1841.

SOUTHERN CHURCHMAN

Richmond, Jan. 2, 1835–1839 (?); Alexandria, Va., "soon after 1839"–May 24, 1861; Richmond, Nov. 22, 1861–March 29, 1865. Jan. 2, 1835–March 29, 1865.[1] Weekly. Folio, 4 pp., 5-7 cols.[2] $2.50-$20 a year. 1,250 subscribers.[3]

Editors: William F. Lee, Jan. 2, 1835–May, 1837; Lucius M. Purdy, June–Aug., 1837; Z. Mead, Sept., 1837–1843; E. R. Lippitt, 1843–March 1848; George A. Smith, June, 1848–Sept. 27, 1855; D. Francis Sprigg, Oct. 5, 1855–March 29, 1865.[4]

Proprietors: Lee and others.[5]

In launching the *Southern Churchman* as an organ of the Protestant Episcopal Church, William F. Lee wrote of his determination to use the power of the press in "forming and controlling public sentiment" to help correct "the evils" confronting society. He was especially interested in arresting the spread of demoralizing doctrines and in arousing readers "in behalf of the benighted and enthralled heathen."[6] A general family religious newspaper, the *Southern Churchman* became the South's leading Episcopal weekly. It contained theological discussions, church news and proceedings, a literary department, essays, editorials, and miscellany.

U.L.S., 2nd ed., p. 2646; Cappon, *Virginia Newspapers,* p. 184.

Other holdings: NcU Aug. 5, 1836; June 2, 1838; Jan. 24, 31, Feb. 14, March 7, 22, 1862. VU [1856-1858, 1860].

[1] Resumed in Alexandria Aug. 31, 1865; now published in Richmond.

[2] Half-sheets of two pages appeared during most of the war.

[3] This was the average circulation. The issue for Jan. 4, 1861, reported 2,500.

[4] After the early death of Lee (1804-1837) other local Episcopal ministers carried on the paper. Smith, native of England and former editor of the *Episcopal Recorder,* Philadelphia, conducted a boys' school near Alexandria. See *Southern Episcopalian,* Charleston, II (Sept., 1855), 276. Sprigg, a native of Maryland and author of *Aids to Those Who Pray in Private,* was Rector of Grace Church, Alexandria. See Allibone's *Dictionary of Authors,* II, 2213.

[5] The ownership cannot always be established. Originally, Lee, who was connected with a printing office, owned the paper, but it was stated editorially in the issue of Jan. 11, 1855, that the publication was the property of the Diocese of Virginia. At the close of Smith's editorship the *Southern Churchman* was in the hands of a stock company, and the trustees of the Theological Seminary of Virginia, who owned a majority of the stock, appointed Sprigg his successor. See *Southern Churchman,* Aug. 23, 1855.

[6] *Southern Churchman,* Jan. 2, 1835.

Southern Episcopalian

Charleston. April (?), 1853–March 7, 1863, or later.[1] Semimonthly; monthly.[2] Octavo, 48-56 pp. $2 a year. 750 subscribers.

Editors and proprietors: G. P. Gadsden, J. H. Elliott, and Joseph A. Shanklin.[3]

The founders announced as their purpose making the *Southern Episcopalian* "a useful vehicle and register of ecclesiastical intelligence, and as circumstances may require, defender of the interest of Christian truth, as held in the Church of which we are part." The magazine, despite the high quality of most articles, was never self-sustaining and had to rely on special donations.[4] It contained church history, stories, theology, poetry, church news and proceedings, biographical sketches, editorials, and book reviews.

U.L.S., 2nd ed., p. 2648; (1), p. 992. Hoole, *Charleston Periodicals,* pp. 62-63.

Other holdings: NcD June, 1861.

[1] Superseded the *Charleston Gospel Messenger, and Protestant Episcopal Register.* Suspended Jan.–Nov., 1862.

[2] Founded as a semimonthly folio, the *Southern Episcopalian* became a monthly of octavo size in April, 1854.

[3] Shanklin, rector of St. Peter's Church, Charleston, joined the editorial staff in Jan., 1855, and died of yellow fever in Sept., 1856. Gadsden and Elliott, likewise Episcopal clergymen, edited the remaining volumes. After April, 1855, the magazine was printed and published by A. E. Miller, 3 State Street.

[4] *Southern Episcopalian,* I (April, 1854), 46; V (Feb., 1859), 600; VIII (June, 1861), 168.

Southern Evangelical Intelligencer
Southern Intelligencer[1]

Charleston. March 27, 1819–April 1, 1826.[2] Weekly. Quarto, 8 pp., March 27, 1819–Dec. 29, 1821; folio, 4 pp., 5 cols., Jan., 1822–April 1, 1826. $3–$4 a year.

Editors and proprietors: B. M. Palmer and George Reid, March 27, 1819–Dec. 29, 1821;[3] William Riley, Oct., 1822–April 1, 1826.[4]

With the motto "And many shall run to and fro, and knowledge shall be increased," this Presbyterian newspaper was designed primarily to communicate news of the progress of benevolent enterprises. The editors relied heavily on material selected from American and English periodicals. The content included news of churches and proceedings of benevolent societies, foreign and domestic secular news, editorials, poetry, letters, and miscellany.

U.L.N., p. 641. U.L.S., 2nd ed., p. 2648; (1), p. 992.

Other holdings: VRT March, 1819–March, 1820.

[1] The first title, of which *Southern Christian Intelligencer* was a variation, remained in use through 1821, the second thereafter.

[2] Superseded by the *Charleston Observer.*

[3] Palmer and Reid were local Presbyterian ministers. W. P. Young printed vol. 1, W. C. Young, vol. 2. The issue for April 7, 1821, announced that new printers, Gould and Riley, equipped with new type just in from New York had taken over the printing.

[4] An editorial announcement Dec. 29, 1821 (vol. 3, no. 39), stated that the next number would appear in January on an enlarged sheet and be numbered vol. 4, no. 1. There was also to be a new editor who would be able to devote his entire time to the task. Apparently the plan for a full-time editor did not develop and one of the printers had to take over. Riley, layman, librarian of the Charleston Religious Tract Society, and proprietor of a printing office, formally assumed the editorship in Oct., 1822. See *Southern Intelligencer,* April 1, 1826.

SOUTHERN EVANGELIST

Charleston. 1834–May 5, 1838.[1] Semimonthly, 1834-1836; weekly, July 2, 1836, or earlier–May 5, 1838. Quarto, 8 pp., 2-3 cols.[2] $2.50 a year.

Editors: L. F. W. Andrews, 1834–July 2, 1836; Theophilus Fisk, July 9, 1836–Oct. 1, 1836, or later; John Gregory, (?)–May 5, 1838.[3]

Proprietors: Andrews, 1834–July 2, 1836; Trustees of the Charleston Universalist Society, July 9, 1836–(?); Gregory and C. A. Hall, (?)–May 5, 1838.

The editor wrote on July 9, 1836, that since the *Southern Evangelist* was the only Universalist journal and the only "liberal paper" in the entire South, it must be sustained. Under the motto "Do the work of an Evangelist—Putting on the Breast-Plate of Faith and Love, and for a Helmet, the hope of Salvation," this paper printed sermons, religious news, editorials, reviews, letters, and poetry in support of Universalism.

Not listed U.L.S.

Holdings: NcD Feb. 3–May 5, 1838. ScChC July 9, 23, 30, Aug. 6, 27, Sept. 3, 24, Oct. 1, 1836.

[1] The prospectus, dated April 4, 1834, announced that L. F. W. Andrews, a Universalist minister and native Southerner, would launch the *Southern Evangelist* in Montgomery, Ala., in May. This he did. See *Southern Pioneer and Gospel Visiter,* Baltimore and Richmond, May 10, June 21, 1834. Before the close of the year Andrews had moved his paper to Charleston. See Eddy, *Universalism in America,* II, 593. The *Evangelical Universalist,* founded in Macon, Ga., in 1838 superseded the *Southern Evangelist* as the unofficial organ of Southern Universalists.

[2] The proprietors announced Oct. 1, 1836, that at the beginning of 1837 the publication would be enlarged to folio. Vol. 4, no. 32, was the last folio issued. The remaining 19 nos. were quarto, 8 pp., 3 cols.

[3] Fisk, a Universalist minister, announced in the issue for July 9, 1836, that he was assuming his duties without previous experience as an editor. H. F. Stearns and S. J. McMorris were listed as nonresident corresponding editors. A notice in the issue for Oct. 1, 1836, stated that Andrews would become joint editor at the beginning of the next volume. Gregory was a Universalist minister.

SOUTHERN FAMILY VISITOR

Newton County, Ga. 1850(?).[1] Weekly. 1,000 subscribers.

No copy known.

[1] Listed in Kennedy, "Catalogue of Newspapers and Periodicals" (1850), as a religious publication having 1,000 subscribers.

SOUTHERN FRIEND

Richmond. Tenth Month, 1864–Third Month, 1865.[1] Semi-monthly. Octavo, 16 pp. $20 a year.

Editor and proprietor: John Bacon Crenshaw.[2]

This Quaker magazine was established as a substitute for the Philadelphia *Friend* and the *Friend's Review* and not in opposition to them.[3] Eight pages of each number, paged separately, were used to reprint Thomas Clarkson's *A Portraiture of Quakerism.* The remaining eight dealt with religious, literary, agricultural, and secular subjects, and emphasized Confederate military regulations relating to Quakers. Obituaries, marriages, and church proceedings also appeared.

U.L.S., 2nd ed., p. 2648.

[1] Publication resumed Tenth Month, 1865, and ceased with the completion of twenty-four numbers, Third Month, 1866.

[2] Crenshaw (1820-1889), a native Virginian, was minister of the Richmond Meeting. See Cartland, *Southern Heroes,* p. 347.

[3] *Southern Friend,* Tenth Month 1, 1864.

SOUTHERN INTELLIGENCER. *See* SOUTHERN EVANGELICAL INTELLIGENCER

SOUTHERN LIGHT, AN INDEPENDENT RELIGIOUS AND LITERARY JOURNAL

Edgefield, S. C. Jan.–Dec., 1856, or later.[1] Monthly. Octavo, 40 pp. $2 a year.

Editor and proprietor: E. L. Whatley.

This journal, published independently of the South Carolina Baptist State Convention by a Baptist preacher, was "Set for the Defence of Truth, and Devoted to the Diffusion of Knowledge." It tended to be outspoken on religious matters and the editor's views often did not conform to those generally held by Baptists. Although Whatley opposed theological seminaries and denounced systematic theology, he was not an Old School Baptist. The *Southern Baptist,* organ of the South Carolina Baptist State Convention, criticized Whatley for printing a Universalist sermon by Hosea Ballou.[2]

U.L.S., 2nd ed., (1), p. 992.

Other holdings: NcD Feb., June–Aug., Oct.–Dec., 1856. ScU Feb.–Dec., 1856.

[1] Whatley resigned as pastor of the Baptist Church at Edgefield in Dec., 1856, and removed to the Low Country. He expected to enlarge and con-

tinue the *Southern Light* but no further numbers are known. See *Southern Light,* I (Dec., 1856), 477.

[2] *Southern Baptist, Charleston,* July 22, 1856. *Southern Light,* I (Aug., 1856), 308-310.

SOUTHERN LUTHERAN

Charleston, Aug. (?), 1861–Aug. 15, 1863, or later; Columbia, S. C., Oct. 4, 1863, or earlier–Sept. 4, 1864, or later. Aug. (?), 1861–Sept. 4, 1864, or later.[1] Weekly. Folio, 4 pp., 5-7 cols. $2-$8 a year. 2,800 circulation.[2]

Editors: "A Committee of the Synod of South Carolina," 1861-1863; N. Aldrich and John Bachman, Aug. 1, 1863–1864;[3] A. R. Rude, 1864.

Proprietor: Robert G. Chisolm.[4]

The *Southern Lutheran* was the only Lutheran newspaper published in the Confederacy. Under the motto "Endeavoring to keep the unity of the spirit in the bond of peace," the editors worked for a Southern Lutheran Church including every synod in the Confederate States whether it had formerly been connected with the old General Synod or not. As a family religious newspaper, the *Southern Lutheran* contained editorials, secular and religious news, poetry, selections, communications, obituaries, marriages, advertisements, and miscellany.

U.L.S., 2nd ed., (1), p. 993.

[1] Several issues were missed because of wartime conditions. One editor was a chaplain, another belonged to a rifle company, and all the printers were volunteers. After Nov. 16, 1861, only unfolded half-sheets of two pages appeared. The *Southern Lutheran* was not revived after the war. In 1866 the *Evangelical Lutheran* began publication in Charlotte, N. C., and the *Lutheran Visitor* in Staunton, Va. They were combined in 1868 to form the *Lutheran and Visitor,* Columbia, S. C., with A. R. Rude, last editor of the *Southern Lutheran,* as editor. See *Lutheran Visitor,* III (June, 1868), no. 6, and *Lutheran and Visitor,* April 1, 1869.

[2] This was the number of copies printed on Aug. 25, 1864. About half went to regular subscribers, the remainder to Confederate soldiers. In 1862 the committee of editors had asked the Synod of South Carolina to provide funds for copies for the army. They were, the committee wrote, made "necessary by the continued urgent application made for the paper by our soldiers both upon the seaboard and in other parts of the Confederacy. . . . Your committee have learned from authentic sources that the paper is eagerly sought after by the soldiers of the various regiments, and read by numbers to whom a tract would only be considered as so much waste paper." See Evangelical Lutheran Church, *Minutes of the Annual Convention of the Synod of South Carolina,* 1862, p. 13.

[3] Apparently Aldrich and Bachman were the chief editors from the beginning. Editorials were often signed either "A" or "B," and the *North Carolina Presbyterian,* Fayetteville, Nov. 23, 1861, referred to Bachman as

the editor. Bachman (1790-1874), a naturalist and Lutheran clergyman, was born in New York but spent most of his life in Charleston. He became the recognized leader of his denomination in South Carolina. See *Dictionary of American Biography,* I, 466-467. A committee of the Synod of South Carolina named the editors.

[4] Chisolm was listed as "Financial Agent." A Lutheran historian states, however, that he assumed the entire financial responsibility for the publication. See Hallman, *Evangelical Lutheran Synod of South Carolina,* p. 93. By 1863 the paper had become the property of the General Synod of the Confederate States. See Evangelical Lutheran Church, *Minutes of the Annual Convention of the Synod of South Carolina,* 1863, p. 27. James Phynney was the printer in Charleston, Evans and Cogswell in Columbia.

SOUTHERN METHODIST

Macon, Ga. 1859 (?).[1]

Editor and proprietor: James Stewart.

Founded at the time Joseph Walker was publishing the *Baptist Champion* in Macon, Stewart proposed to "pierce the helmet and break the javelin of this daring young warrior of aquatic proclivities."[2] Although Stewart announced that he would defend the Methodist Church, bishops and elders, whom he had not consulted in advance, were soon saying that he "did not have the right to publish the Southern Methodist without the consent of Conference." Stewart then spoke out boldly for independence. "We have," he wrote, "learned one thing. Within ten years the Methodist Church has undergone a great change, and is now the grandest monopoly the world ever knew, so far as publishing interests are concerned. All effort to do good through the Press on the part of private individuals is crushed down, and every Methodist enterprise is put under ban, whose honors do not go to Conference officials, and whose profits do not fall into the coffers of the Church!"[3]

No copy known.

[1] Nos. 1-6 were mentioned in the *Baptist Champion,* Macon, Ga., between Aug. 1 and Oct. 1, 1859.

[2] Quoted in *Baptist Champion,* Aug. 1, 1859.

[3] Quoted in *Baptist Champion,* Oct. 1, 1859.

SOUTHERN METHODIST

Rome, Ga. 1849 (?).[1] Weekly. Folio.

Editor and publisher: Russell Reneau.[2]

Motto: "Methodism is Religion Mounted on Horse-back!"

No copy known.

[1] The issue for Jan. 27, 1849, is quoted in the *Arminian Magazine,* Rome, Ga., I (June, 1849), 329.

[2] Reneau also edited and published the *Arminian Magazine* of Rome.

SOUTHERN METHODIST ITINERANT

Parkersburg, Va. (now W. Va.). 1856-1860 (?).[1] Semimonthly; weekly (?).

Editor and proprietor: W. Kennedy.[2]

No copy known.

[1] Referred to in the *Richmond Christian Advocate,* Oct. 2, 1856, and in Kenny, *American Newspaper Directory* (1860), p. 72.

[2] Kennedy, a Methodist clergyman, was a member of the Western Virginia Conference. See *Richmond Christian Advocate,*Oct. 2, 1856.

SOUTHERN METHODIST PULPIT

Richmond, June, 1848–Dec., 1850; Greensboro, N. C., Jan., 1851–Dec., 1852. June, 1848–Dec., 1852.[1] Monthly. Octavo, 32 pp. $1 a year. 2,200 subscribers.[2]

Editor and proprietor: Charles F. Deems.[3]

Desiring to encourage the development of Southern literature, Deems founded the magazine "to disprove what has already been said, that neither for love nor money could we secure a dozen sermons a year from Southern Methodist preachers."[4] In addition to the sermons which filled about half of each number, this monthly contained biographical sketches, editorials, church proceedings, essays, and reviews of secular and religious books.

U.L.S., 2nd ed., p. 2652; (1), p. 993.

Other holdings: NcU [1849-1850, 1852].

[1] Superseded the *Southern Pulpit,* Macon, Ga. Between July and Dec., 1850, the size of each monthly number was doubled in order to complete vol. 3 in 6 months.

[2] Upon the demise of the *Southern Pulpit* in 1848 its list of 900 subscribers was transferred to the *Southern Methodist Pulpit.* This gave the latter more than 2,200 subscribers, most of whom were retained. See *Southern Methodist Pulpit,* I (1849), 172. Deems was one of the few Southern editors who claimed any degree of financial success. In his valedictory he wrote, "We do not die of neglect," and that he was discontinuing publication because of his "laborious and responsible position" as president of Greensboro Female College. See *Southern Methodist Pulpit,* V (Dec., 1852), 379.

[3] Deems (1820-1895), a native of New York, entered the methodist ministry after graduation from Dickinson College. He taught at the University of North Carolina, 1842-1848, Randolph-Macon College, 1848-1849, and was president of Greensboro Female College, 1850-1854. After the war he returned to New York as an independent preacher. See *Dictionary of American Biography,* V, 192-193.

[4] *Southern Methodist Pulpit,* I (1848), 19.

SOUTHERN PIONEER AND GOSPEL VISITER[1]

[1] Superseded the newly founded *Gospel Visiter,* Baltimore. About the time the *Gospel Visiter* was established, Universalist leaders in Richmond issued

proposals for the *Southern Pioneer.* Before the first number of the latter appeared, the two were combined. See *Southern Pioneer and Gospel Visiter,* I (Oct., 1831), 23.

SOUTHERN PIONEER AND PHILADELPHIA LIBERALIST[2]

Baltimore and Richmond.[3] Oct., 1831–April, 1837 (?).[4] Monthly, octavo, 24 pp., $1 a year, Oct., 1831–Oct., 1832; semimonthly, quarto, 8 pp., $1 a year, Nov. 17, 1832–Oct. 18, 1834; weekly, quarto, 8 pp., $1.50 a year, Oct. (?), 1834–April, 1837 (?). 1,700 subscribers.[5]

Editors and proprietors: "An Association of Gentlemen," Oct., 1831–Nov. 9, 1833; Otis A. Skinner, S. P. Skinner, and L. F. W. Andrews, Nov. 23, 1833–Dec. 21, 1833; Otis A. Skinner, Jan. 4, 1834–(?).[6]

Otis A. Skinner supplied the driving force behind this pioneer Southern Universalist periodical. Of the fifteen Universalist publications in the United States in 1832 it was the only one issued south of the Mason and Dixon line.[7] Under the motto "Behold I bring you good tidings of great joy which shall be unto all people," the editors advanced the teaching that "God will have all men to be saved and to come unto the knowledge of the truth." They centered their attacks on the doctrine of endless misery as taught by the "limitarians" or "partialists" who formed other denominations. The content included many polemical discussions of theological questions, letters, accounts of the founding of new Universalist societies, miscellany, and, as a weekly, a record of passing political events.

U.L.S., 2nd ed., p. 391, as *Baltimore Southern Pioneer and Richmond Gospel Visiter.*

Other holdings: VU Nov. 17, Dec. 1, 1832–Oct. 5, 1833.

[2] In 1835 the *Philadelphia Liberalist* was united with the *Southern Pioneer and Gospel Visiter* under the above title. See Eddy, *Universalism in America,* II, 592. The new title is listed in U.L.S., 2nd ed., p. 2652, as *Southern Pioneer and Evangelical Liberalist,* Philadelphia.

[3] This periodical was "published simultaneously in Baltimore and Richmond." Vol. 1 was dated from Richmond and printed by William Wooddy, Baltimore. Vol. 2, likewise dated from Richmond, was printed by Thomas Boothby, Baltimore. Vol. 3, dated alternately at irregular intervals from Richmond and Baltimore, was also printed by Boothby.

[4] Superseded by the *Universalist Union,* New York. See Eddy, *Universalism in America,* II, 592.

[5] *Southern Pioneer and Gospel Visiter,* III (Dec. 21, 1833), 39.

[6] Otis A. Skinner, Baltimore, was the principal editor. Others composing the "Association of Gentlemen" were J. B. Pitkin, Richmond; L. F. W. Andrews,

Augusta, Ga.; S. Streeter, Boston; and S. P. Skinner, Baltimore. All the editors were Universalist ministers. Eddy, *Universalism in America,* 11, 592, lists Andrews, George C. McCune, and Robert Smith as editors of the weekly.

[7] *Southern Pioneer and Gospel Visiter,* I (May, 1832), 167.

SOUTHERN PREACHER (proposed)

New Bern, N. C. 1837. Monthly. $1 a year.

Editor and publisher: Thomas Meredith.[1]

The content was to consist of sermons collected over the South.[2]

No copy known.

[1] See section on *Biblical Recorder* for sketch of Meredith.

[2] The prospectus, dated March 15, 1837, appeared in the *Southern Christian Herald,* Cheraw, S. C., May 19, 1837. No evidence has been found that the first number ever appeared.

SOUTHERN PRESBYTERIAN

Milledgeville, Ga., Aug. 25, 1847–May 2, 1849; Milledgeville and Charleston, May 11, 1849–July 5, 1850; Milledgeville, July 11, 1850–Dec. 30, 1852; Charleston, Feb. 24, 1853–Sept. 29, 1860; Columbia, S. C., Nov. 2, 1860–June (?), 1864; Augusta, Ga., Oct. 6, 1864–April 6, 1865. Aug. 25, 1847–April 6, 1865.[1] Weekly.[2] Folio, 4 pp., 6-7 cols. $2.50-$20 a year. 4,000 subscribers.[3]

Editors: Washington Baird, Aug. 25, 1847–April 6, 1854;[4] John Lycan Kirkpatrick, April 13, 1854–July 4, 1857;[5] Kirkpatrick and Bazile E. Lanneau, July 11, 1857–1858; H. B. Cunningham, Dec. 4, 1858, or earlier–Sept. 29, 1860; Abner A. Porter, Nov. 2, 1860–April 6, 1865.

Proprietors: Baird, Aug. 25, 1847–Aug. 25, 1853; Baird and John M. Frazer, Sept. 1, 1853–April 6, 1854; J. S. Chambers, W. Harral, Frazer, and others, April 13, 1854–June (?), 1856; Archibald Campbell and Company, June 21, 1856–Oct. 31, 1857; James and Williams, Nov. 14, 1857–Sept. 15, 1860; Robert Jones, Sept. 22-29, 1860; Elam Sharpe and Company, Nov. 2, 1860–Jan. 18, 1862; Porter and Company, Jan. 25, 1862–April 6, 1865.[6]

The migration of the *Charleston Observer* to Richmond in 1845 left the Southeastern synods without a weekly religious newspaper. Washington Baird, responding to overtures from ecclesiastical bodies in that area, founded the *Southern Presbyterian* as a general family denominational paper. The prospectus declared that the publication would be "Southern in its design and its spirit; decidedly Presbyterian in its principles." The content included communications, foreign correspondence, editorials, religious and secular news, marriages, deaths, markets, book reviews, departments for various members of the family, and miscellany.

U.L.S., 2nd ed., p. 2653; (1), p. 993. Hoole, *Charleston Periodicals,* pp. 51-54.

Other holdings: GaU Nov. 3, 1864. NcU [1855-1859, 1863]. PPPrHi [1847-1860]. VRT [1861].

[1] After vol. 4, no. 27 (N. S.) had been reached in Columbia in June, 1864, publication was suspended until Oct. 6, 1864, when vol. 4, no. 28, appeared in Columbia. Half-sheets of two pages were published much of the time between 1862 and 1864. The suspension at the close of the war lasted until Dec. 28, 1865, when James Woodrow and Company began another new series in Columbia. Still published as one of several journals forming the *Presbyterian of the South,* Richmond.

[2] During some sessions of the General Assembly extras were issued daily. In Dec., 1861, for example, eleven numbers of *The Assembly Reporter, The Southern Presbyterian, Extra,* were published by Elam Sharpe and Company in Augusta, and in May, 1863, A. A. Porter and Company got out seven numbers of the *Daily Southern Presbyterian* in Columbia. NcMHi and VRT have files.

[3] Although there were 4,000 subscribers at the time, publication had to be suspended in the summer of 1864 for lack of funds for operating expenses. Too many subscribers had failed to pay. See *Southern Presbyterian,* Oct. 6, 1864.

[4] Baird, born about 1807 in Pennsylvania, became a Presbyterian minister after graduation from Jefferson College. His work included teaching and missionary activities in Florida. See Synod of Georgia, *Minutes,* 1869, pp. 10-11.

[5] Kirkpatrick, a North Carolinian, was a graduate of Hampden-Sydney and pastor of Glebe Street Presbyterian Church, Charleston, from 1854 until 1860, when he became president of Davidson College. See Nevin, *Encyclopaedia of the Presbyterian Church,* p. 1172.

[6] A committee appointed by the Synod of Georgia helped launch the *Southern Presbyterian,* but it was privately owned and published. The printer in Milledgeville is unknown. When Baird moved the paper to Charleston, Feb. 24, 1853, W. Y. Paxton, who was listed as "publisher," became printer. In 1856 Archibald Campbell became "associated in the ownership and conduct" of the paper, and from then on the proprietors owned printing establishments.

Southern Presbyterian Pulpit
Southern Pulpit[1]

Richmond. May, 1853–May, 1854, or later. Monthly. Octavo, 16 pp., May, 1853–April (?), 1854; duodecimo, 24 pp., May, 1854–(?). $1 a year.

Editor and proprietor: William Potter.

Each number contained one long original sermon by a Southern minister and a small amount of miscellaneous selected material.

U.L.S., 2nd ed., p. 2653.

[1] The first title appeared until Jan., 1854, or later; the second was used in May, 1854. There may possibly have been two publications. An advertise-

ment of the *Southern Pulpit* in the *Southern Churchman,* Richmond, April 13, 1854, declared that the second volume would be devoted mostly to sermons by Episcopal clergymen of the South. If the *Southern Presbyterian Pulpit* and the *Southern Pulpit* constitute a single publication, Potter had probably decided to make it nonsectarian.

Southern Presbyterian Review

Columbia, S. C. June, 1847–April, 1864.[1] Quarterly. Octavo, 152-172 pp. $3 a year.

Editors and proprietors: An Association of Ministers.[2]

This was the principal religious quarterly review published in the South Atlantic States before 1865. It differed from monthly magazines in that the leading articles tended to be much longer, more often developed serious doctrinal themes, and frequently exhibited a greater interest in the problems of church organization. The book notices and accounts of the meetings of General Assemblies in the *Southern Presbyterian Review* resembled those in weekly newspapers and monthly magazines. This periodical, files of which are available in many libraries, constitutes a valuable source for material relating to the history of the Presbyterian Church in the South.[3]

U.L.S., 2nd ed., p. 2653; (1), p. 993.

[1] No issue appeared between April, 1856, and April, 1857. No. 3 of vol. 16 was published in April, 1864, after which publication ceased until March, 1866, when no. 4 appeared. The publication came to a close in Dec., 1885, with vol. 36.

[2] The original members were George Howe, Benjamin M. Palmer, and James H. Thornwell, all distinguished Presbyterian clergymen. Howe was professor of Biblical literature at Columbia Theological Seminary for over fifty years and author of the outstanding *History of the Presbyterian Church in South Carolina.* Palmer, a nephew of the Benjamin M. Palmer who edited the *Southern Evangelical Intelligencer* in Charleston, left pastorates in South Carolina in 1856 to become pastor of the First Presbyterian Church of New Orleans. Thornwell, one-time president of the South Carolina College, is regarded as the outstanding Presbyterian theologian of the day. Sketches of all three editors appear in the *Dictionary of American Biography.*

When publication was resumed in 1857, John B. Adger replaced Palmer on the staff. James Woodrow came into control in the early 1860's and served as editor and publisher throughout the remainder of the periodical's life. The printers before 1864 were I. C. Morgan (vols. 1-3, 6-9); A. S. Johnston (vols. 4-5); E. H. Britton (vol. 10); R. W. Gibbes (vols. 11-12); and C. P. Pelham (vols. 13-16). By 1857 the association had paid out for printing $1200 more than the total receipts from subscribers. See *Southern Presbyterian Review,* X (April, 1857), 2.

[3] Spence, "Southern Presbyterian Reviews," p. 9.

SOUTHERN PULPIT

Macon, Ga. July, 1848–April, 1849.[1] Monthly. Octavo, 16-24 pp. $1 a year. 900 subscribers.

Editor and proprietor: Josiah Fletcher Askew.[2]

Printer: B. F. Griffin.

In an effort to eliminate Southern dependence on the North for literature, Askew solicited sermons for publication from living ministers of all evangelical denominations. He opposed the "ruinous errors" of Atheism, Deism, Universalism, Romanism, Rationalism, Transcendentalism, Antinomianism, and Arianism.[3]

U.L.S., 2nd ed., (1), p. 994.

[1] Beginning in May, 1849, the *Southern Methodist Pulpit,* Richmond, was sent to the 900 former subscribers to the *Southern Pulpit.* See *Southern Methodist Pulpit,* I (May, 1849), 172.

[2] Askew (1814-1848), a native North Carolinian, was graduated from Randolph-Macon College before beginning a short career as a teacher and Methodist preacher in Georgia. See *Southern Pulpit,* I (Nov., 1848), 9-11.

[3] *Southern Pulpit,* I (July, 1848), back cover.

SOUTHERN PULPIT. *See* SOUTHERN PRESBYTERIAN PULPIT

SOUTHERN RELIGIOUS TELEGRAPH. *See* VISITOR AND TELEGRAPH

SOUTHERN SABBATH SCHOOL ADVOCATE: A FIRE-SIDE COMPANION FOR THE FAMILIES OF BAPTISTS (proposed)

Whiteville, Ga. 1844. Semimonthly. Quarto, 8 pp. $1 a year.

Editor and proprietor: Thomas M. Slatghter.[1]

The prospectus stated that the publication would fill the place of a teacher in families denied the advantages of Sabbath Schools. A contemporary editor expressed the hope "that Christians of all denominations in the South, will patronize this work. Why should we depend upon the North for Sabbath School Journals."[2]

No copy known.

[1] He was also editor of the *Youth's Companion,* Whiteville, Ga.

[2] Joseph S. Baker in the *Christian Index,* Penfield, Ga., Feb. 9, 1844. The prospectus was dated Dec. 26, 1843, and first appeared in the *Christian Index,* Jan. 5, 1844. Publication was to begin in May, but no evidence has been found that the first number ever appeared.

SOUTHERN UNIVERSALIST

Macon, Ga. 1838.[1] Weekly. Folio.

Editor and proprietor: L. F. W. Andrews.

No copy known.

[1] Immediately after Andrews, a Universalist minister, issued his prospectus

and sent specimen numbers to 600 potential subscribers, John Gregory, editor of the *Southern Evangelist,* Charleston, proposed consolidating the two papers. See *Southern Evangelist,* March 17, 1838. This was done on April 7, 1838, the new paper being called *Evangelical Universalist.*

SOUTHERN WATCHMAN AND GENERAL INTELLIGENCER. *See* SOUTHERN BAPTIST AND GENERAL INTELLIGENCER

SPIRITUALIST

Richmond. 1844-(?).[1] Semimonthly. $2 a year.

Editor and proprietor: John T. Walsh.[2]

The prospectus declared that the periodical would be devoted to "Primitive Christianity," which, in this case, meant the principles of the Disciples of Christ. The first number was filled with original articles on the differences between the beliefs of John Thomas and those of Alexander Campbell.

No copy known.

[1] The *Religious Herald,* Richmond, reproduced the prospectus (dated Sept. 6, 1844), on Oct. 3, 1844, and two weeks later reviewed the first number.

[2] See section on *Christian Friend,* Wilson, N. C., for sketch of Walsh.

SPIRITUALIST. *See* CHRISTIAN SPIRITUALIST

STAR OF THE SOUTH

Milledgeville, Ga. 1826-(?). Quarto.

Editor: Michael Smith.[1]

Alexander Campbell described this new Universalist periodical as follows: "This is one of the luminaries of the day, just adapted for the relaxing influence of a southern climate; for the editor is busily employed in relaxing the sanctions of the gospel. He has reasoned himself into the belief that all men will be saved, and is now employed in teaching the readers of his paper that no man will be punished in hell."[2]

No copy known.

[1] Smith, a Universalist minister from New England, reprinted large portions of the *Religious Inquirer,* Hartford, Conn. See Eddy, *Universalism in America,* II, 590.

[2] *Christian Baptist,* Buffaloe Creek, Va., ninth ed., IV (Oct., 1826), 280.

SUNDAY SCHOOL PAPER FOR THE SOUTH (?)

South Carolina. 1861 (?).[1]

No copy known.

[1] "The South Carolina Sunday School Union has issued the first number." See *Christian Observer,* Philadelphia and Richmond, June 20, 1861.

SUNDAY SCHOOL VISITOR

Charleston.[1] Jan. 1, 1851–1855. Semimonthly, Jan.–June, 1851; Monthly, July, 1851–1855. Folio, 8-16 pp., 3-4 cols. 50¢ a year.

Editor: Thomas Osmond Summers.[2]

Proprietor: Methodist Episcopal Church, South.[3]

The General Conference of the Methodist Episcopal Church, South, adopted measures in 1850 providing for the publication of a Sunday school paper to take the place of the *Sunday School Advocate,* published in the North.[4] Illustrated with engravings and adapted to the needs of children, the *Sunday School Visitor* contained letters, stories, poems, announcements, and miscellany.

U.L.S., 2nd ed., p. 2713. Hoole, *Charleston Periodicals,* pp. 60-61.

[1] Although the first four numbers bore the designation "issued simultaneously at Charleston, S. C., and Nashville, Tenn.," the work was actually published in Charleston from the beginning until 1855, when it was transferred to Nashville. Receipt of the first number published in Nashville was acknowledged by the *Weekly Message,* Greensboro, N. C., Sept. 13, 1855. Hoole's *Charleston Periodicals,* pp. 60-61, sketches the history of the publication in Nashville.

[2] Summers, a native of England and a prolific author, served for years as general book editor of the Methodist Episcopal Church, South. See Simpson, *Cyclopaedia of Methodism,* 4th rev. ed., pp. 838-839.

[3] John Early, book agent of the Methodist Episcopal Church, South, was listed as publisher and handled all financial matters; C. Canning did the printing.

[4] *Sunday School Visitor,* Jan. 1, 1851.

SUNDAY VISITANT: OR, WEEKLY REPOSITORY OF CHRISTIAN KNOWLEDGE

Charleston.[1] Jan. 3, 1818–Dec. 25, 1819. Weekly. Quarto, 4 pp. $2.50-$3 a year.

Editor and proprietor: Andrew Fowler.[2]

This Episcopal periodical, advertised as proper to be read on the Lord's day, attempted to instruct all members of the family. There were discussions of church government, theology, and cases of conscience; biographical sketches; church proceedings; and prayers.

U.L.S., 2nd ed., p. 2713; (1), p. 1015.

Other holdings: ScChC [1818-1819].

[1] Although dated from Charleston, vol. 1 was printed at the office of the *Winyaw Intelligencer,* Georgetown, S. C. T. B. Stephens printed vol. 2 in Charleston.

[2] Fowler (1760-1850), a native of New England who attended Yale and

spent his last forty years in South Carolina, was the first missionary sent out by the Society for the Advancement of Christianity in South Carolina. He also founded Charleston's first Sunday schools and conducted an academy. See *Charleston Gospel Messenger, and Protestant Episcopal Register,* XXVII (Feb., 1851), 441-443.

UNION CHRISTIAN INTELLIGENCER. *See* CHRISTIAN INTELLIGENCER

UNITARIAN CHRISTIAN

Augusta, Ga. March–Sept., 1831. Quarterly. Duodecimo, 48 pp. $1 a year.

Editor not given.[1]

In his "Introductory Observations" the editor questioned why one should launch a periodical "in a cause so unpopular as that of Unitarianism." Answering he wrote, "We, like every other sect of Christians, believe that religion is held in greater purity of doctrine among ourselves than elsewhere."[2] Many of the articles discussed some aspect of the conflicting beliefs of Unitarians and Trinitarians. Biographical sketches, selections, and poems also appeared.

U.L.S., 2nd ed., p. 2827.

[1] Printed by W. Lawson for the Augusta Unitarian Book Association. The first of the three numbers contained an address by the Reverend Samuel Gilman of Charleston.

[2] *Unitarian Christian,* I (March, 1831), 1.

UNITARIAN DEFENDANT

Charleston. June 22–Nov. 16, 1822. Semimonthly.[1] Quarto, 4 pp.

Editor not given.[2]

Containing theological discussions, essays, and miscellany, this magazine was designed primarily to defend Unitarians against the assaults of Trinitarians.

U.L.S., 2nd ed., p. 2827.

[1] The eleven numbers appeared irregularly at intervals of about two weeks.

[2] Samuel Gilman probably edited the publication. See Hoole, *Charleston Periodicals,* p. 25. Gilman (1791-1858), eminent author and Unitarian clergyman, moved to Charleston in 1819. See *Dictionary of American Biography,* VII, 305-306.

UNITED STATES CATHOLIC MISCELLANY
(CHARLESTON CATHOLIC MISCELLANY[1]

Charleston. June 5, 1822–Dec., 1861.[2] Weekly. Quarto, 8 pp., 3 cols., 1822; Octavo, 16 pp., 1824-1825; Large quarto, 8 pp., 3-4 cols., 1826-1861. $4-$3 a year. 800 subscribers.

Editor: John England, 1822-1842.[3]

Proprietor: Diocese of Charleston.[4]

Bishop England hoped to make this newspaper, the first Catholic periodical founded in the United States, a national organ, but was unable to win the necessary support from the hierarchy.[5] He did, however, have at least a few subscribers in each of twenty states by 1830. The official organ of the Diocese of Charleston, the *United States Catholic Miscellany,* contained pastoral letters, addresses of the bishop, announcements, encyclicals, church news, editorials, book notices, biographical sketches, poetry, selections, and advertisements.

U.L.S., 2nd ed., p. 2833.

Other holdings: NcD vol. [7]. NcU June 24, 1854; July 12, Aug. 9, Dec. 27, 1856; Jan. 17, March 21, Sept. 26, 1857; March 27, May 3, 15, Nov. 13, 1858; [1859-1860]; April 27, Aug. 24, Sept. 7, 1861.

[1] Name adopted immediately after the secession of South Carolina on Dec. 20, 1860.

[2] Suspended Jan.–Dec., 1823, and Jan.–June, 1826. (Vol. I of 31 nos. was completed at the close of 1822. Vol. II, no. 1, total no. 32, appeared Jan. 7, 1824.) Publication ceased when the great fire of Dec. 11, 1861, destroyed about one-half of Charleston, including the office of the *Charleston Catholic Miscellany.*

[3] Although the editors were not named in the paper, they can often be identified. England (1786-1842) was the founder and for twenty years the principal editor. A native of Ireland, he became Bishop of the Diocese of Charleston in 1820. Authorities regard him as the ablest Catholic clergyman in the United States during his time. See Guilday, *England,* I, 473; *Dictionary of American Biography,* VI, 161; and Maynard, *American Catholicism,* chap. xiii. England was assisted, especially during his long periods of absence from Charleston, by John McEnroe, John Bermingham, Timothy McCarthy, J. F. McNeill, J. M. Cool, John Fielding, and other Catholic clergymen of Charleston. The bishops who succeeded England likewise served as editors. They were Richard S. Baker, Ignatius Reynolds, and, at the time of the Civil War, the prominent Patrick N. Lynch.

[4] The *United States Catholic Miscellany* was the property of the Diocese of Charleston, but England himself financed the first volume at a loss of $500. (See issue for Jan. 7, 1824.) During 1823, while the paper was suspended, he sold shares to several members of the diocese. They, however, received no return on their investments, for the paper never became self-supporting. Its long career was made possible by a steady stream of gifts from interested persons.

[5] Maynard, *American Catholicism,* p. 239. See also Foik, *Catholic Journalism,* p. 75.

VIRGINIA AND NORTH CAROLINA CONFERENCE JOURNAL. *See* CHRISTIAN SENTINEL

VIRGINIA AND NORTH CAROLINA PRESBYTERIAN PREACHER
PRESBYTERIAN PREACHER[1]

Fayetteville, N. C. Jan., 1828–July, 1829, or later.[2] Monthly. Octavo, 16-24 pp. $1 a year.

Editor and publisher: Colin McIver.[3]

Since at that time most editors preferred not to indicate their denomination in the title, McIver explained that it was no part of the design of his publication to attack the doctrines taught in other branches of the Christian Church, but to maintain and illustrate those which Presbyterians believed.[4] Each number contained one or two sermons, with notices and advertisements limited to the covers or provided for by the addition of extra pages. Six of those who contributed sermons were from Virginia, five from North Carolina, and five from other states.

U.L.S., 2nd ed., p. 2889; (1), pp. 854, 1079.

Other holdings: NcMHi April–May, Oct., 1828.

[1] In Jan., 1829, the scope was enlarged to include sermons from any American Presbyterian minister and the title changed accordingly. A new volume numbering also began at that time.

[2] July, 1829, is the latest issue known and it is unlikely that many more numbers appeared.

[3] See section on *Evangelical Museum* for sketch of McIver.

[4] *Virginia and North Carolina Presbyterian Preacher,* I (Jan., 1828), cover.

VIRGINIA BAPTIST

Fredericksburg, Va.[1] May 1, 1858–Oct., 1860, or later.[2] Weekly. Folio, 4 pp., 6 cols. $2 a year.

Editors: William Rufus Powell, May 1, 1858–July, 1859;[3] John Churchill Willis, July 21, 1859–Oct., 1860, or later.[4]

Proprietors (?).[5]

The *Virginia Baptist* was, according to its prospectus, founded to oppose the course of the *Religious Herald,* the leading Baptist paper in Virginia, relative to "Test Churches." These were congregations which made total abstinence from the use of alcoholic beverages a test of church membership. The *Virginia Baptist* favored both "Test Churches" and "Old Landmarkism"; the *Religious Herald* opposed both.[6] The *Virginia Baptist* was also "anti-Board," maintaining that each Baptist Association rather than the Southern Baptist Convention's boards should conduct missionary activities. This weekly, with its emphasis on temperance, contained editorials, communications, book notices, poetry, selections, miscellany, and advertisements.

U.L.S., 2nd ed., (1), p. 1079.

Other holdings: VRB July 21, Aug. 11, 1859

[1] The *American Christian Record* (p. 694), Kenny, *American Newspaper Directory,* 1860 (p. 73), and Cappon, *Virginia Newspapers* (p. 189), list a weekly called the *Virginia Baptist* published in Richmond in 1860. No copy is known. This may possibly be another paper, the Fredericksburg publication may have been transferred to Richmond, or these references may be incorrect citations of the Fredericksburg *Virginia Baptist.*

[2] The last notice of this paper examined appeared in the *Southern Baptist Messenger,* Lexington, Ga., Nov. 1, 1860.

[3] Powell (1808-1859), a Virginian, attended old-field schools, read law, and taught school before he entered the Baptist ministry. He became an outstanding advocate of total abstinence as a test of church membership. See Taylor, *Virginia Baptist Ministers,* series 3, pp. 13-17. Powell's obituary is in the *Virginia Baptist,* July 21, 1859.

[4] Willis (1824-1894), born in Virginia, became a successful country preacher and farmer. See Taylor, *Virginia Baptist Ministers,* series 4, pp. 222-226.

[5] The owners and printers cannot be clearly identified. Cappon, *Virginia Newspapers* (p. 92), states that the *Virginia Baptist* was "established" by Powell; *Zion's Advocate,* Front Royal, Va., June 5, 1858, lists Joseph Billingsley as publisher; while the *Virginia Baptist* itself gives John A. Billingsley as publisher in the issue for March 10, 1859. After the death of Powell, Willis listed himself as publisher, remarking, "the present is the first issue from our press." See *Virginia Baptist,* July 21, 1859.

[6] *Zion's Advocate,* Front Royal, Va., June 5, 1858; *Union Christian Intelligencer,* Charlottesville, Va., June 5, 1858.

Virginia Baptist Preacher, Original Monthly
Baptist Preacher, Original Monthly[1]

Richmond. Jan., 1842–Jan., 1859 (?).[2] Monthly. Octavo, 20 pp. (average). $1 a year. 1,600 subscribers.[3]

Editor and proprietor: Henry Keeling.[4]

The plan for this publication originated among a group of Richmond ministers who were interested in developing a Baptist literature. Although at first only Virginia ministers were encouraged to contribute, after 1844 subscribers and contributors from the entire country were solicited with considerable success. The periodical contained editorials and sermons, all of which were said to be written expressly for it.

U.L.S., 2nd ed., p. 397; (1), p. 164, as *Baptist Preacher, Original Monthly.*

Other holdings: Nc 1846-1847. NcW 1842–Jan., 1856. VRB 1842-1855.

[1] Title used after Jan., 1844.

[2] Listed annually in the *American Baptist Almanac* through 1862 and in Kenny, *American Newspaper Directory* (1860), p. 70, but no copies later than 1859 are known.

[3] Keeling stated in the *Baptist Preacher, Original Monthly,* II (Jan., 1843), 1, that he had 2000 subscribers. Kennedy, "Catalogue of Newspapers and Periodicals," gave 1,250 for 1850.

[4] See section on *Evangelical Inquirer* for sketch of Keeling.

Virginia Evangelical and Literary Magazine
Evangelical and Literary Magazine, and Missionary Chronicle
Literary and Evangelical Magazine[1]

Richmond. Jan., 1818–Dec., 1828.[2] Monthly. Octavo, 48-56 pp. $3 a year.

Editors: John Holt Rice, 1818-1827; Amasa Converse, 1827-1828.[3]

Proprietors: Rice, 1818-1820; Nathan Pollard, 1821-1823; Pollard and Charles Goddard, 1824-1825; Pollard, 1826; Pollard and Converse, 1827; Converse, 1828.[4]

Explaining why he was founding a periodical, Rice wrote that he recognized the "pre-eminent and inexpressible importance" of religion and felt "bound by every obligation" to promote it to the full extent of his power.[5] Regardless of the wording of the title at any particular time, this Presbyterian magazine was more religious than literary throughout its career. There were discussions of theological questions, essays on morals, education, and discipline, book reviews, missionary news, and church proceedings. The term "literary" was used to include essays on agriculture, inland navigation, the construction of roads, and education. Nearly all of the material was written expressly for the magazine.

U.L.S., 2nd ed., p. 1594; (1), p. 607, as *Literary and Evangelical Magazine.*

Other holdings: PPPrHi 1821-1828. VRB 1818-1823, 1825.

[1] First title used 1818-1820; second, 1821-1823, but the words "and Missionary Chronicle" were dropped after one year; third, adopted Jan., 1824, and used thereafter.

[2] Superseded the *Christian Monitor,* Richmond. The *Family Visitor,* established in Richmond in 1822 by Nathan Pollard, cut into the prosperity of Rice's magazine, leaving it fewer subscribers in 1828 than formerly. See *Literary and Evangelical Magazine,* XI (Nov., 1828), 605-611. Amasa Converse, who became owner of both publications in 1828, discontinued the magazine.

[3] See section on *Christian Monitor* for sketch of Rice. He was assisted as editor by several clergymen and laymen, among whom were Moses Hoge, John D. Blair, George A. Baxter, Conrad Speece, Matthew Lyle, William

Hill, John Matthews, and Samuel B. Wilson. See Alfred J. Morrison, "The Virginia Literary and Evangelical Magazine, Richmond, 1818-1828," *William and Mary College Quarterly Historical Magazine,* XIX (April, 1911), 266-272. See section on *Christian Observer* for sketch of Converse.

[4] William W. Gray was the first printer. By 1820, Pollard, proprietor of the Franklin Press, had become the printer.

[5] *Virginia Evangelical and Literary Magazine,* I (Jan., 1818), 1.

Virginia Religious Magazine

Lexington, Va. Oct., 1804–Dec., 1807. Bimonthly. Octavo, 64 pp. $1.50 a year. 350 subscribers.

Editors and proprietors: A group of ministers under the patronage of the Synod of Virginia.[1]

When, in 1804, the Synod of Virginia of the Presbyterian Church declared that it considered a vehicle of communication necessary to the prosperity of the church, a small group of ministers undertook privately the publication of a magazine.[2] It contained domestic and foreign religious intelligence, theological discussions, essays on morals, literary criticism, biographical sketches, poetry, and stories.

U.L.S., 2nd ed., p. 2891.

Other holdings: NcW Oct.–Nov., 1805.

[1] The group consisted of Archibald Alexander, Matthew Lyle, Samuel Houston, Samuel Brown, Daniel Blain, and George A. Baxter. The printer was Samuel Walkup. See *Virginia Religious Magazine,* I (1804), title page.

[2] *Virginia Religious Magazine,* II (1806), Preface.

Virginia Telescope

West Columbia, Va. (now W. Va.). Nov. (?), 1854 (Jan. 25, 1855, is vol. 1, no. 8)–May 23, 1855, or later.[1] Weekly. Folio, 4 pp., 6 cols. $1 a year.

Editor: W. M'K. Cain.[2]

Proprietor: M. Michael.

The *Religious Telescope* (Dayton, Ohio), official organ of the United Brethren, offended Virginia readers by printing abolition material, whereupon they established the *Virginia Telescope* as their unofficial organ.[3] Although definitely classed as a religious newspaper, it contained a larger proportion of secular matter than most. There were essays on theology and morals, communications, selections, philosophical quotations, secular and religious news, market prices, discussions on agriculture, family departments, and advertisements.

U.L.N., p. 751.

Other holdings: NcD Jan. 25, March 7, May 23, 1855.

[1] A notice signed "Sanders and Murrell" stated that the subscription books of the *Messenger* had been transferred to M. Michael, who would henceforth send the *Virginia Telescope* to its subscribers. See *Virginia Telescope,* Jan. 25, 1855.

[2] Cain was a minister of the Church of the United Brethren in Christ.

[3] Drury, *History of the Church of the United Brethren,* pp. 575-576.

Visitor and Telegraph
Southern Religious Telegraph[1]

Richmond. Jan. 6, 1827–Jan. 9, 1839.[2] Weekly. Folio, 4 pp., 5-7 cols. $2.50 a year. 2,000 subscribers.

Editors and proprietors: Nathan Pollard, Jan. 6–Feb. 10, 1827; Pollard and Amasa Converse, Feb. 17, 1827–June 28, 1828;[3] Converse, July 5, 1828–Jan. 9, 1839.

Although Converse remained neutral while the Presbyterian schism of the thirties was developing, he cast his lot with the New School in the summer of 1837, declaring, "there can be neutrality no longer in any part of the church."[4] This caused the loss of about 25 per cent of his subscribers, including nearly all those from North Carolina, and precipitated removal to Philadelphia in 1839.[5] A family religious weekly, the *Southern Religious Telegraph* contained church and secular news, editorials, essays, letters, poetry, marriages, deaths, advertisements, specialized departments, and miscellany.

U.L.N., p. 710. U.L.S., 2nd ed., p. 2653, and, as *Christian Observer,* p. 680; (1), p. 275. Cappon, *Virginia Newspapers,* p. 185.

Other holdings: NcMHi [Jan. 2, 1830–Jan. 9, 1839]. NcU June 6, 1838. PPPrHi 1828-1838.

[1] First title used Jan. 6, 1827–Dec. 25, 1829; second, Jan. 2, 1830–Jan. 9, 1839.

[2] Pollard, already publishing the *Richmond Family Visitor,* purchased the subscription list of the *North Carolina Telegraph,* Fayetteville, and consolidated the two papers under the title *Visitor and Telegraph.* (The *North Carolina Telegraph,* Dec. 29, 1826, contained notice of the sale of its subscription list.) The volume numbering of the Richmond publication was continued. Immediately after the issue for Jan. 9, 1839, Converse combined the *Southern Religious Telegraph* with the *Philadelphia Observer* to form the *Religious Telegraph and Observer.* This paper, with the name changed in 1840 to *Christian Observer,* was published in Philadelphia until 1861, when Richmond again became the place of publication.

[3] See section on *Christian Observer* for sketch of Converse.

[4] Quoted in *Southern Christian Herald,* Cheraw, S. C., July 7, 1837.

[5] A North Carolina clergyman wrote the editor of the *Southern Christian Herald* (see issue for Aug. 18, 1837) that the "Southern Religious Telegraph

has lost its influence among us; it will not be able to do much more mischief in this Synod."

WATCHMAN AND HARBINGER

Greensboro, N. C. 1863-1865 (?).[1] Weekly. Folio, 2 pp., 6 cols. $10 a year.

Editor: J. L. Michaux.[2]

Proprietor: North Carolina Conference of the Methodist Protestant Church.

A wartime religious newspaper advertised as "Devoted to the Interests of the Methodist Protestant Church, and to General Intelligence: Containing Moral and Literary Essays, Poetry, etc.," the *Watchman and Harbinger* included church news, secular news, obituaries, ministerial appointments, advertisements, and selections.

U.L.N., p. 502.

Other holdings: NcU Feb. 17, 1865.

[1] The *North Carolina Christian Advocate,* Raleigh, July 22, 1863, contained notice that J. L. Micheaux [*sic*] would begin the *Weekly Harbinger* in Sept., 1863. The last issue examined is dated Feb. 17, 1865 (vol. 2, no. 16).

[2] Michaux (1827-1898), an outstanding Methodist Protestant minister, was a native Virginian and a member of the North Carolina Conference. See Drinkhouse, *History of Methodist Reform,* II, 681. The conference appointed a publishing committee consisting of R. H. Wills and T. H. Pegram to exercise general supervision.

WATCHMAN AND OBSERVER

WATCHMAN AND OBSERVER OR CENTRAL PRESBYTERIAN[1]

Richmond. Aug. 21, 1845–Dec. 27, 1855.[2] Weekly. Folio, 4 pp., 6 cols. $3 a year. 2,000 subscribers.[3]

Editor and proprietor: Benjamin Gildersleeve.[4]

Shortly after Gildersleeve purchased the *Watchman of the South,* Richmond, and combined his *Charleston Observer* with it, many of his former supporters in South Carolina and Georgia subscribed to the newly founded *Southern Presbyterian* of Milledgeville, Georgia. Gildersleeve's paper remained, nevertheless, the leading Old School Presbyterian journal of the South. It contained church proceedings and news, essays, editorials, theological discussions, obituaries, marriages, poetry, secular news, miscellany, and advertisements.

U.L.S., 2nd ed., p. 2922. (The NcMHi and PPPrHi files, although listed as complete, lack scattering numbers.) Cappon, *Virginia Newspapers,* p. 191.

Other holdings: NcU Oct. 26, 1848.

[1] Second title adopted Aug. 9, 1855, and used thereafter.

[2] Formed by consolidating the *Charleston Observer* with the *Watchman of the South,* Richmond, the *Watchman and Observer* appeared weekly without interruption until Gildersleeve retired and his paper was superseded by the *Central Presbyterian* of Richmond.

[3] Kennedy, "Catalogue of Newspapers and Periodicals," 1850.

[4] See section on *Central Presbyterian* for sketch of Gildersleeve. When he retired on Dec. 27, 1855, he had completed thirty-seven years as an editor. From Aug. 21, 1845, until Jan. 20, 1848, John B. Martin and William W. Dunnavant printed the *Watchman and Observer.* After this no printer was listed, only the address of the office on Main Street appearing among the business announcements.

WATCHMAN OF THE SOUTH

Richmond. Aug. 31, 1837–Aug. 14, 1845.[1] Weekly. Folio, 4 pp., 5-6 cols. $3 a year. 4,200 subscribers.[2]

Editor and proprietor: William S. Plumer.[3]

In the summer of 1837, when Amasa Converse, editor of the *Southern Religious Telegraph* of Richmond, announced his support of the New School branch of the Presbyterian Church, Plumer promptly founded the *Watchman of the South* as the organ of the Old School. The subtitle declared the paper's devotion to the promotion of practical piety, the diffusion of religious and general intelligence, and the propagation of the distinctive tenets and institutions of the Presbyterian Church. One of the outstanding religious weeklies published in the South, Plumer's paper included secular and religious news, editorials, essays, communications, church proceedings, book notices, advertisements, and miscellany.

U.L.S., 2nd ed., p. 2922. Cappon, *Virginia Newspapers,* p. 192.

Other holdings: NcU May 16, 1839.

[1] Plumer announced on the dates given herein the purchase of the following papers: *Southern Christian Herald,* Cheraw, S. C., Dec. 20, 1838; *American Presbyterian,* Nashville, Tenn., Aug. 29, 1839; *New Orleans Observer,* April 16, 1840. On July 10, 1845, Plumer announced the sale of his paper to Benjamin Gildersleeve, editor of the *Charleston Observer,* who, after Aug. 14, combined the two publications to form the *Watchman and Observer,* Richmond.

[2] The *Watchman of the South,* April 23, 1840, with over four thousand subscribers, claimed a longer list than any political or any other religious paper in Virginia.

[3] Plumer (1802-1880), a native of Pennsylvania and a graduate of Princeton Seminary, was pastor of the First Presbyterian Church, Richmond, during

the period of his editorship. See Nevin, *Encyclopaedia of the Presbyterian Church,* p. 622, and *Dictionary of American Biography,* XV, 13-14. The printers employed by Plumer were B. R. Wren, Aug. 31, 1837–March 25, 1841, and John B. Martin and William W. Dunnavant, April 1, 1841–Aug. 14, 1845.

WEEKLY MESSAGE

Greensboro, N. C. Oct. 30, 1851–1865.[1] Weekly. Folio, 4 pp., 6 cols. $1 a year.

Editor and proprietor: Sidney D. Bumpass, Oct. 30–Dec., 1851; Frances M. Bumpass, 1852-1865.[2]

Although not the organ of an annual conference, the *Weekly Message* was devoted to the interests of Methodism, especially the promotion of piety and morality. The proprietress declined an opportunity to sell her subscription list to the committee appointed to establish the *North Carolina Christian Advocate,* preferring to retain the publication because it afforded a small income.[3] This newspaper contained moral and religious essays, poetry, stories, dialogues, news, announcements, church proceedings, editorials, obituaries, markets, family departments, and advertisements. Many of the selections came from the *Guide to Holiness* of Boston.

Not listed U.L.S.

Holdings: Nc July 7, 1853. NcD July 13, Oct. 5, 1854; Sept. 13, 1855; May 29, 1856; April 25, June 20, 1859; July 27, Oct. 5, 1860; March 29, Aug. 31, 1861. NcR July 19, 1855; April 10, 1856; Jan. 27, Feb. 20, 26, 1857; Dec. 25, 1858. NcU [1851-1865].

[1] After only a short suspension at the close of the war, the *Weekly Message,* with the name changed first to *Message* and later to *Olive Branch,* was published until 1871.

[2] Sidney D. Bumpass, Methodist minister and founder of the paper, died Dec. 12, 1851. James Jamieson served as editor for a few months, but during most of its life the *Weekly Message* was both owned and edited by Bumpass's widow. Orin Churchill and others served as printers. Methodist ministers secured subscribers. See *Southern Methodist Pulpit,* Greensboro, N. C., V (April, 1852), 113; *Weekly Message,* July 7, 1853; and Ethel Troy, "Methodist Preacher in Old Raleigh Kept Busy," *News and Observer* (Raleigh, N. C.), May 4, 1952.

[3] Deems, *Annals of Southern Methodism for 1856,* p. 174.

WESLEYAN JOURNAL

Charleston. Oct. 1, 1825–March 3, 1827.[1] Weekly. Folio, 4 pp., 5 cols. $3 a year.

Editors: A committee of the South Carolina Conference.[2]

Proprietors: The South Carolina Conference of the Methodist Episcopal Church.

This Methodist paper, as official organ of the South Carolina Conference, contained church proceedings, news, and notices. Editorials, theological discussions, poetry, domestic and foreign secular news, market prices, miscellany, and advertisements also appeared. In offering reasons for the union of their publication with the *Christian Advocate,* the South Carolina Conference declared the need of a "general paper" in order to avoid the "danger of collision" which existed when there were many separate papers.[3]

U.L.S., 2nd ed., p. 2933. Hoole, *Charleston Periodicals,* p. 28.

Other holdings: ScSW complete file.

[1] The *Wesleyan Journal* was the second oldest Methodist newspaper in the United States, being antedated only by *Zion's Herald,* Boston, 1823. See Crum, *History of the Southern Christian Advocate,* p. 24. In 1827 the *Wesleyan Journal* was consolidated with the *Christian Advocate,* published in New York by the Methodist Book Concern, to form the *Christian Advocate and Journal,* New York. See *Wesleyan Journal,* March 3, 1827, for details of the merger.

[2] Stephen Olin, appointed first editor by the South Carolina Conference, was prevented by ill health from accepting the position. See *Wesleyan Journal,* Oct. 1, 1825. The committee appointed in his place consisted of William Capers, J. O. Andrew, H. Bass, N. Laney, and S. J. Wagner. Capers actually did most of the editorial work. See *Wesleyan Journal,* March 3, 1827, and Wightman, *Life of Bishop Capers,* pp. 249-250. See section on *Southern Christian Advocate* for sketch of Capers.

[3] *Wesleyan Journal,* March 3, 1827.

Western Baptist

Buchanan, Va. 1842 (?)-1845 (?).[1] Weekly. $2.50 a year.

Editor and proprietor: William H. Hughart.

When it first appeared, Baptist editors greeted this publication as an advocate of their views, but it turned out to be a Disciples of Christ newspaper.[2]

No copy known.

[1] Mentioned in the *Christian Index,* Penfield, Ga., Jan. 12, 1843, as recently founded, and in the *Christian Intelligencer,* Charlottesville, Va., Aug. 11, 1845, as about to suspend.

[2] Recommended by Joseph S. Baker, editor of the Baptist *Christian Index,* Jan. 12, 1843, and listed in the *Almanac and Baptist Register,* 1844, p. 36. A Disciples editor declared, however, that Hughart was attempting to plant "the cause" in Southwestern Virginia. When Hughart abandoned his paper because of the financial loss it entailed, this same editor recommended his own paper to the Valley Co-operation, a Disciples organization, as a substitute (James W. Goss in the *Christian Intelligencer,* June 16, Aug. 11, 1845). Alexander Campbell's *Millennial Harbinger,* I (April, 1844), 185, endorsed Hughart's publication.

WESTERN VIRGINIA BAPTIST

Buchanan, Va. 1857 (?).[1] Weekly.

No copy known.

[1] "A new paper, styled the *Western Virginia Baptist,* has just been commenced in Buchanan, Botetourt Co., Va." Notice in *Southern Baptist,* Charleston, Jan. 27, 1857. Listed in *American Baptist Almanac,* 1858, p. 31.

YOUTH'S COMPANION

Whiteville, Ga. (?).[1] 1843 (?).[2] Monthly.

Editor: Thomas M. Slatghter.

Baptist.

No copy known.

[1] The only evidence that Whiteville was the place is the fact that Slatghter issued the prospectus for another publication, the *Southern Sabbath School Advocate,* from that address.

[2] This date is based on a notice in the *Christian Index,* Penfield, Ga., Feb. 9, 1844, stating that the *Youth's Companion,* "though highly commended by the press, was discontinued for want of adequate patronage."

YOUTH'S REPERTORY AND CHILD'S MAGAZINE

Macon, Ga. Sept., 1831.[1] Monthly. Duodecimo, 36 pp.

Editor and proprietor: G. Capers.

A Methodist periodical designed especially for Georgia young people, this magazine contained a biographical sketch of William Henry Drayton, essays, poetry, and selected miscellany.

Not listed U.L.S.

Hoole, *Charleston Periodicals,* p. 33.

[1] Information regarding this magazine appeared in another of Capers's periodicals, the *Georgia Christian Repertory,* Macon. On Dec. 15, 1831, he requested friends and agents who had subscriptions for the *Youth's Repertory* to forward them immediately so he would know how many copies of the second number to print. Later he returned the money of those who had subscribed, remarking March 7, 1832, that there were not enough subscribers to warrant a second number. Hoole, *Charleston Periodicals,* p. 33, lists the *Youth's Repertory and Child's Magazine* and locates the one known copy. It includes, however, no title-page showing place or printer, so Hoole very appropriately expresses his lack of conviction that this was a Charleston magazine.

YOUTH'S SUNDAY CASKET

Richmond. 1842-(?).[1] Semimonthly. Quarto. 50¢ a year.

"Publisher": A. T. Maddox.

Designed for children and illustrated with engravings, this publication sought to promote the Sunday school movement.

No copy known.

[1] A favorable notice of the current number appeared in the *Christian Index,* Penfield, Ga., July 29, 1842.

ZION'S ADVOCATE

Front Royal, Va. Jan. 7, 1854–1865.[1] Semimonthly.[2] Octavo, 16 pp. $1 a year. 2,500 subscribers.[3]

Editor and proprietor: John Clark.[4]

This Old School Baptist periodical was established to oppose the *Signs of the Times,* Middletown, New York, which, according to Clark, introduced "heresies more abominable, and foreign from the truth of the gospel, than anything that can be found . . . in our country." Clark claimed his followers were a "separate and distinct people" from those Old School Baptists who accepted the leadership of Gilbert Beebe.[5] The content of *Zion's Advocate* continued largely theological and controversial, with some church news and proceedings, advertisements, and miscellany. Editorial material enjoyed considerable prominence.

U.L.S., 2nd ed., p. 43, as *Advocate and Messenger.*

Other holdings: NcD [1859]. NcW Jan. 2, 1858–Dec. 17, 1859. VRB 1854, 1857.

[1] Continued after the Civil War until superseded by the *Advocate and Messenger,* which is now edited at Kimball, Va., and printed at Front Royal, Va.

[2] Listed incorrectly in Kenny, *American Newspaper Directory,* 1860, p. 72, as weekly.

[3] Subscribers were located primarily in Va., Mo., Ohio, Tenn., and Ga. See *Zion's Advocate,* Dec. 4, 1858.

[4] Clark (1804-1882), a Virginian, left his trade as a bridge builder to become a minister, and by self-application gained a fair education. In great demand as a preacher, he traveled widely and many regarded him as the leading Old School minister in Virginia. See Pittman, *Biographical History of Primitive or Old School Baptist Ministers,* pp. 64-65.

[5] *Zion's Advocate,* Jan. 3, 1857.

Titles Arranged Chronologically

1800-1809

1802

Georgia Analytical Repository. 1803.[1]

1804

Virginia Religious Magazine. 1807.

1807

(Georgia Express). 1808.

1810-1819

1810

Lynchburg Evangelical Magazine. 1811.

1814

Christian Mirror. 1814.

1815

Christian Monitor. 1817.

Lay-Man's Magazine. 1816.

1816

Monthly Visitant; Or, Something Old. 1816.

1818

Sunday Visitant: Or, Weekly Repository of Christian Knowledge. 1819.

Virginia Evangelical and Literary Magazine. 1828.

1819

Missionary. 1825.

Southern Evangelical Intelligencer. 1826.

1820-1829

1821

Roanoke Religious Correspondent; Or, Monthly Evangelical Visitant. 1823.

[1] Beginning and closing dates are included. When no closing date is given publication has continued to the present.

1822

Family Visitor. 1826.

Unitarian Defendant. 1822.

United States Catholic Miscellany. 1861.

1823

Christian Baptist. 1830.

1824

Gospel Messenger and Southern Christian Register. 1853.

1825

Christian Journal (proposed).

Wesleyan Journal. 1827.

1826

Evangelical Inquirer. 1827.

Georgia Reporter and Christian Gazette. 1826.

North Carolina Telegraph. 1826.

Liberalist. 1828.

Star of the South. 1826.

1827

Charleston Observer. 1845.

Visitor and Telegraph. 1839.

1828

Evangelical Museum. 1828.

Religious Herald.

Virginia and North Carolina Presbyterian Preacher. 1829.

1829

Evangelical Port-Folio (proposed).

1830-1839

1830

Millennial Harbinger. 1870.

1831

Georgia Christian Repertory. 1832.

Southern Pioneer and Gospel Visiter. 1837.

Unitarian Christian. 1831.

Youth's Repertory and Child's Magazine. 1831.

1832

Christian Sentinel. 1900.

Messenger of Peace (proposed).

1833

Christian Index.

Evangelical Lutheran Preacher, and Pastoral Messenger. 1835.
North Carolina Baptist Interpreter. 1834.

1834

Apostolic Advocate. 1839.
Banner of the Cross. 1834.
Methodist Sunday-School Recorder. 1834.
Southern Christian Herald. 1838.
Southern Evangelist. 1838.

1835

Biblical Recorder.
Christian Telescope. 1835.
Southern Baptist and General Intelligencer. 1838.
Southern Churchman.

1836

Christian Publisher. 1843.
Primitive Baptist. 1879.
Signs of the Times. 1840.

1837

Georgia Christian Sentinel. 1837.
Morning Watch. 1840.
Southern Christian Advocate.
Southern Preacher (proposed).
Watchman of the South. 1845.

1838

Evangelical Universalist. 1840.
Southern Universalist. 1838.

1839

Southern Baptist Preacher, Or, Sermons by Living Baptist Ministers in the South. 1841.
Southern Baptist Pulpit or Monthly Sermons. 1840.
Southern Christian Sentinel. 1841.

1840-1849

1840

Baptist Chronicle and Monthly Monitor. 1841.
Evangelical Miscellany and Ecclesiastical Review (proposed).
Methodist Protestant Banner. 1840.

1842

Baptist Expositor and South-Western Intelligencer. 1842.
Christian Warrior. 1845.

Southern Christian Repository. 1842.
Virginia Baptist Preacher, Original Monthly. 1859.
Western Baptist. 1845.
Youth's Sunday Casket. 1842.

1843
Christian Magazine of the South. 1851.
Episcopal Protestant. 1845.
Southern Baptist Advocate. 1844.
Youth's Companion. 1843.

1844
Christian Intelligencer. 1862.
Christian Sun.
Southern Sabbath School Advocate (proposed).
Spiritualist. 1844.

1845
Carolina Baptist, A Monthly Magazine. 1846.
Herald of the Future Age. 1847.
Watchman and Observer. 1855.

1846
Calvinistic Magazine. 1850.
Carolina Baptist. 1860.
Southern Baptist Missionary Journal. 1851.

1847
Baptist Guardian. 1848.
Baptist Recorder. 1849.
Periodical Library. 1847.
Southern Presbyterian.
Southern Presbyterian Review. 1885.

1848
Arminian Magazine. 1849.
Christian Banner. 1862.
Southern Methodist Pulpit. 1852.
Southern Pulpit. 1849.

1849
Baptist Messenger. 1851.
Commission. 1851.
Monthly Miscellany. 1849.
Religious and General Intelligencer. 1850.
Southern Baptist Review. 1849.
Southern Methodist. 1849.

1850-1859

1850

Erskine Miscellany. 1862.
Mountain Messenger and Baptist Recorder. 1859.
Southern Advocate. 1850.
Southern Family Visitor. 1850.

1851

Home and Foreign Journal. 1861.
North Carolina Baptist. 1853.
Parish Visitor. 1856.
Southern Baptist Messenger. 1861.
Sunday School Visitor. 1855.
Weekly Message. 1871.

1852

Christian Repository. 1852.

1853

Carolina Baptist. 1858.
Christian Friend. 1860.
Carolina Intelligencer. 1855.
Southern Episcopalian. 1863.
Southern Presbyterian Pulpit. 1854.

1854

Virginia Telescope. 1855.
Zion's Advocate.

1855

American Baptist Memorial. 1856.
Christian Union Magazine. 1855.
Family Christian Album. 1855.
Herald of Truth. 1856.

1856

Central Presbyterian. 1908.
Christian Union. 1858.
Christian Union and Religious Review. 1856.
Commission; Or, Southern Baptist Missionary Magazine. 1861.
Florida Baptist Union. 1857.
North Carolina Christian Advocate.
Semi-Monthly Progressionist. 1859.
Southern Light, an Independent Religious and Literary Journal. 1856.
Southern Methodist Itinerant. 1860.

1857

Pastor's and People's Journal. 1858.
Western Virginia Baptist. 1857.

1858

North Carolina Presbyterian. 1931.
Virginia Baptist. 1860.

1859

Baptist Champion. 1860.
Baptist Telescope. 1860.
Carolina Progressionist. 1860.
Christian Spiritualist. 1860.
Landmark Banner and Cherokee Baptist. 1865.
North Western Virginia Baptist. 1861.
Southern Methodist. 1859.

1860-1864

1860

Church Intelligencer. 1866.
Family Visitor. 1860.

1861

Christian Observer.
Evangelical Pulpit. 1862.
Herald of Truth (proposed).
Southern Lutheran. 1864.
Sunday School Paper for the South. 1861.

1862

Children's Friend. 1915.
Child's Index. 1865.
Confederate Baptist. 1865.

1863

Army and Navy Herald. 1865.
Army and Navy Messenger. 1865.
Children's Guide. 1865.
Confederate Baptist Review (proposed).
Nazarene Banner. 1864.
Soldier's Friend. 1864.
Soldier's Paper. 1865.
Soldier's Visitor. 1865.
Watchman and Harbinger. 1865.

1864

Pacificator. 1865.
Southern Friend. 1866.

Titles Arranged Alphabetically by Denominations

BAPTIST

American Baptist Memorial, Richmond.
Banner and Baptist. See *Landmark Banner and Cherokee Baptist.*
Baptist Banner. See *Landmark Banner and Cherokee Baptist.*
Baptist Champion, Macon, Ga.
Baptist Chronicle and Monthly Monitor, Columbus, Ga.
Baptist Expositor and South-Western Intelligencer, Columbus, Ga.
Baptist Guardian, Richmond.
Baptist Messenger, Elizabeth City, N. C.
Baptist Preacher, Original Monthly. See *Virginia Baptist Preacher, Original Monthly.*
Baptist Recorder, Fairmont, Va.
Baptist Telegraph, Jacksonville, Fla.
Baptist Telescope, Hendersonville, N. C.
Biblical Recorder, New Bern, N. C.
Carolina Baptist, Charleston.
Carolina Baptist, Hendersonville, N. C.
Carolina Baptist, A Monthly Magazine, Greenville, S. C.
Carolina Intelligencer, Shelby, N. C.
Child's Index, Macon, Ga.
Christian Banner, Fredericksburg, Va.
Christian Index, Washington, Ga.
Christian Repository, Atlanta.
Christian Telescope, Montpelier, N. C.
Commission, Richmond.
Commission; Or, Southern Baptist Missionary Magazine, Richmond.
Confederate Baptist, Columbia, S. C.

Confederate Baptist Review (proposed), Columbia, S. C.
Evangelical Inquirer, Richmond.
Evangelical Miscellany and Ecclesiastical Review (proposed), Petersburg, Va.
Florida Baptist Union, Thomasville, Ga.
Georgia Analytical Repository, Savannah.
Home and Foreign Journal, Richmond.
Landmark Banner and Cherokee Baptist, Rome, Ga.
Lone Baptist and Christian Investigator (proposed), Jacksonville, Fla.
Messenger of Peace (proposed), Raleigh, N. C.
Monthly Miscellany; A Religious and Literary Review, Richmond, Atlanta, New Orleans.
Mountain Messenger and Baptist Recorder, Morgantown, Va.
Nazarene Banner, Atlanta.
North Carolina Baptist, Asheville, N. C.
North Carolina Baptist Interpreter, Edenton, N. C.
North Western Virginia Baptist, Grafton, Va.
Periodical Library, Penfield, Ga.
Primitive Baptist, Tarboro, N. C.
Religious and General Intelligencer, Wilmington, N. C.
Religious Herald, Richmond.
Roanoke Religious Correspondent; Or, Monthly Evangelical Visitant, Danville, Va.
Signs of the Times, Alexandria, Va.
Soldier's Friend, Atlanta.
Southern Baptist. See *Carolina Baptist,* Charleston.
Southern Baptist Advocate, Charleston.
Southern Baptist and General Intelligencer, Charleston.
Southern Baptist Messenger, Lexington, Ga.
Southern Baptist Missionary Journal, Richmond.
Southern Baptist Preacher, or, Sermons by Living Baptist Ministers in the South, Washington, Ga.
Southern Baptist Pulpit, Or, Monthly Sermons, Fayetteville, N. C.
Southern Baptist Review, Raleigh, N. C.
Southern Christian Repository, Raleigh, N. C.
Southern Light, An Independent Religious and Literary Journal, Edgefield, S. C.
Southern Preacher (proposed), New Bern, N. C.

Southern Watchman and General Intelligencer. See *Southern Baptist and General Intelligencer.*
Virginia Baptist, Fredericksburg, Va.
Virginia Baptist Preacher, Original Monthly, Richmond.
Western Virginia Baptist, Buchanan, Va.
Youth's Companion, Whiteville, Ga.
Zion's Advocate, Front Royal, Va.

CATHOLIC

Charleston Catholic Miscellany. See *United States Catholic Miscellany.*
Pacificator, Augusta, Ga.
United States Catholic Miscellany, Charleston.

CHRISTADELPHIAN

Advocate for the Testimony of God, as it is Written in the Books of Nature and Revelation. See *Apostolic Advocate.*
Apostolic Advocate, Richmond.
Herald of the Future Age, Richmond.

CHRISTIAN

Christian Sun, Hillsboro, N. C.

DISCIPLES OF CHRIST

American Christian Preacher and Disciples' Miscellany. See *Christian Friend.*
Carolina Christian Monthly. See *Christian Friend.*
Christian Baptist, Buffaloe Creek, Va.
Christian Baptist. See *Christian Friend.*
Christian Friend, Wilson, N. C.
Christian Intelligencer, Charlottesville, Va.
Christian Preacher. See *Christian Friend.*
Christian Publisher, Charlottesville, Va.
Christian Union, Augusta, Ga.
Christian Union and Religious Review, King William Court House, Va.
Disciples' Advocate. See *Christian Friend.*
Family Visitor, N. C.
Millennial Harbinger, Bethany, Va.
Morning Watch, Evergreen, S. C.
Spiritualist, Richmond.

Union Christian Intelligencer. See *Christian Intelligencer.*
Western Baptist, Buchanan, Va.

EPISCOPAL

Charleston Gospel Messenger and Protestant Episcopal Register. See *Gospel Messenger and Southern Christian Register.*
Church Intelligencer, Raleigh, N. C.
Episcopal Protestant, Charleston.
Gospel Messenger and Southern Christian Register, Charleston.
Lay-Man's Magazine, Martinsburg, Va.
Parish Visitor, Richmond.
Southern Churchman, Richmond.
Southern Episcopalian, Charleston.
Sunday Visitant; Or, Weekly Repository of Christian Knowledge, Charleston.

LUTHERAN

Evangelical Lutheran Preacher, and Pastoral Messenger, Winchester, Va.
Southern Lutheran, Charleston.

METHODIST

Arminian Magazine, Rome, Ga.
Army and Navy Herald, Macon, Ga.
Children's Guide, Macon, Ga.
Christian Sentinel, Richmond.
Georgia Christian Repertory, Macon, Ga.
Georgia Christian Sentinel, Covington, Ga.
Herald of Truth, Hendersonville, N. C.
Methodist Christian Sentinel. See *Christian Sentinel.*
Methodist Protestant Banner, Charleston.
Methodist Sunday-School Recorder, Richmond.
North Carolina Christian Advocate, Raleigh, N. C.
Richmond Christian Advocate. See *Christian Sentinel.*
Soldier's Paper, Richmond.
Southern Christian Advocate, Charleston.
Southern Methodist, Macon, Ga.
Southern Methodist, Rome, Ga.
Southern Methodist Itinerant, Parkersburg, Va.
Southern Methodist Pulpit, Richmond.
Southern Pulpit, Macon, Ga.

Sunday School Visitor, Charleston.
Virginia and North Carolina Conference Journal. See *Christian Sentinel.*
Watchman and Harbinger, Greensboro, N. C.
Weekly Message, Greensboro, N. C.
Wesleyan Journal, Charleston.
Youth's Repertory and Child's Magazine, Macon, Ga.

PRESBYTERIAN

Banner of the Cross, Columbia, S. C.
Calvinistic Magazine, Abingdon, Va.
Central Presbyterian, Richmond.
Charleston Observer, Charleston.
Children's Friend, Richmond.
Christian Magazine of the South, Columbia, S. C.
Christian Monitor, Richmond.
Christian Observer, Richmond.
Due West Telescope. See *Erskine Miscellany.*
Erskine Miscellany, Due West, S. C.
Evangelical and Literary Magazine and Missionary Chronicle. See *Virginia Evangelical and Literary Magazine.*
Evangelical Museum, Fayetteville, N. C.
Evangelical Port-Folio (proposed), Fayetteville, N. C.
Georgia Reporter and Christian Gazette, Sparta, Ga.
Literary and Evangelical Magazine. See *Virginia Evangelical and Literary Magazine.*
Missionary, Mount Zion, Ga.
North Carolina Presbyterian, Fayetteville, N. C.
North Carolina Telegraph, Fayetteville, N. C.
Pastor's and People's Journal, Macon, Ga.
Presbyterian Preacher. See *Virginia and North Carolina Presbyterian Preacher.*
Soldier's Visitor, Richmond.
Southern Christian Herald, Columbia, S. C.
Southern Christian Sentinel, Charleston.
Southern Evangelical Intelligencer, Charleston.
Southern Intelligencer. See *Southern Evangelical Intelligencer.*
Southern Presbyterian, Milledgeville, Ga.
Southern Presbyterian Pulpit, Richmond.
Southern Presbyterian Review, Columbia, S. C.

Southern Pulpit. See *Southern Presbyterian Pulpit.*
Southern Religious Telegraph. See *Visitor and Telegraph.*
Virginia and North Carolina Presbyterian Preacher, Fayetteville, N. C.
Virginia Evangelical and Literary Magazine, Richmond.
Virginia Religious Magazine, Lexington, Va.
Visitor and Telegraph, Richmond.
Watchman and Observer, Richmond.
Watchman of the South, Richmond.

QUAKER

Southern Friend, Richmond.

SPIRITUALIST

Carolina Progressionist, Cross Anchor, S. C.
Christian Spiritualist, Macon, Ga.
Progressionist. See *Carolina Progressionist.*
Spiritualist. See *Christian Spiritualist.*

UNITARIAN

Unitarian Christian, Augusta, Ga.
Unitarian Defendant, Charleston.

UNITED BRETHREN

Virginia Telescope, West Columbia, Va.

UNIVERSALIST

Christian Warrior, Richmond.
Evangelical Universalist, Macon, Ga.
Liberalist, Wilmington, N. C.
Semi-Monthly Progressionist, Newnan, Ga.
Southern Evangelist, Charleston.
Southern Pioneer and Gospel Visiter, Richmond.
Southern Universalist, Macon, Ga.
Star of the South, Milledgeville, Ga.

NONSECTARIAN

Army and Navy Messenger, Petersburg, Va.
Christian Journal (proposed), Richmond.
Christian Mirror, Charleston.
Christian Union Magazine, Va.
Evangelical Pulpit, Forsyth, Ga.

Family Christian Album, Richmond.
Family Visitor, Richmond.
Herald of Truth (proposed), Newton, N. C.
Lynchburg Evangelical Magazine, Lynchburg, Va.
Monthly Visitant; Or, Something Old, Alexandria, Va.
Richmond Family Visitor. See *Family Visitor.*
Southern Sabbath School Advocate (proposed), Whiteville, Ga.

DENOMINATION UNKNOWN

(*Georgia Express*), Athens, Ga.
Religious Magazine.
Southern Advocate, Raleigh, N. C.
Southern Family Visitor, Newton County, Ga.
Sunday School Paper for the South, S. C.
Youth's Sunday Casket, Richmond.

Titles Arranged Alphabetically According to Place of Publication

FLORIDA

Jacksonville

Baptist Telegraph

Lone Baptist and Christian Investigator (proposed)

GEORGIA

Athens

(*Georgia Express*)

Atlanta

Christian Repository

Landmark Banner and Cherokee Baptist

Monthly Miscellany; A Religious and Literary Review

Nazarene Banner

Soldier's Friend

Augusta

Baptist Banner

Christian Union

Pacificator

Southern Christian Advocate

Southern Presbyterian

Unitarian Christian

Columbus

Baptist Chronicle and Monthly Monitor

Baptist Expositor and South-Western Intelligencer

Covington

Georgia Christian Sentinel

Southern Baptist Messenger

Forsyth

Evangelical Pulpit

Lexington

Southern Baptist Messenger

Macon

Army and Navy Herald

Baptist Champion

Children's Guide

Child's Index

Christian Index

Christian Spiritualist

Evangelical Universalist

Georgia Christian Repertory

Pastor's and People's Journal

Southern Methodist

Southern Pulpit

Southern Universalist

Youth's Repertory and Child's Magazine

Milledgeville

Southern Presbyterian

Star of the South

Mount Zion

Missionary

Newnan

Semi-Monthly Progressionist

Newton County

Southern Family Visitor

Penfield

Christian Index

Periodical Library

Southern Baptist Preacher, Or, Sermons by Living Baptist Ministers in the South

Rome

Arminian Magazine

Landmark Banner and Cherokee Baptist

Southern Methodist

Savannah

Georgia Analytical Repository

Sparta

Georgia Reporter and Christian Gazette

Thomasville

Florida Baptist Union

Washington

Christian Index

Southern Baptist Preacher, Or, Sermons by Living Baptist Ministers in the South

Whiteville

Southern Sabbath School Advocate (proposed)

Youth's Companion

NORTH CAROLINA

Asheville

North Carolina Baptist

Charlotte

Church Intelligencer

Edenton

North Carolina Baptist Interpreter

Elizabeth City

Baptist Messenger

Fayetteville

Evangelical Museum

Evangelical Port-Folio (proposed)

North Carolina Presbyterian

North Carolina Telegraph

Southern Baptist Pulpit or Monthly Sermons

Virginia and North Carolina Presbyterian Preacher

Goldsboro

Christian Friend

Greensboro

Southern Methodist Pulpit

Watchman and Harbinger

Weekly Message

Hendersonville

Baptist Telescope

Carolina Baptist

Herald of Truth

Hillsboro

Christian Sun

Hookerton

Christian Friend and Bible Unionist

Kinston

American Christian Preacher and Disciples' Miscellany

Milton

Roanoke Religious Correspondent; Or, Monthly Evangelical Visitant

Montpelier

Christian Telescope

New Bern

Biblical Recorder

North Carolina Baptist Interpreter

Southern Preacher (proposed)

Newton

Herald of Truth (proposed)

Pittsboro

Christian Sun

Raleigh

Biblical Recorder

Christian Sun

Church Intelligencer

Messenger of Peace (proposed)

North Carolina Christian Advocate

Primitive Baptist

Southern Advocate

Southern Baptist Review

Southern Christian Repository

Shelby

Carolina Intelligencer

Tarboro

Primitive Baptist

Wilmington

Liberalist

Religious and General Intelligencer

Wilson

Christian Friend

——?

Family Visitor

SOUTH CAROLINA

Charleston

Carolina Baptist

Carolina Baptist, a Monthly Magazine
Charleston Observer
Christian Mirror
Episcopal Protestant
Gospel Messenger and Southern Christian Register
Methodist Protestant Banner
Southern Baptist Advocate
Southern Baptist and General Intelligencer
Southern Christian Advocate
Southern Christian Sentinel
Southern Episcopalian
Southern Evangelical Intelligencer
Southern Evangelist
Southern Lutheran
Southern Presbyterian
Sunday School Visitor
Sunday Visitant: Or, Weekly Repository of Christian Knowledge
edge
Unitarian Defendant
United States Catholic Miscellany
Wesleyan Journal

Cheraw
Southern Baptist Pulpit or Monthly Sermons
Southern Christian Herald

Columbia
Banner of the Cross
Christian Magazine of the South
Confederate Baptist
Confederate Baptist Review (proposed)
Southern Christian Herald
Southern Lutheran
Southern Presbyterian
Southern Presbyterian Review

Cross Anchor
Carolina Progressionist

Due West
Erskine Miscellany

Edgefield
Southern Light, an Independent Religious and Literary Journal

Evergreen

Morning Watch

Greenville

Carolina Baptist, a Monthly Magazine

Winnsboro

Christian Magazine of the South

——?

Sunday School Paper for the South

VIRGINIA

Abingdon

Calvinistic Magazine

Alexandria

Monthly Visitant; Or, Something Old

Signs of the Times

Southern Churchman

Bethany (now W. Va.)

Millennial Harbinger

Buchanan

Western Baptist

Western Virginia Baptist

Buffaloe Creek (now W. Va.)

Christian Baptist

Charlottesville

Christian Intelligencer

Christian Publisher

Danville

Roanoke Religious Correspondent; Or, Monthly Evangelical Visitant

Fairmont (now W. Va.)

Baptist Recorder

Fredericksburg

Christian Banner

Virginia Baptist

Front Royal

Zion's Advocate

Grafton (now W. Va.)

North Western Virginia Baptist

King William Court House

Christian Union and Religious Review

Lexington
Virginia Religious Magazine

Lynchburg
Lynchburg Evangelical Magazine

Martinsburg (now W. Va.)
Lay-Man's Magazine

Morgantown (now W. Va.)
Mountain Messenger and Baptist Recorder

Parkersburg (now W. Va.)
Southern Methodist Itinerant

Petersburg
Army and Navy Messenger
Christian Sun
Evangelical Miscellany and Ecclesiastical Review (proposed)

Richmond
American Baptist Memorial
Apostolic Advocate
Baptist Guardian
Central Presbyterian
Children's Friend
Christian Intelligencer
Christian Journal (proposed)
Christian Monitor
Christian Observer
Christian Sentinel
Christian Warrior
Commission
Commission; Or, Southern Baptist Missionary Magazine
Evangelical Inquirer
Family Christian Album
Family Visitor
Herald of the Future Age
Home and Foreign Journal
Methodist Sunday-School Recorder
Monthly Miscellany; A Religious and Literary Review
Parish Visitor
Religious Herald
Soldier's Paper
Soldier's Visitor
Southern Baptist Missionary Journal

Southern Churchman
Southern Friend
Southern Methodist Pulpit
Southern Pioneer and Gospel Visiter
Southern Presbyterian Pulpit
Spiritualist
Virginia Baptist Preacher, Original Monthly
Virginia Evangelical and Literary Magazine
Visitor and Telegraph
Watchman and Observer
Watchman of the South
Youth's Sunday Casket

Scottsville
Christian Intelligencer

Suffolk
Christian Sun

West Columbia (now W. Va.)
Virginia Telescope

Winchester
Evangelical Lutheran Preacher, and Pastoral Messenger

——?
Christian Union Magazine

Bibliography of Works Cited

Agnew, Samuel. "History of Town of Due West [S. C.]." [n.d.]. MS in Erskine College Library.

Alexander, J. E. *A Brief History of the Synod of Tennessee, from 1817 to 1887.* Philadelphia, 1890.

Allen, I. M. *The United States Baptist Annual Register and Almanac. 1833.* Philadelphia, 1833.

———. *The Triennial Baptist Register. No. 2–1836.* Philadelphia, 1836.

Allibone, S. Austin. *A Critical Dictionary of English Literature and British and American Authors.* 3 vols. Philadelphia, 1881.

Almanac and Baptist Register, 1841-1846; *Baptist Almanac and Annual Register,* 1847-1850; *Baptist Almanac,* 1851-1853; *American Baptist Almanac,* 1854-1864. Philadelphia, 1841-1864.

American Baptist Almanac. See *Almanac and Baptist Register.*

American Christian Record: Containing the History, Confession of Faith, and Statistics of Each Religious Denomination in the United States and Europe. New York, 1860.

"Articles of Agreement between H. K. Ellyson and the Board of Managers for Foreign Missions of the Southern Baptist Convention." [*ca.* 1846]. MS now in possession of the Foreign Mission Board of the Southern Baptist Convention, Richmond.

Autobiography of Rev. James Boyce, D.D. Edited by H. T. Sloan. Abbeville, S. C., 1892.

Baptist Almanac. See *Almanac and Baptist Register.*

Baptist Almanac and Annual Register. See *Almanac and Baptist Register.*

Barrett, J. Pressley (ed.). *The Centennial of Religious Journalism, 1808-1908.* 2nd ed. Dayton, Ohio: Christian Publishing Association, 1908.

Beebe, Gilbert. *A Compilation of Editorial Articles, Copied from the Signs of the Times.* Middletown, N. Y., 1868.

Benedict, David. *Fifty Years among the Baptists.* New York, 1860.

Brantley, Rabun Lee. *Georgia Journalism of the Civil War Period.* "Contributions to Education of George Peabody College for Teachers," no. 58. Nashville, Tenn.: George Peabody College for Teachers, 1929.

Brigham, Clarence S. *History and Bibliography of American Newspapers, 1690-1820.* 2 vols. Worcester, Mass.: American Antiquarian Society, 1947.

Broadus, John A. *Memoir of James Petigru Boyce.* New York, 1893.

Cappon, Lester J. *Virginia Newspapers 1821-1935; A Bibliography with Historical Introduction and Notes.* "Guide to Virginia Historical Materials," pt. 1. New York: D. Appleton-Century Company, 1936.

Carroll, H. K. *The Religious Forces of the United States Enumerated, Classified, and Described. . . .* New York: C. Scribner's Sons, 1912.

Cartland, Fernando G. *Southern Heroes; or, The Friends in War Time.* Cambridge, Mass., 1895.

Cathcart, William (ed.). *The Baptist Encyclopaedia: A Dictionary of the Doctrines, Ordinances, Usages, Confession of Faith. . . .* Philadelphia, 1881.

Charleston [S. C.] *Courier.* Oct. 25, 1813–Jan. 16, 1814.

Coggeshall, William Turner. *The Newspaper Record, Containing a Complete List of Newspapers and Periodicals in the United States. . . .* Philadelphia, 1856.

Crum, Mason. *The Southern Christian Advocate: An Historical Sketch.* Mason Crum, Duke University, 1945.

Deems, Charles F. (ed.). *Annals of Southern Methodism for 1856.* Nashville, Tenn., 1857.

———. *Annals of Southern Methodism for 1857.* Nashville, Tenn., 1858.

Dictionary of American Biography. 21 vols. New York: C. Scribner's Sons, 1928-1944.

Drinkhouse, Edward J. *History of Methodist Reform, Synoptical of General Methodism, 1703 to 1898. . . .* 2 vols. Baltimore, Md., 1899.

Drury, A. W. *History of the Church of the United Brethren in Christ.* Dayton, Ohio: The Otterbein Press, 1924.

Eddy, Richard. *Universalism in America: A History.* 2 vols. Boston, 1891-1894.

Foik, Paul J. *Pioneer Catholic Journalism.* "United States Catholic Historical Society, Monograph Series," no. 11. New York: The United States Catholic Historical Society, 1930.

Fortune, Willard A. *The Disciples in Kentucky.* [n.p.], 1932.

Gilmer, Gertrude C. *Checklist of Southern Periodicals to 1861.* "Useful Reference Series," no. 49. Boston: F. W. Faxon Company, 1934.

Gregory, Winifred (ed.). *American Newspapers 1821-1936: A Union List of Files Available in the United States and Canada.* New York: The H. W. Wilson Company, 1937.

——— (ed.). *Union List of Serials in Libraries of the United States and Canada.* 2nd ed. New York: The H. W. Wilson Company, 1943.

Guilday, Peter. *The Life and Times of John England, First Bishop of Charleston.* 2 vols. New York: The American Press, 1927.

Hallman, S. T. *History of the Evangelical Lutheran Synod of South Carolina, 1824-1924.* Columbia, S. C., 1924.

Hastings, James (ed.). *Encyclopaedia of Religion and Ethics.* 13 vols. New York: Charles Scribner's Sons, 1913-1927.

History of the Baptist Denomination in Georgia: with Biographical Compendium. . . . Compiled for the Christian Index. 2 parts. Atlanta, 1881.

Holcombe, Henry. *The First Fruits, in a Series of Letters.* Philadelphia, 1812.

Hoole, William Stanley. *A Check-List and Finding-List of Charleston Periodicals, 1732-1864.* Durham, N. C.: Duke University Press, 1936.

Howe, George. *History of the Presbyterian Church in South Carolina. Prepared by Order of the Synod of South Carolina.* 2 vols. Columbia, S. C., 1870, 1883.

Hull, Henry. *Sketches from the Early History of Athens, Georgia, 1801-1825.* Edited by A. L. Hull. Athens, Ga., 1884.

Johnson, Guion Griffis. *Ante-Bellum North Carolina: A Social History.* Chapel Hill: University of North Carolina Press, 1937.

Journal of the Convention of the Protestant Episcopal Church, in the Diocese of Virginia, 1848.

"Keeping the Record Straight, Religious Journalism in America." *Christian Observer.* Louisville, Feb. 19, 1936.

Kennedy, Joseph Camp Griffith. "Catalogue of the Newspapers and Periodicals Published in the United States, Showing the Town and County in which the Same are Published, how often Issued, their Character and Circulation. Compiled from the United States Census Statistics of 1850." *Livingston's Law Register for 1852.* New York, 1852.

Kenny, Daniel J. (comp.). *The American Newspaper Directory and Record of the Press.* New York, 1861.

McLean, Frank. "Periodicals Published in the South before 1880." Unpublished Ph.D. dissertation, University of Virginia, 1928.

Malikoff, Gabrielle E. (ed.). *Union List of Serials in Libraries of the United States and Canada.* 2nd ed. Supplement, January 1941–December 1943. New York: The H. W. Wilson Company, 1945.

Maynard, Theodore. *The Story of American Catholicism.* New York: The Macmillan Company, 1943.

Mercury. Charleston, July 24, 1854.

Minutes of the Evangelical Lutheran Synod and Ministerium of South Carolina and Adjacent States, October 1862, 1863.

Minutes of the General Assembly of the Presbyterian Church in the Confederate States of America, 1863.

Minutes of the General Assembly of the Presbyterian Church in the United States of America, 1851.

Minutes of the State Convention of the Baptist Denomination in South Carolina, 1835, 1843, 1844, 1858.

Minutes of the Synod of Georgia, 1869.

Minutes of the Synod of North Carolina, for September, 1837, with an Appendix, 1837.

Minutes of the Synod of South Carolina held in the Second Presbyterian Church, Charleston, 1901.

Minutes of the Synod of Virginia, 1867, 1869, 1894.

Morrison, Alfred J. "The Virginia Literary and Evangelical Magazine, Richmond, 1818-1828." *William and Mary College Quarterly Historical Magazine,* XIX (April, 1911), 266-272.

Mott, Frank Luther. *A History of American Magazines, 1741-1885.* 3 vols. Vol. 1, New York: D. Appleton and Company, 1930.

Vols. 2 and 3, Cambridge, Mass.: Harvard University Press, 1938.

National Cyclopaedia of American Biography.... 36 vols. New York: J. T. White Co., 1893-1950.

Neese, J. Everette. "The First Half Century of the Christian Denomination in the South." Unpublished B.A. thesis, Elon College, 1936.

Nevin, Alfred (ed.). *Encyclopaedia of the Presbyterian Church in the United States of America.* Philadelphia, 1884.

North Carolina Baptist Almanac for the Year 1893.

Oates, John Alexander. *The Story of Fayetteville and the Upper Cape Fear.* [Charlotte, N. C.: Dowd Press, 1950].

Pittman, R. H. (ed.). *Biographical History of Primitive or Old School Baptist Ministers of the United States. . . .* Anderson, Ind.: Herald Publishing Co., 1909.

Power, Frederick D. *Sketches of Our Pioneers.* Chicago, 1898.

Proceedings of the Southern Baptist Convention, 1849, 1851.

"Report of H. K. Ellyson to the Foreign Mission Board of the Southern Baptist Convention, April 30, 1847." MS in Foreign Mission Board of the Southern Baptist Convention, Richmond.

Roorbach, Orville A. *Bibliotheca Americana. Catalogue of American Publications. . . . Together with a List of Periodicals Published in the United States.* New York, 1852.

Richardson, Lyon A. *A History of Early American Magazines, 1741-1789.* New York: Thomas Nelson and Sons, 1931.

Richardson, Robert. *Memoirs of Alexander Campbell.* 2 vols. Cincinnati, 1897.

Shaw, Cornelia Rebekah. *Davidson College: Intimate Facts.* New York: Fleming H. Revell Press, 1923.

Shipp, Albert M. *The History of Methodism in South Carolina.* Nashville, 1884.

Simpson, Matthew (ed.). *Cyclopaedia of Methodism.* 4th rev. ed., Philadelphia, 1881.

Spence, T. H., Jr. "Southern Presbyterian Reviews." Reprinted from *The Union Seminary Review,* February, 1945.

Taylor, George Braxton. *Virginia Baptist Ministers.* 3rd-6th series. Lynchburg, Va.: J. P. Bell Co., 1912-1935.

Taylor, James B. *Lives of Virginia Baptist Ministers.* 2nd ed. rev. and enl. Richmond, 1838.

———. *Virginia Baptist Ministers.* Series 2. Philadelphia, 1859.

Tupper, H. A. *The Foreign Missions of the Southern Baptist Convention.* Philadelphia, 1880.

Tyler, J. Z. *Rise of the Reformation in Richmond and the Distinctive Peculiarities of the Disciples.* Richmond, 1882.

United States Census. Manuscript Returns, 1860. Georgia, Social Statistics, Bibb and Fulton Counties. Duke University Library.

Ware, Charles Crossfield. *North Carolina Disciples of Christ.* St. Louis: Christian Board of Publication, 1927.

Wightman, William May. *Life of William Capers.* Nashville, 1859.

Index